THE BISHOP PIKE AFFAIR

The William Stringfellow Reprint Series
Consulting Editor, Bill Wylie-Kellerman

The Ethics Trilogy
Conscience and Obedience
An Ethic for Christians and Other Aliens in a Strange Land
Instead of Death
(series foreword by Bill Wylie-Kellerman)

The Autobiographical Trilogy
My People is the Enemy
A Second Birthday
A Simplicity of Faith
(series foreword by Scott Kennedy)

The Dissent Trilogy
Dissenter in a Great Society
Suspect Tenderness
(coauthor, Anthony Towne)
The Politics of Spirituality
(series foreword by Daniel Berrigan)

The Foundations Quartet (forthcoming)
A Private and Public Faith
Count it all Joy
Free in Obedience
Imposters of God

Also (with coauthor Anthony Towne):
The Bishop Pike Affair
The Death and Life of Bishop Pike

THE BISHOP PIKE AFFAIR

Scandals of Conscience and Heresy, Relevance and Solemnity in the Contemporary Church

WILLIAM STRINGFELLOW
ANTHONY TOWNE

Wipf & Stock
PUBLISHERS
Eugene, Oregon

". . . *for the whole state of Christ's Church*"

Wipf and Stock Publishers
199 W 8th Ave, Suite 3
Eugene, OR 97401

The Bishop Pike Affair
Scandals of Conscience and Heresy, Relevance
and Solemnity in the Contemporary Church
By Stringfellow, William, and Towne, Anthony
Copyright©1967 by The Stringfellow Trust
ISBN 13: 978-1-55635-326-0
ISBN 10: 1-55635-326-X
Publication date 3/8/2007
Previously published by Harper & Row, 1967

It is a sad reflection upon the sincerity of Christian discipleship that so often in the history of the Church controversy has been conducted with bitterness and has been associated, as both cause and effect, with personal animosity. It is truly said that to become bitter in controversy is more heretical than to espouse with sincerity and charity the most devastating theological opinions; and by this standard the "orthodox" are condemned as grievously as their opponents. Progress in apprehension of the truths of the Gospel must chiefly come by the intercourse of minds united in friendship, so that they can do that most difficult thing to which St. Paul refers as though it ought to come naturally—"speaking the truth in love."

—WILLIAM TEMPLE
late Archbishop of Canterbury[1]

---

[1] October 1, 1937, while he was still Archbishop of York, and chairman of the Commission on Christian Doctrine appointed by the Archbishops of Canterbury and York in 1922, Temple so introduces the Commission's Report: *Doctrine in the Church of England* (London: Society for Promoting Christian Knowledge, 1938).

Foreword to the 2007 Edition

Treasure in an Earthen Vessel

> But we have this treasure in earthen vessels, to show that the transcendent power belongs to God and not to us. We are afflicted in every way, but not crushed; perplexed, but not driven to despair; persecuted, but not forsaken; struck down, but not destroyed.
>
> —2 Corinthians 4:7–12 RSV

> The credibility of the resurrection as an ultimate promise for humanity rests upon specific trumps over the power of death which occur in common life. Death, in many guises, pursued Bishop Pike relentlessly, and in many instances did Pike live in the resurrection, transcending death's power.
>
> —William Stringfellow & Anthony Towne, *The Death and Life of Bishop Pike*

Anthony Towne and William Stringfellow bore witness to the gospel and to America.

For the small and normally soft-spoken lawyer Stringfellow and the bear-like but even more soft-spoken poet Towne such witness was the essence of their Christian vocation. As life partners and co-authors, fellow polemicists and theologians, Towne and Stringfellow discerned the scope and power of death manifest in the culture in which they lived. More importantly, they lifted up the people whose very lives challenged death's omnipotence in this life and bore witness to the power of life—both in this life and over death.

Foreword to the 2007 Edition

Stringfellow and Towne's vocational collaboration was made evident in their notorious choice to publicly support anti-war activist Father Daniel Berrigan. The Jesuit priest, his brother Philip Berrigan, and seven others had burned Selective Service files with homemade napalm at a draft board office in Catonsville, Maryland in 1968. The prophetic protest against the war in Vietnam resulted in felony charges and a trial for "the Catonsville Nine." The federal court found them guilty of destruction of U.S. property, destruction of Selective Service files, and interference with the Selective Service Act of 1967 and sentenced them to several years in prison.

Stringfellow attended the trial of the Catonsville Nine as defense counsel and spoke out on behalf of the defendants. During Dan Berrigan's months-long flight underground from federal authorities following his conviction, he was clandestinely hosted by Towne and Stringfellow at their Block Island, Rhode Island home. The pair described apprehension of the fugitive priest by FBI "bird watchers" in their book *Suspect Tenderness*. Stringfellow and Towne identified Daniel Berrrigan's life, work, and civil disobedience as signs of the presence and power of what they understood to be the word of God breaking into human history—resisting, challenging, and overcoming the power of death.

The Nixon White House conspicuously confirmed the potential consequence of such vocation and witness by threatening felony prosecution of Stringfellow and Towne for extending hospitality to Berrigan. Their legal defense was disarmingly straightforward: hospitality is simply a Christian responsibility; abiding by the dictates of a lie-telling, rights-suppressing, and war-making nation is not. When Rhode Island's Episcopal bishop, not known for his radical views, joined others protesting their prosecution, the U.S. backed off "the Block Island Two," dropping the case against Towne and Stringfellow. The nature of Stringfellow and Towne's vocation was also conspicuously confirmed in their choice to write about the late Episcopal bishop James Albert Pike. This foreword serves to reintroduce these books: *The Bishop Pike Affair*, originally published in 1967, and *The Death and Life of Bishop Pike* (1976).

Foreword to the 2007 Edition

The Bishop Pike Affair describes the convoluted sequence of events spanning the years following charges of heresy against Pike by several fellow bishops. Towne and Stringfellow wrote their account soon after the culmination of the heresy charges at the 1966 meeting of the House of Bishops in Wheeling, West Virginia. At that meeting, the Episcopal bishops adopted a "compromise" statement in what proved to be the vain hope of derailing momentum towards a full-blown public heresy trial. The book's cover promises a "documented behind-the-sanctuary report on a battle for belief that rages in the American Church today." The story ends inconclusively, however. Before the final gavel sounded, Pike and two other bishops brought everybody up short with their last-minute demand for due process and an investigation of the "rumors, reports, and allegations, affecting [Pike's] personal and official character."

A number of bishops clearly found Pike's public ministry—as Dean of the Cathedral of St. John the Divine in New York City in the 1950s and later as Bishop of California in San Francisco—an outrage that threatened their worldview and the faith. They considered accusations of heresy against Pike momentous and seriously overdue. Stringfellow and Towne argue persuasively in this book that opposition to Pike had little to do with theology. Rather than regard for doctrinal niceties or theological truths, accusations against Pike hinged on his "social radicalism" on issues such as "birth control, the liberation of women, the racial crisis, McCarthyism, capital punishment, abortion, fair housing, the plight of farm workers, censorship, civil liberties, the Vietnam war, [and] resistance to illegitimate authority, among a host of others."

The church establishment was primarily concerned with preserving what they thought to be the church's image. They viewed a public trial for heretical beliefs against one of the nation's most prominent churchmen an embarrassment to be avoided at all costs. Unfortunately, as the authors spell out in great detail, among the costs sustained by the church leadership were demonstrations for Pike's right to a fair hearing.

Foreword to the 2007 Edition

For perhaps too few others, including Towne and Stringfellow, the heresy debacle was a foreboding taste of an impending reality in the American churches. While the pursuit of heresy charges against Pike met with mixed success, the forces arrayed against him were flexing muscles that only grew in strength in the coming years. McCarthy-era techniques and economic bullying succeeded in removing from power the very presiding bishop who oversaw attempts to diffuse the heresy controversy, an unanticipated cost of attempted compromise. Political and economic reactionaries would come to exercise enormous power within and control over the Episcopal church and would eventually hijack Protestant Christianity in the United States. Stringfellow and Towne describe those reactionaries as "substantially unconcerned with theology as such," and "very absorbed in maintaining or turning back the status quo in every respect, socially, racially, politically, scientifically, educationally, religiously." They speak ominously of a group that "possesses an economic influence and a mental temperament to further these aims." Forces of political reaction and supposed religious orthodoxy continue to wield enormous influence over the American church and public life, with ever-appearing and disastrous consequence.

Stringfellow and Towne's account of this lurid heresy affair includes their penetrating and at times humorous observations. The appendix consists of many relevant documents and public and private statements and correspondence. The Bishop Pike Affair describes how "the most controversial ecclesiastical personality of the times," attracted attention and concern because people both inside and outside of the church "at least recognize in the bishop a Christian, and an ecclesiastic at that, who is living in the present century." In other words, his example was viewed sympathetically by many people in the United States and around the world. Pike provided Stringfellow and Towne a particularly edifying example of a Christian living their faith at the intersection of the gospel and America.

The Death and Life of Bishop Pike takes up the matters foreshadowing Pike's vocation, his prominent place in the twentieth-century American church, and the unusual events surrounding his death.

For the biographers "doing theology" was part and parcel of a Christian's vocation. Doing theology meant seeking out and understanding death's reach into all of our lives, including numerous mundane and banal expressions such as earning a livelihood and suffering illness. Doing theology also encompassed elevating those signs of life overcoming death, moments in which sanity is preserved, conscience asserted, and peoples' humanity defended. Their writings, including these two volumes on Bishop Pike, affirm these dual realities—the ubiquitous reach of death and the steadfast triumph of life.

Towne and Stringfellow saw the reign of death as daunting in its all-encompassing reach, but they also affirmed that life has the final word. Death's power may be consuming, restricting, and dehumanizing, but those who would follow Christ are unfettered in their humanity and their freedom. Stringfellow and Towne grounded this powerful assertion in the lives of ordinary people and the lives of sometimes not-so-ordinary persons such as Bishop James A. Pike.

Writing about Pike was not simply a matter of biography or historiography. For Towne and Stringfellow Pike's death and life illumine the gospel. These men understood that the revolutionary nature and contagious power of Christian faith locate in and emanate from the message that death does not have the final word.

From that perspective, they assess Pike's childhood and especially the maternal influence on his growing up and maturation. They appraise Pike's rapid ascendancy in the field of law, in the church, and in American public life. They detail a life ensnared in controversy, both public and private. They provide the fullest account in print of Bishop Pike's three marriages and what the authors describe as Pike's "moral ambiguities," including the disturbing circumstance of a paramour's suicide. They offer insight into the personality that beguiled, outraged, or inspired so many both within and beyond the church. They considered Bishop Pike "remarkably obtuse politically," a person constantly attributing "high motives to his enemies and detractors, minimizing or overlooking evidence to the contrary."

Foreword to the 2007 Edition

Nevertheless, in their final analysis, Pike possessed truly catholic interests and extraordinarily variegated talents. This was a man who did not tire of his mind or the use of it: of asking questions, of seeking more knowledge of every sort, of changing, of growing, of listening, of thinking, of learning about everything and about anything. He had a restless, relentless, questing, insatiable curiosity for living. He was an open, intuitive, risking, audacious spirit. Bishop Pike has been frequently called a prophet; we consider that not quite precise; we think his genre is pioneer.

In 1968, as a first year student at the University of California at Santa Cruz, I had the great blessing to travel to Israel and Europe with Bishop Pike. This was because my sister Diane Kennedy and Jim Pike fell in love and worked together the final three years of his life. I worked as a research assistant and "gofer" for both of them the last year and a half of Bishop Pike's life and with Diane for several years after his death. My views of these two books are heavily influenced by this brief but intense experience. Reading Towne and Stringfellow's work, I learned a great deal about how the charges of heresy against Pike fit into his life as a whole. Most of the conclusions that have been drawn from a broader study of Pike's life were confirmed by my experience of Jim Pike. We share several impressions, including uncertainty about purported communication between the Bishop and his deceased son.

On a few points, however, my views differ from the authors. For example, the question of communication with the dead assumes too great a place in the public's understanding of Bishop Pike and, so far as I am concerned, takes up too much space in the Stringfellow and Towne biography. The popular press may well have portrayed that psychic communication with his son, Jim Jr., obsessed the bishop in his last years, or that such obsession drove the bishop mad. During what turned out to be his last years, I had occasion to closely watch this very public figure and I consider these impressions ill founded. I saw Pike use his visibility and considerable energy and skills to oppose the war in Vietnam and to help people, including clergy, who found themselves leaving or being forced out of the institutional church.

I vividly recall Pike's excitement when he telephoned Diane and me from the Baltimore trial of the Catonsville Nine in October 1968. Pike was extremely proud that Stringfellow had arranged for him to join as legal counsel at the defense table. He complained that—except for Protestant theologian Harvey Cox and Dorothy Day, founder of the Catholic Worker movement—no bishops or church leaders were present at the trial to support the defendants. Standing alongside and speaking on behalf of the Berrigans and other anti-war protesters was for Bishop Pike a natural and compelling extension of his pastoral, teaching, and prophetic ministries. I often heard Pike say during the final eighteen months of his life that he was far more concerned with "life after birth" than "life after death." As Towne and Stringfellow wrote, "Resurrection . . . has to do with life, and indeed, the fulfillment of life, before death." Contrary to widely held opinions, my observations confirmed that Pike's dedication to life after birth guided how he apportioned his time, energy, and formidable gifts.

Stringfellow and Towne describe how controversy swirled about Jim Pike's marriage to Diane Kennedy. Following their marriage, which took place in our family's Methodist church in San Jose, California, in December 1968, Bishop Pike was effectively barred from his public ministry by his successor, the new Bishop of California. This prompted a public announcement of Jim and Diane Pike's decision to leave the church, made April 1969 in a national magazine. But this decision was perhaps too greatly influenced by Jim Pike's concern for the impact of continuing controversy on his marriage to Diane. He wrote to the presiding bishop the following September, saying that he was not yet foreswearing his demand for a full investigation of charges against him, leaving open the question of his staying in the church. Pike sent the letter immediately before embarking to the Middle East on a belated honeymoon. Soon after arriving in Israel, Jim and Diane Pike sojourned in a small rental car into the desert east of Bethlehem. Their destination was the wilderness above Qumran where the Dead Sea Scrolls were discovered and where they believed Jesus fasted, prayed, and withstood his "temptations."

Through a series of mishaps, the Pikes were forced to abandon their car in the desert. Diane miraculously survived an overnight ordeal, hiking through rugged terrain to reach the Dead Sea and find help. Stringfellow and Towne were among the millions of people waiting for word of Pike's fate. I was with the search party that, nearly a week later, discovered Pike's body in Wadi Mashash, west of the Dead Sea. He had died of a fall and exposure to the elements on a craggy canyon wall. I clambered up the steep canyon wall to join Diane, who was waiting in an Israeli army vehicle above, as Bishop Pike's body was lifted by a helicopter from the steep wall of the desert canyon.

My first exposure to Towne and Stringfellow was reading Stringfellow's *Instead of Death*, a gift from Diane, as a high school church summer camper in the mid 1960s. Jim Pike spoke often of William Stringfellow and Anthony Towne. One of his favorite stories—recounted with great energy, waving of arms, and reenacting of ritual—recalled his anointing Stringfellow with borrowed petroleum jelly in the hospital while Stringfellow was recuperating from a life-threatening operation. I met Stringfellow and Towne personally in 1969 following Pike's death. Diane and I visited Block Island to reaffirm Pike's request that they write his biography. As part of their preparation for this assignment, we four traveled together in Israel and the occupied West Bank of Palestine in 1970. In October 1972 Stringfellow and Towne invited me to New York City to join with anti-war activists from around the country to "talk about the Gospel and America." I was living on the California coast so we joked about having America surrounded. I helped with research on the Pike biography. I continued close contact until Towne's death in 1980 and Stringfellow's in 1986. Jim Pike was a common bond of friendship and source of inspiration for the three of us.

Their strong affinity with Bishop James A. Pike stretched back a decade and a half at the time of Pike's death in 1969. This affinity cannot be understood only by the peculiar combination of being both lawyer and theologian that Stringfellow and Pike shared. Nor can it be explained by Stringfellow and Towne also being Episcopalians or aligned with Pike on social issues. Surely there were plenty of lawyers, theologians, even lawyers and theologians, as well as Episcopalians and social activists, with whom Towne and Stringfellow felt no particular affinity and for whom they lacked the deep affection they felt for Bishop Pike. Rather, their bond stems from Stringfellow's and Towne's comprehension that a great deal was at stake in the ways in which the gospel and America intersected in the life and vocation of Pike. It implicated the whole body of Christ:

> Whatever happens to Bishop Pike, or to his enemies and detractors, or to his friends and followers, does not matter nearly as much as what is done about the issues—as much for the world as for the Church—which have become stark and, so to speak, incarnate in the case of Bishop Pike. (*The Bishop Pike Affair*)

Pike's demand for an investigation of the charges against him surprised his accusers and the church leadership. His place in the church was left unresolved at the end of "The Bishop Pike Affair," due to his demand for an investigation of charges against him. Ironically, his status as bishop was also left unresolved when he died in the Judean wilderness nearly three years later.

In their many written and spoken words Stringfellow and Towne argued that the gospel is not about religion, rituals, beliefs, or behaviors by which believers will somehow win favor in God's eye. They railed against the idolatry of false religiosity—patently manifest in American racism, militarism, and poverty. Towne and Stringfellow contrasted "American religiosity" with "biblical faith or theology." They understood that death itself was arrayed against Bishop Pike. It was the same battle they fought standing beside Daniel Berrigan when "the target of that assault was our humanity—the very *esse* [sic] of our humanness: sanity and conscience." It is no wonder that

Foreword to the 2007 Edition

their biography of Pike highlights an early incident in his life, the first episode of which there is detailed knowledge in which Pike ventured his own intelligence against prevalent authority, in which he sought to redeem his conscience against conformity, in which he risked approbation and success for the sake of conviction, in which his independence broke through and his talent to question and problem challenge and search took clarity as his vocation. As both friends and enemies of James A. Pike concur, this became at once his most admirable and engaging and his most irritating and provocative characteristic. They summarize these various traits as evidence of Pike's "capacity for courage."

Anthony Towne and William Stringfellow appreciated at the deepest level that the forces of life and death contended within, around, and over Jim Pike. His triumph was recognition that "Life is a gift" and that "Faith . . . the acceptance, honoring, rejoicing in that gift . . . freedom from moral bondage to death . . . enables a person to live humanly and to die at any moment without concern."

According to Stringfellow and Towne, Bishop Pike "moved—through a lifetime—from church dogmatics to confession of the gospel, from 'smooth orthodoxy' to personal faith, from—in his own words—the 'ontological' to the 'existential.'"

Quitting the church . . . represented a penultimate act of faith for him. This was the issue of religion vs. the gospel, ecclesiology vs. theology, doctrinal recitals vs. confession, authority vs. conscience, the Church vs. Jesus, idolatry vs. faith. As James A. Pike became less and less religious, it can be said that he became more and more Christian.

By their witness to the transformation of Bishop James Pike in these two works, William Stringfellow and Anthony Towne say more about healing and forgiveness than about conflict and controversy.

Scott Kennedy
Easter 2007
Santa Cruz, California
kenncruz@pacbell.net

Acknowledgments

This book could not have been written but for the particular cooperation of the Right Reverend James A. Pike and the Right Reverend Henry I. Louttit. Each of these bishops received the authors with cordiality and candor and each has been indispensable in making available documents pertinent to the subject of the book. They both have the earnest gratitude of the authors.

Appreciation is due to virtually all the other incumbent bishops of the Episcopal Church as well. Every bishop was requested to furnish information deemed relevant and, with but few exceptions, the response from the bishops was ready and helpful.

The authors personally interviewed nearly a hundred individuals in the course of the research and preparation of this book. It is impractical to list them all here, and, in some instances, it would be indiscreet to do so. They know who they are and their assistance is in this way thankfully acknowledged.

Of those interviewed, specific mention is made of the Most Reverend John E. Hines, the Presiding Bishop, for his generous consideration in granting the authors so much of his time.

The authors wish also to thank the editors of *The New York Times*, *Time* magazine, *Newsweek*, Richard Philbrick of *The Chicago Tribune*, Willmar Thorkelson of *The Minneapolis Star*, and Lester Kinsolving of *The San Francisco Chronicle* for access to their files or other sources, and to acknowledge the cooperation of the Dean and the Librarian of The General Theological Seminary in New York City in obtaining material. The same is true for Messrs. Ronald Barlow and E. Allen Kelly of Morehouse Barlow, Inc. and the Reverend Canon Charles Guilbert, Secretary to the House of Bishops.

Barton Lidicé Beneš is the extraordinarily perceptive artist who executed the end papers for this book. The authors regard his contribution to the book as genius.

Stanton Putnam and Ray Karras have been accomplices of the authors in the research required. Both confess that this work has greatly edified them as to the estate of the contemporary Church. Both have the authors' sincere appreciation and a hope that their edification is adequate recompense for their diligence.

While it remains the belief of the authors that authors should not thank publishers, they do acknowledge the especial technical aid which the publishers, here, have afforded the authors, specifically in reproducing certain documents and tapes. Perhaps, therefore, the final acknowledgment published should be for Xerox and Sony.

—WILLIAM STRINGFELLOW
—ANTHONY TOWNE

Contents

End Papers: An Impression of the Bishops in Session at Wheeling, 1966—Barton Lidicé Beneš

xiii *Foreword:* Of the Intent of This Book at This Time
    The Problem of Objectivity
    The Right to Know the Truth
    The Anatomy of Heresy Trials
    A Quaint Episode

1 Part One: The Chronicle of a Controversy
    The Evolution of a Bishop
    The Evolution of a Theologian
    The Evolution of a "Heretic"
    The Evolution of a Pastor
    The Evolution of Candor
    The Convention in St. Louis
    The Intervention of a Poetaster
    The Case of the Reverend Mrs. Phyllis Edwards
    The Baptism of Luci Baines Johnson
    The Bishop Takes a Sabbatical
    The Death of the Bishop's Son

x   CONTENTS

   The Incident at O'Hare
   The Worker Priest in the Purple
   The Months of Transition
   The Conference for Disturbed Clergy
   The Evolution of a Born Fighter
   The Presentment of the Charges
   The Appointment of the Dun Committee
   The Agitation of a Fraternity
   The Dealings at Wheeling
   The Bishop is for Burning
   An Ecumenical Interlude
   A Night to Remember
   A Rhapsody in Purple
   An Anticlimax Ends in Grace

93 PART TWO: Exegesis of a Controversy

94 *First*—Dogma, Doctrine and Discipline

   What is Heresy?
   Orthodoxy or Conformity?
   Orthodoxy or Semantics?

115 *Second*—Heresy and Due Process

   An Inherent Profanity
   Procedural Defects in the Pike Affair
   The Anatomy of Expedience
   Due Process, Episcopal Style
   Bishop Pike's Ploy

139 *Third*—The Fraternity of Bishops
   The Ethics of Episcopal Fraternity
   The Notoriety and Naïveté of Pike
   Vanity and Vulgarity

161 *Fourth*—Social Radicalism and Heresy
   A Matter of Malice?
   A Bishop without a Cause?
   Bishops with Causes or Causes with Bishops?
   A Problem of Appeasement?
   An Ominous Portent?

195 *A Homily*— The Humor of Heresy

198 *Appendix*
   I. The Arizona Charges and the Glacier Park Detente
   II. The Presentment Papers of Bishop Louttit
   III. The Louttit-Pike Correspondence
   IV. The Wheeling Documents
      —The majority statement censuring Bishop Pike
      —A statement of the minority
      —Bishop Pike's demand for investigation
      —The Stokes resolution
   V. The Roll Call of Bishops on Pertinent Matters
   VI. Relevant Provisions of the Constitution and Canons of the Episcopal Church
   VII. Data on the "Bayne Committee"
      —The Presiding Bishop's mandate
      —Bishop Pike's response
      —Bishop Bayne's interpretation of the Committee's task
   VIII. Bibliography of Works of James A. Pike

251 *Notes*

FOREWORD

Ninety per cent of the people want me to pour boiling oil on you with the Bishop of Florida [the Right Reverend E. Hamilton West] pulling your fingernails out at the same time. Ten per cent think that's what we're doing now.

> —The Right Reverend Henry I. Louttit, Bishop of South Florida: addressing Bishop Pike during a joint press conference in Wheeling, West Virginia.[1]

I understand well the will of this House to adopt this document. I regret this deeply. I speak here against this statement, not as a Bishop, not even as a Christian, just as—just as a man. The substance I would not wish to argue. The whole process by which a man is publicly tried, excoriated really, and condemned—condemned in some deep sense to death—by God!—heresy is nothing to what we call him here. Heresy! I'm pretty kosher, but heresy is nothing to what we say about this man!

> —The Right Reverend Daniel Corrigan, Director of the Home Department, Episcopal Church: during the censure debate.[2]

---

[1] At the House of Bishops meeting, October 23–27, 1966, as reported in *The Vancouver Sun*, November 5, 1966, p. 10.

[2] As transcribed, live, by the Canadian Broadcasting Corporation, October 25, 1966, at Wheeling, West Virginia.

Of the Intent of This Book at This Time

It would be simple to write about the recurrent accusations of heresy against Bishop James A. Pike, the censure of him by a majority of his peers and his subsequent demand for an ecclesiastical trial, in a fashion which exploits the passions aroused and the confusions occasioned by the affair.

It would be easy to dwell upon the diverse and versatile frailties of bishops, both in general and in the particular, in a way that would titillate those who subsist vicariously on hearsay or gossip or exposé. Any who anticipate such morbid entertainments in this book will be, we trust, disappointed and frustrated.

In one of our letters, addressed to all the bishops of the Episcopal Church, while the book was being written, there is this paragraph:

One bishop has raised with us the question of why we have undertaken this book. Let it be known, therefore, that the initiative in the matter was entirely that of the publisher, but that it also became clear that some book would be written by somebody. One of the principal reasons that we agreed, to the sacrifice of other commitments, to do this book was a conviction that we could do a responsible job and prevent some piece of slick journalism being published to exploit this controversy, to the detriment of all concerned and to the disrepute of the Church.

Whether the book succeeds in this purpose is now for others to assess, but we want to reiterate here what our purpose has been and is.

It would be possible, without indulging in muckraking, to write a partisan book on the Bishop Pike affair—an apologetic for Pike's accusers or a brief in his defense or an alibi for those bishops caught in the ambiguous regions between the principal adversaries. This book attempts none of these things. We have tried to write a book that is fair to all parties and viewpoints and that is fastidiously accurate as to the facts presently ascertainable so that the facts may speak for themselves within a context which has some historical reference and theological literacy and which admits a concern for the destiny of the Church of Christ in contemporary culture.

The Problem of Objectivity

This is not to claim that this book is objective in the sense of neutrality. On the contrary, we are convinced that neutrality is neither a viable nor responsible option on any of the substantive issues of theology and of the Church's mission in society. Nor are we empty-headed, without positions and opinions, and, our views, which frequently are not coincident or complimentary, have elsewhere been published in other books and in periodicals. Moreover, we are both Episcopalians: one by birth, as it were, later ratified by choice, the other by a decision made in adulthood. It is scarcely to be expected that any Episcopalian would not have some convictions at stake in the Bishop Pike affair. In a less immediate way, the same can be said of any Christian of any tradition, denomination or sect and, for that matter, it can also be affirmed by multitudes of people who remain outside the precincts of the inherited churchly institutions familiar on the American scene.

Yet if objectivity, in a connotation of either neutrality or blandness, is not possible or appropriate, it *is* nonetheless still feasible to secure all the facts that can be obtained and to relate them with accuracy and fairness. In pursuit of the facts in this controversy, the accounts of various news media, the availability of films, photographs and tapes, interviews with numerous persons, access to correspondence, documents and official records have yielded an enormous quantity of research material. Most of this data was capable of being verified from one or more sources independent of that from which it was originally obtained and we have done just that. It is not to be expected that everyone, or even anyone, will attribute the same weight or relevance to certain facts that we have or that there will be a consensus among others about inferences which we have drawn from the facts. We do not concur in some instances about these things between ourselves.

We recognize, too, the limitations on any book written about a heated and complex dispute while the matter is still unresolved and is unlikely to be resolved quickly. On the other hand, if the history of Christendom is taken seriously, in one sense, the essential issues which have come to a focus in the present time in the Bishop Pike affair can never be settled this side of the eschaton. If this book sheds a little light upon what actually happened in the Bishop Pike case, subject as it is to the amendments of subsequent events or disclosures, it will have honored the intent of its author and, we hope, may be not only edifying but healing.

Let it be admitted that we are aware of another sort of factor which affects the objectivity of this book. While we have tried to forbear dealing in personalities—we are writers, one a lawyer, the other a poet, neither one a psychiatrist—and while we have attempted to refrain from judgment about motives beyond recognizing that the motivations of all directly concerned are mixed, we have made one assumption with specific respect to all of the bishops involved in accusing, censuring, or defending Bishop Pike. We assume that they are all adults, responsible actors who readily accept the consequences of their decisions and actions. Anyone wishing to attack this book has the gratuitous counsel to challenge us for making what may be a frivolous assumption. In any event, while *speculation* as to motives may now and then creep in, *judgment* of motives has, we trust, been rigorously suppressed.

The Right to Know the Truth

There has been, as the acknowledgments recognize and as the book itself evidences, a helpful if not always enthusiastic cooperation from bishops, and from many others, in our research for this book. But there have been some emphatically hostile to the effort. One bishop, in response to inquiries submitted to him, wrote:

> It is quite presumptuous of you or any publishing house to feel you have the right to canvass every Bishop of the House of Bishops, asking them to report how they voted, and why, on a particular situation. I resent the whole project rather seriously.

This appears to us an anomalous attitude in view of the fact that the House of Bishops decided to conduct its debate about the censure of Bishop Pike in public before television cameras and legions of journalists and galleries packed with clergy and laity and interested non-churchmen. But, beyond that, this seems to us an exceedingly un-Anglican sentiment to be suffered by an Episcopal bishop. We hold the view that everything of public consequence that bishops decide and do should be decided and done in the open and subject to questions by churchmen, both clergy and laymen. That, we understand, is an elementary tradition stemming from the English Reformation, reflected in the Articles of Religion of the Episcopal Church, and, before all that, precedented in the conduct of the earliest congregations of the Church as witnessed, to cite an instance not wholly dissimilar from the current strife, though without pressing the citation as a literal analogy, in the dispute about the authenticity of Saint Paul's credentials as an Apostle. (Acts 9. 26–30; 15; II Corinthians 11. 1–12)

One of us, being a lawyer, is, perhaps, peculiarly biased in favor of the right to know what goes on in the sanctum of the House of Bishops because of a more general disposition favoring open and straightforward inquiry in all public affairs, and because of an esteem for such openness as part of the genius of Anglo-Saxon jurisprudence. The other, being a poet, just enjoys the truth for its own sake and hence opposes the condescensions of any who obstruct the right to know it. Both of us, in other words, uphold inquisitiveness, though by the very same token, we be against inquisitions.

This is not a concern which is asserted only in our own names. We believe that the Bishop Pike affair embodies issues of such vital importance for both the Church and society that everybody both within and outside the Church has the right to know what

Bishop Pike has said and done, what prompted accusations of heresy against him, what occasioned his censure by his fellow bishops, and what seems more likely than not to eventuate in a trial.

In precisely that connection, one does not have to dig very deeply to discern that there is much in the mass media reports of the whole matter, through the years, which has lent itself to distortion, false or erroneous impressions, confusion at least thrice compounded, and widespread consternation among churchmen. If, as seems to us the case, at the same time the Bishop Pike affair has alternately amused and bemused secular folk and, in either circumstance, tarnished the image of the Church or inhibited any outside the Church from taking the Gospel seriously, then so much the more cogent is the purpose and, we trust, the service this book represents.

The public dimensions of the controversy surrounding Bishop Pike and the consequent non-contingency of the right to know and publish the facts can be, perhaps, illuminated by recalling another situation in which vested claims of orthodoxy collided with those of conscience. We refer, of course, to the Scopes trial. In that matter, the personal disposition of the accused became, in our view, much less important than the engagement of issues which the trial enabled. What happened to the prosecutor or to the defendant was not as significant as the confrontation in the proceedings between religious fundamentalism and elemental science. Whatever the eventual outcome of the Bishop Pike affair, whatever the fate of Bishop Pike or of any other bishops privy to the ruckus, the more essential consideration is that Bishop Pike's position in both the Church and society has now become a symbol and focus, in the present day, of a whole portfolio of challenges and concerns with which the Church is being accosted and assaulted. Whatever happens to Bishop Pike, or to his enemies and detractors, or to his friends and followers, does not matter nearly as much as what is *done* about the issues—as much for the world as for the Church—which have become stark and, so to speak, incarnate in the case of Bishop Pike.

The good bishops of the Episcopal Church may, if they choose, ignore, evade, temporize about, or sacrifice Bishop Pike. That is, relatively, of little consequence. The real problem is not this man. The actual peril concerns whether or not the Church, in its prevailing mode of life, has *both* facility with the world and integrity in the Gospel of Jesus Christ to thus *both* survive and be worthy of survival.

Having this strenuously upheld the right of all to know, let it be recorded that the documentation which we have gathered and utilized in writing this book, while not in an ultimate sense exhaustive, is, at this stage of the matter, we are confident, definitive, so much so, that, at one time in our labor we, teasingly, proposed to the publisher that we write a ten page book with a 1,000-page Appendix of pertinent items and leave the readers to their own devices in reconstructing events and making an exegesis of them. Since we failed to persuade Harper & Row to accede to this inspired suggestion, we have instead selected the most evidently vital documents for the Appendix of this book. They, of course, stand on their own, but, we want to point out that they also are a means by which the reader can reach his own conclusions both about the immediate controversy attending Bishop Pike and about this book.

In the Appendix, as Table V, there is a reconstruction of the vote of the bishops on the censure of Bishop Pike, together with related items. When the hour came for the vote, despite the public character of the act and the great notoriety attaching to it because of the *en masse* presence of the press, television, radio, and people in the galleries, it was ruled that a roll call vote would not be taken. Only numbers, but no names, of voting bishops were recorded. We candidly state our view that this was a ridiculous ruling bound to evoke suspicious questions to the effect: "What do the bishops have to hide?" or "Are any bishops shamed by their vote?"

Thus we have attempted in Table V, by polling the bishops and by resort to other documentary sources, to reconstruct the actual roll call on the censure. One bishop, who refused to admit his vote, forbade us to print his name in this book. But, since that would be equivalent to ignoring his existence, we have ignored his forbiddance, instead. Despite extraordinary diligence and care, the Table referred to is not complete in every detail. One difficulty, for example, has been merely establishing which bishops attended the Wheeling, 1966, meeting of the House of Bishops since, incredible though it seems, the registration roster of those in attendance has been destroyed. Table V, therefore, represents as accurate a reconstruction of the roll call that did not take place as, under the circumstances, has been capable of being made and verified.

The Anatomy of Heresy Trials

Few people, including churchmen, and, notably, bishops, are knowledgeable about heresy trials and the proceedings canonically incident thereto. The Appendix of this book contains a section which can remedy such illiteracy. Let it only be noted here that such ecclesiastical proceedings are intricate, cumbersome, and protracted in the Episcopal Church, though that is not a unique attribute of the Episcopal Church. Yet the obscurity associated with the procedures and, some would argue, the neglect of reforming those procedures so that they could be conducted with competence and dispatch should not be construed as proof of the novelty or rareness of heresy trials. In the last decade of the nineteenth century through the first three of the present century, there were several trials and threats of trials in the Episcopal Church, including the well known case of Bishop William Montgomery Brown in 1924 and the celebrated trial of the Reverend Algernon S. Crapsey, who prematurely styled himself "the last of the heretics," in 1906. In other churches during approximately the same period there were a good many trials, and as recently as 1953 three Lutheran pastors were tried.

One of the paradoxes of heresy proceedings is that the trial apparatus does not usually allow substantive consideration of theology. Thus, in the trial of Bishop Brown, expert testimony from professional theologians as to the confessional latitude of the Anglican Communion was excluded. And in the present controversy about Bishop Pike, the Presiding Bishop ruled at the outset of the public debate that theology was not to be discussed, but only whether to adopt, reject or modify the censure of Bishop Pike.

If theological issues are not commonly dealt with in heresy

proceedings or in the preliminaries thereto, factors which would generally be regarded as non-theological are certainly very much in the foreground. All sorts of extra-mural social, psychological, and political pressures, institutional dynamics, personality conflicts, fraternal loyalties, protocol problems, along with miscellaneous virtues and vices, enter the scene and influence events. As one newsman who witnessed the happenings at Wheeling remarked—"The House of Bishops turned into the biggest 'group life lab' the Episcopalians have ever had"— an allusion to the enthusiasm in some quarters of the Episcopal Church for group dynamics experimentation.

A Quaint Episode

Finally, a word of admonition to the reader is in order.

If this were a work of fiction—a novel the plot of which we had invented and the characters of which we had created in our own imaginations—we doubt that the book would be published.

There is just too much in the Bishop Pike affair which taxes credibility.

In recounting these scandals of conscience and heresy, relevance and solemnity in the contemporary Church, in this still unfinished episode, we have found ourselves, as some readers surely will also, alternately outraged and ashamed, amused and bewildered, admiring and cynical, proud and repelled, grateful and chastened. There is much in this account fraught with irony, some that documents stupidity, some which discloses malice, some which glimpses tragedy, some which displays pomposity, some that is filled with humor, some that demonstrates betrayal, and a little which witnesses the power, as well as the need, of forgiveness.

William Stringfellow
Anthony Towne

Maundy Thursday, 1967
New York City

PART ONE

THE CHRONICLE OF A CONTROVERSY

Having taken this position regarding a trial, nevertheless, we feel bound to reject the tone and manner of much that Bishop Pike has said as being offensive and highly disturbing within the communion and fellowship of the Church. And we would disassociate ourselves from many of his utterances as being irresponsible on the part of one holding the office and trust he shares with us.

His writing and speaking on profound realities with which Christian faith and worship are concerned are too often marred by caricatures of treasured symbols and at the worst, by cheap vulgarizations of great expressions of faith.

> —Excerpt from a Statement adopted by a majority of the House of Bishops at the Wheeling meeting.[1]

Bishop Pike has been disturbing, admittedly. Often in his dialogues with the faithless, with youth, with adherents of other religious faiths he has spoken precipitously and with some risk. He would have preferred more time for consideration, but the pace of our day does not allow us such time. We believe it is more important to be a sympathetic and self-conscious part of God's action in the secular world than it is to defend the positions of the past, which is a past that is altered with each new discovery of truth.

> —Excerpt from a Supplemental Statement endorsed by a minority of the House of Bishops at the Wheeling meeting.[2]

---

[1] Minutes of the House of Bishops, Wheeling, West Virginia, October 25, 1966, p. 27.
[2] Minutes of the House of Bishops, Wheeling, West Virginia, October 25, 1966, p. 31.

The Chronicle of a Controversy

LATE one bleak January afternoon in 1953 three eminent prelates of the Protestant Episcopal Church in the United States of America began, over sherry, a conversation that has continued to this day and has come to enlist the whole membership of that church and much of the general public.

The conversation took place in the Cathedral Heights residence of the Bishop of New York, Horace W. B. Donegan. His guests were Henry I. Louttit, then as now Bishop of South Florida, and James A. Pike, then Dean of the Cathedral of St. John the Divine. The two guests were meeting for the first time.

It was the beginning of a warm friendship that has survived many vicissitudes and strange events and persists even now despite Bishop Louttit's decision in the fall of 1966 to initiate charges of heresy against his old friend who was by that time the Resigned Bishop of California, and the most controversial ecclesiastical personality of the times.

The conversation that afternoon, as Bishop Louttit now remembers it—Bishop Pike has no distinct recollections of it—touched upon a controversy involving the University of the South (Sewanee), an institution owned by 21 Episcopal dioceses in 10 Southern states. The trustees of the university had rejected the previous spring a recommendation of the Synod of the Province of Sewanee that Negro students be admitted to its School of Theology, an action that precipitated the resignation of the school's dean and eight of its faculty.

Dean Pike mentioned that he had learned that he was soon to be offered an honorary degree (Doctor of Divinity) by the university and would also be invited as baccalaureate speaker for the following June's commencement exercises. He was, he said, reluctant to accept because he had the impression that the trustees did not seriously intend to desegregate the seminary. Bishop Louttit, himself at that time one of those trustees, assured the Dean that action would shortly be taken that would lead to full integration of the institution, over a period of time. It was his opinion that Dean Pike accepted his assurance, and would, therefore, accept the honor and the invitation.

A few weeks later the university announced the appointment of a new dean of the School of Theology and of replacements for four of the resigned faculty. At about the same time it also announced cancellation of a special meeting of the trustees, scheduled for February, which a number of Southern bishops had requested to discuss the university's policy on race. Instead, the announcement said, a committee of trustees would consider the matter and report at the regular June meeting of the full board.

On February 12, 1953, Dean Pike released to the press a letter to the university's President, Dr. Edward N. McCrady, in which he declined the offer of a degree and refused the invitation to be baccalaureate speaker. He could not, he said, "accept a degree in white divinity." He gave these reasons for his decision:

By deferring consideration of the matter until this June and proceeding first to the procurement of a set of instructors who were willing to fill the ranks without any change in the race policy against which the present faculty witnessed by their resignations, you have for the time being—neatly relieved yourself of the necessity of facing the issue.

I cannot but see in these two events, taken along with certain of your own recent statements, a determination to avoid a reversal or modification of the apartheid policy adopted last June.[1]

This letter of Dean Pike's apparently crossed in the mail a letter from the university formally offering the degree and inviting the Dean to speak. Bishop Louttit regarded this action as a violation of trust, and he has lately said that it was the first of a series of events that established what he calls a "pattern of untrustworthiness" on the part of his friend.²

In June of 1953 the trustees of the University of the South did, in fact, take action that led to the admission of the first Negro student to its School of Theology in the fall of 1954, somewhat more than a year later.

The day after Dean Pike's declination appeared in the press, that year's graduating class of the Sewanee School of Theology sent him the following telegram:

> CONGRATULATIONS ON YOUR DEFENSE OF CHRIST'S CHURCH. FAITH CAN MOVE "MOUNTAINS."³

Sewanee is the Indian word for "mountains."

The Evolution of a Bishop

James Albert Pike was born on February 14, 1913. His mother raised him a Roman Catholic, first in Oklahoma City and later, when the father had died, in Hollywood, California. Devout and conventional in his faith, young Pike served as acolyte, and when the time came, chose as his college the Jesuit University of Santa Clara. He entertained the possibility of studying to become a priest.

He early discerned conflicts between what he was taught in science courses and what was expounded in philosophy classes. When, in a course on apologetics, the Church's teaching on birth control arose he found he could not accept it, and on reflection saw that the doctrine of papal infallibility was at stake. On his own he undertook a study of the biblical and historical arguments pro and con that doctrine, concluding that he should align himself with the minority of bishops at Vatican Council I who could not go along with papal infallibility and so signified by voting "non placet." His doubts were sufficient to persuade him against the priesthood, and following his sophomore year he transferred to U.C.L.A. By 1936 he had received his degrees in Arts and in Law from the University of Southern California, and shortly thereafter was admitted to the bar in California. In 1938, having served as a

Sterling Fellow, he was awarded a degree of Doctor of Sciences of Law from Yale University.

During this secular education Pike became agnostic. "I wasn't antichurch"; he has said, "I just dropped out."[4] Following Yale he accepted appointment as an attorney with the Securities and Exchange Commission in Washington, D.C. By then a "fervent humanist" Pike regarded his assignment as an opportunity for "saving widows and orphans from being robbed by Wall Street."[5] He also got married in 1938 to a girl he had known in Hollywood, but the marriage was not successful, and they were divorced two years later.

His work in Washington led to membership in the bar of the United States Supreme Court, and also to an appointment to the faculty of the George Washington University Law School. One of his students—to whom he gave an A—was Esther Yanovsky, also an agnostic. The two were married in 1942, having composed their own wedding service, strictly legal and utterly without reference to God. The judge who performed the service, however, ignored their wishes, being (as it turned out) a devout Methodist, and he used a service the same as that found in the Episcopal *Book of Common Prayer*.

During most of the war years Pike served in the Navy as an officer, first with Naval Intelligence and later as an attorney for the United States Maritime Commission and the War Shipping Administration. At the same time he experienced a renewed interest in the Church, dropping in occasionally for services at the Episcopal National Cathedral. While still in uniform, in 1944, Pike was ordained a deacon—and later made a curate—at St. John's Church on Lafayette Square near the White House. Admiral Land, then the young deacon's military superior, issued an exceptional order that permitted Pike to wear clerical street attire when appropriate.

In addition to his service at St. John's, Pike also developed a Church-related program for students at Georgetown University. Working with the Reverend Elwyn Smith, Presbyterian campus minister, and the Reverend Howard Johnson (who was later to serve under him as Canon Theologian at St. John the Divine, New York) he soon had a group of students numbering close to one hundred involved in activities that on the campus, at least, stirred up much publicity, and which may have been, therefore, the first of Pike's long series of ecclesiastical spectaculars.

After the war Pike continued at St. John's for a year, attending at the same time, full time, classes at Virginia Theological Seminary just across the Potomac. He then moved to New York City to attend a double summer session at Union Theological Seminary, taking up a residence at General Theological Seminary, where, the following fall, he became both Tutor and Fellow. He studied in both seminaries, but principally Union from which he received his Bachelor of Divinity degree *magna cum laude*. He had not, however, followed a typical academic program. Since he had prepared, under tutors, for canonical examination for ordination as deacon in Washington, he stressed, at Union, advanced courses in theology and ethics under such men as the late Paul Tillich (with whom he maintained a close friendship until the latter's death in 1966), Reinhold Niebuhr and John Bennett. He omitted courses in so-called "practical theology" such as preaching, religious education and parish administration.

In 1946 James A. Pike was ordained to the priesthood by the Bishop of Washington, Angus Dun. Not long afterwards he became rector of Christ Church, Poughkeepsie, New York, a post he held for somewhat more than two years, and during which time he served also as the first chaplain to Episcopal students at Vassar College. Christ Church was a moribund parish when its new priest burst upon the scene, and was anything but that when he left. In the course of a brief, vigorous ministry Pike cultivated the gifts for preaching and apologetics that have distinguished his public ministry ever since.

In 1949 he accepted a call to become chaplain of Columbia University, New York City, and chairman of its Department of Religion, which was non-existent when he came and had a curriculum of 32 courses, an undergraduate major and a master of arts program when he left. His service at Columbia was typically enthusiastic and largely successful (he persuaded, for example, the late Paul Tillich and Georges Florzski to join the faculty as adjunct professors). His attachment to Columbia was to survive his departure from those positions, in that he continued as adjunct professor in religion and law during his tenure as Dean of the Cathedral of St. John the Divine.

In the fall of 1952 Pike became, upon the invitation of the Bishop of New York, Horace W. B. Donegan, dean of the largest Protestant church (and cathedral) in the world. (St. John the Divine is, technically, the largest of all cathedrals, given that St. Peter's in Rome, principal edifice of the Roman Catholic Church, is not officially a cathedral, but a mere—if vast—church.) The post of dean at St. John the Divine had been vacant for twelve years, Bishop Donegan's predecessors, Bishops Manning and Gilbert, having fulfilled the office of dean with the aid of canons.

The Very Reverend James A. Pike, as he was now styled, was to fill that vacancy with remarkable intensity for some six years until his election, in 1958, as Bishop of California.

Only some few months after he assumed the deanship Pike was to meet, as we have said, for the first time and in the apartments of the Bishop of New York, his friend and later nemesis the Bishop of South Florida, Henry I. Louttit.

The Evolution of a Theologian

While he was still rector of Christ Church, Poughkeepsie, Pike was suggested (by Dean Lawrence Rose of General Theological Seminary) to Dr. John Heuss, then Director of the Department of Christian Education of the National Council of the Episcopal Church, as a possible member of the Authors' Committee for *The Church's Teaching*, a projected series of six volumes designed to explicate for adult laymen the faith of the Episcopal Church.

Pike did participate in the work of the first two volumes: *The Holy Scriptures*, the author of which was Dr. Robert Claude Denton, and *Chapters in Church History*, the author of which was Dr. Powel Mills Dawley.

For the third volume the committee first secured a draft from Dr. Pike and Dr. Frederick Q. Shafer, and then assigned the writing of the volume to Dr. W. Norman Pittenger, instructor and later professor of Apologetics at General Theological Seminary and to Dr. Pike, by that time chaplain at Columbia. This volume, which dealt with doctrine, was the most difficult to write (it passed through some ten drafts) and to secure agreement upon, and indeed there was some feeling in the committee that such a work could not be written.

In those days as to a lesser extent now, following the pattern of the "mother" Anglican Church of England, the Episcopal Church in the United States was loosely divided into three parts: "high church," meaning Anglo-Catholic and traditional; "low church," meaning Protestant and evangelical; and "broad church," meaning something that fell somewhere between the others. Pittenger and Pike encountered enormous difficulty reconciling the points of view of the three factions on a matter so sensitive as the central doctrines of the Episcopal faith, and, on occasion, they experienced difficulty agreeing between themselves.

The result was that *The Faith of the Church*, as the third volume was called, proffered what Bishop Pike has recently described as "smooth orthodoxy," and on the more controversial doctrinal issues the authors found, in good Anglican fashion, a formula of words that left room for conflicting interpretations.

The Faith of the Church, first published in 1951, has enjoyed a wide popularity among clergy and laity ever since, having gone through innumerable printings, in hard cover and paperback, and standing even today as a sort of quasi-official reference book for laymen concerned to know what Episcopal doctrines are and mean.[6]

Pike's theological position in 1951, then, was nothing more or less or other than the conventional, generally accepted teachings of the Episcopal Church as they had been received. He did not question whether those teachings were adequate, but only how they might be expounded meaningfully to the faithful. He has said that when he entered the ministry he remained a lawyer who had merely changed clients. He was engaged in forensic apologetics for the orthodox teachings of the Church he served.

Dean Pike exercised the same role as preacher at the Cathedral of St. John the Divine, where his lively sermons on church doctrine—and his provocative sermons on controversial social issues—frequently attracted congregations of 4,000, an achievement seldom matched before or since his six-year incumbency, and on special liturgical occasions filled the church to its capacity of 10,000. He became during those years something of an unofficial spokesman for the Episcopal Church on doctrinal and on social issues, and in the process also became an ecclesiastical celebrity, rivaled in fame only by Roman Catholic Bishop Fulton J. Sheen. His celebrity, in fact, assumed nationwide proportions when he conducted for some years a successful weekly TV program, "The Dean Pike Show."

During his years as dean Pike published (sometimes in collaboration with others) a series of short books for laymen on subjects of general interest—marriage, anxiety—which tended to be self-help books that outlined a problem and attempted to give the answer as derived from the orthodox teaching of the church.[7] In nothing that he wrote or said during the decade 1950–1960, whatever other attack might have been made upon him, did even the suggestion of heresy arise. The controversy which increasingly attached to his name derived largely from positions which he took on social issues, beginning with the "white divinity" episode involving the University of the South.

Theologically, Dean Pike could not have been more conventional, and he remained that as Bishop of California during the first year of his episcopate. More and more knowledgeable *about* theology, more and more preoccupied *with* theology, he continued astonishingly undisposed to challenge the doctrines of his church, especially given his bent for inquiry and his lifelong history of intellectual skepticism.

Until 1960, or thereabouts, it is not inexact to say that Pike was not a theologian at all, but rather a man in process of becoming a theologian. Until then his mind did not operate theologically—that is, wondering what is the truth about this or that doctrine, but, rather, worked forensically—that is, assuming this or that doctrine is true how to defend and account for it. Dean Pike was chief attorney for the defense of the faith.

He had not stopped to wonder if his client was innocent.

The Evolution of a "Heretic"

In 1959 *The Christian Century*, a Protestant "ecumenical weekly" periodical, launched a series of articles by prominent churchmen under the general heading "How My Mind Has

Changed."⁸ It was intended that the contributors—including not less a diversity of personalities than, for example, Reinhold Niebuhr, Billy Graham, Martin Luther King, Jr., Will Herberg, Karl Barth, John C. Bennett, *and* James A. Pike—describe how their views had changed radically or otherwise and *theologically* during the decade preceding, roughly the period 1950–1960.

Reflecting recently on his participation in that series, Bishop Pike has said: "In trying to find some ways that my mind had *changed*—trying to, I guess, indicate some growth—I became aware that it *had* changed."

Pike's contribution to the series was entitled "Three-Pronged Synthesis." He concedes that he just "put it down" and "didn't spend much time on it." His executive assistant at the time, the Reverend Richard Byfield, warned him that what he had written was "rather far out," and the Bishop recalls that he revised it in a "somewhat more conservative direction," and then "sent it off."

However much time he spent on it, the article marked a turning point in his theology, containing as it does, seminally, most of the doctrinal skepticism that was to emerge in ensuing years in his public expressions. In the article can be found, tentatively stated, disenchantment with classical doctrine on the Trinity, the Virgin Birth, and Salvation through Christ alone.

He summed up his theological posture at that moment in this paragraph:

(1) I am more broad church, that is, I know less than I used to think I knew; I have become in a measure a "liberal" in theology. (2) I am more low church, in that I cannot view divided and particular denominations as paramount in terms of the end-view of Christ's church, and I do regard the gospel as the all-important and as the *only final* thing. And (3) I am more high church, in that I more value the forms of the continuous life of the Holy Catholic Church as best meeting the needs of people and best expressing the unity of Christ's church. These forms include liturgical expression and the episcopate.⁹

The article was composed in that style of jaunty irreverence and putative vulgarity for which the Bishop has become noted. "I want," he remarks at one point, "to believe in a *big* God"; at another point he introduced one of those phrases that spice his public speeches and infuriate his more fastidious brethren: "The church was centered around the truth of the gospel, but the Bible came along as a sort of *Reader's Digest* anthology."[10] Nonetheless, the piece stands as the first published indication of a disposition on Bishop Pike's part to inquire into the validity of the traditional doctrines and teachings of his church.

After the article was sent in but before its appearance in *The Christian Century*, Bishop Pike attended the 1960 meeting of the House of Bishops in Dallas, Texas. Included in the business to be considered by the House was a proposed Pastoral Letter on doctrine, a draft for which was presented by a committee chaired by Bishop Angus Dun (Bishop Louttit was among the members). The matter was considered in executive session—that is, the discussion is not a part of public record—but it is known that a number of bishops took exception to portions of the draft. Bishop Pike, mindful of his "rather far out" article, was particularly alert to points in the pastoral with which he was not in accord.

The letter as issued on November 16, 1960—and it was not significantly amended from the draft version—is a rigid reaffirmation of the Creeds (especially the Nicene Creed), that is to say, the historic formulations of the fundamental doctrines of the Catholic tradition. Pains were taken by the authors of the letter to distinguish the theological immutability of the Creeds from their susceptibility to cultural mutations, notably changes in understanding occasioned by developments in science. Thus, the letter deems it fitting solemnly to acknowledge:

When the Creeds speak of the "descent" of the Eternal Son to take our manhood into union with Himself, or of the "Ascension" of the risen Incarnate Son, we know that "descent" and "ascent" are movements between God and man and not in inter-stellar space.[11]

The letter further acknowledges a limited authority to historians, and even to photographers:

Historians may correct the biblical and so the creedal description of an historical event as to its date and its photographable details without impugning the revelation of God which breaks through and out of that event.[12]

THE CHRONICLE OF A CONTROVERSY   13

Long, turgid, and tedious, the Dallas Pastoral Letter, as issued, is a proclamation by the House of Bishops that " . . . our Church is irrevocably committed to the historic creeds and regards the Nicene Creed as it was affirmed at the Council of Chalcedon in 451 A.D., as an indispensable norm for the Christian Faith."[13]

No wonder, then, that Bishop Pike, conscious of reservations in his own mind concerning at least three creedal statements, told the House that if the letter was adopted as presented he would be found heretical. (He appears, therefore, to be the first person, certainly the first person in the House, ever to have associated his name with heresy or possible heresy.) He was invited to appear before the committee, and sought, with little success, to have it amended. The committee did insert one sentence that might be construed as a concession of some latitude with respect to St. Luke's (though not St. Matthew's) account of the Virgin Birth:

St. Luke, for instance, was an evangelist more than a historiographer.[14]

Bishop Pike (and some other bishops) were sufficiently displeased with the letter finally brought to the House for a vote that they planned to debate it, and attempt amendments from the floor; if possible they hoped to prevent a vote.

Discussion of the letter, as Bishop Pike recalls it, was severely curtailed, in part because the bishops were anxious to dispose of the business in order to be on time for a party being given in their honor at a country club in Fort Worth. A motion to table—that is, a motion to defer indefinitely any action on the proposal—was narrowly defeated. The Presiding Bishop, Arthur Lichtenberger, entertained a motion on the whole question—that is, a motion to vote the proposal up or down at once. This motion was carried. Those bishops who had planned to debate or to offer amendments were not heard. "So," Bishop Pike recalls, "we were off to Fort Worth—but with a very uncomfortable feeling on the part of a good many of us as to what was affirmed in that pastoral letter."

One month later, on December 21, 1960, "Three-Pronged Synthesis" appeared in *The Christian Century*.

Reaction was swift, widespread, highly publicized, and often vehement. In an editorial on January 16, 1961, *Christianity Today*, a conservative weekly journal, while conceding that Bishop Pike had not explicitly denied the Trinity, the Virgin Birth, or Salvation through Christ alone, sharply rebuked him for his expressed doubts about those doctrines. They seemed especially disturbed that he had suggested it might be a favorable assumption that Joseph was the human father of Jesus.[15] ("Who else?" the Bishop has more recently inquired.)

On January 28, 1961, the Reverend W. Bruce Wirtz, secretary of the Tri-Convocation Clericus of Albany, Dublin, and Thomasville, Georgia, an association of 15 Episcopal clergymen, dispatched a letter to the Bishop of Georgia, Albert R. Stuart. The clericus asserted that Bishop Pike had expressed "disbelief in the Virgin Birth of our Lord, the doctrine of the Holy Trinity as stated by the church and the necessity of salvation through Christ alone." Their letter further alleged that the Bishop had made statements, "in contradiction of the clear and definitive statements" of the Pastoral Letter issued by the House of Bishops in Dallas the previous November. "Such a theological position as the Bishop of California expresses," the letter went on, "calls into grave doubt his suitability for exercising jurisdiction as a bishop of this church."

Bishop Stuart was specifically importuned by the clericus to bring their charges, amounting to charges of heresy, before the next meeting of the House of Bishops "for such action as the bishops, our chief pastors and defenders of the faith, shall see fitting and just."[16] Inasmuch as charges of heresy may be formally lodged against a bishop only by three (or more) of his fellow bishops the matter now reposed directly on the conscience of Bishop Stuart. Heresy charges not having been filed against an Episcopal bishop since the trial and conviction of William Montgomery Brown in 1924, it is not surprising that Bishop Stuart delayed a decision.

In a statement given over the telephone to *The New York Times*, also on January 29, 1961, Bishop Pike responded in this way to the Georgia charges:

Both as a bishop and as a lawyer I can safely say that my comments in *The Christian Century* are within the bounds of doctrinal orthodoxy as judged by such norms as the House of Bishops' recent pastoral letter on doctrine, "The Faith of the Church," officially issued by the National Council of our church, and "Doctrine in the Church of England," the report of the commission appointed by the Archbishops of Canterbury and York.

Our Lord has reminded us that those who do the will of the Father will know the doctrine. It would be interesting for *The New York Times* to inquire of this clericus as to how many of their churches are racially integrated following the clear and official teaching of this church and the Anglican Communion.

The Bible also reminds us that doing the truth is as important as saying the truth.[17]

Neither Bishop Stuart nor Mr. Wirtz, the *Times* reported, could be reached for comment.

On February 2, the Georgia chapter of the American Church Union, an association of conservative—"high church"—clergy, unanimously endorsed the charges made by the clericus and urged Bishop Stuart to lay the charges before the next meeting of the House of Bishops.[18]

The House of Bishops next met in Detroit, Michigan, in late September, 1961; the House of Deputies met concurrently, it being the occasion of a triennial General Convention of the Episcopal Church. Bishop Stuart, after long deliberation, elected not to bring the charges before his brother bishops.

A compromise, instead, was arranged, and on September 20 the deputation (or delegation) of the Diocese of Georgia presented to the House of Deputies the following resolution:

Resolved, The House of Bishops concurring, that this 60th General Convention of the Protestant Episcopal Church do affirm its belief in, and obedience to, the Christian faith as set forth by the Council of Nicea and affirmed at the Council of Chalcedon in 451 A.D., and as represented in the Pastoral Letter issued by the House of Bishops meeting in Dallas in the year of our Lord, 1960.[19]

This was adopted and communicated to the House of Bishops which did concur after accepting an amendment from the Bishop Coadjutor of Alabama striking out the words "Council of Nicea and affirmed at the Council of Chalcedon in 451 A.D." and substituting the words "Apostles' and Nicene Creeds." The deputies concurred.[20]

The supposed affirmation of the Council of Chalcedon had somehow become, apparently, an irrelevance.

On September 27, 1961, a resolution was offered to the House of Deputies by the Reverend Canon Gordon E. Gillett of Quincy (Illinois) which was by implication, though not by name, critical of the theological views of W. Norman Pittenger and James A. Pike. The resolution, however, called merely for the deputies to urge clergy to hold and keep the Christian Faith. The Reverend Morris F. Arnold of Southern Ohio moved to table the resolution, a division was called for, and the vote recorded as: Ayes, 335; Noes, 143. The resolution was tabled.[21]

The charges of the Georgia clericus against the Bishop of California were not, in effect, considered by either House of the 60th General Convention, and there, for the moment, the matter of his alleged heresies rested.

The Evolution of a Pastor

On the occasion of the consecration of James A. Pike as Bishop of California in Grace Cathedral, San Francisco, on Ascension Day, May 15, 1958, a sermon entitled "Bishops—Bound and Free" was preached by Dean Pike's old friend, the Very Reverend John B. Coburn, Dean of the Episcopal Theological School, Cambridge, Massachusetts.

The election of Pike as Bishop of California, even when one assumes the guidance of the Holy Spirit, was something of an exceptional event. (Technically, he was elected bishop coadjutor, the incumbent bishop, Karl Morgan Block, being then near retirement. Bishop Block died September 29—St. Michael and All Angels' Day—1958, and Bishop Pike automatically succeeded as diocesan.)[22]

To be elected bishop a candidate must first of all be chosen by the convention of the diocese, representing clergy and laity alike, according to such rules and procedures as that diocese may prescribe. His election must be confirmed by a majority of the Standing Committees and Bishops of all dioceses. The latter vote is confidential, but it is known that in Pike's case the vote was extremely close.

Opposition to his election among other bishops appears to have been based upon a number of reservations, none of which had to do with theology. A few bishops voted negatively wholly because Pike had suffered a divorce and had subsequently remarried. (One bishop has indicated that he so voted especially because Pike's first spouse then resided in San Francisco and if he became bishop there he would be living in the same city with two wives.[23]) Most of the opposition, however, plainly derived from objection to the controversial positions Pike had taken while Dean of the Cathedral of St. John the Divine on a variety of social and political issues.

Some of this opposition was focussed upon his outspoken support of Negro civil rights agitation, but it seems clear that such opposition was confined to a handful of elder Southern bishops. Dean Pike had taken liberal positions on most of the great social issues of the 1950's: McCarthyism, birth control, censorship, alleged Communism in the churches, and so on. The real opposition to his election as bishop derived from those bishops who are persuaded that the church ought not to involve itself in any way in social or political controversy. In many cases it was not that the negative bishops differed from Pike's views, but only that they objected to his making those views public.

However that may be, Dean Pike was elected and did become the 5th Episcopal Bishop of California.

At the close of his consecration sermon Dean Coburn spoke some particular words to "Brother Jim" which were, in a measure, prophetic, despite the fact that they were, perhaps, prosaic.

Pike was, he said, a missionary of "contagious enthusiasm" and he urged him, as bishop, to direct that enthusiasm to those things which are above, lest he lose it to the world.

Pike was also, he said, a controversial person able to "incarnate" himself in a principle without regard to persons, and he urged him, as bishop, to engage in controversy "as a last resort and not as a first resort."

Pike was finally, he said, now a bishop and a bishop in a particular diocese, and he urged him, as bishop, to bind himself to the clergy and people of that diocese, refraining "with God's help" from all but a few of the calls that would come to him from beyond that diocese.[24]

Dean Coburn had chosen, then, to address some last words of pastoral counsel to a brother clergyman before that clergyman was elevated to the highest pastoral office within the gift of the church. Amidst all that bishops do and have to do in the operation of a diocese in twentieth-century America it is too often overlooked that they are first and foremost chief pastors of the clergy and people of Christ. This was not overlooked by Dean Coburn.

Bishop Pike—either heeding the counsel given him or perhaps merely finding his new responsibilities consuming—did confine himself largely and with "contagious enthusiasm" to the affairs and persons of his diocese during the first year or so of his eight-year incumbency. No controversy whatever appears to have attached to his name outside of his new diocese until more than 15 months later his article on doctrine in *The Christian Century* provoked, more by inadvertence than design on his part, a storm of controversy.

Measured by conventional indices Bishop Pike's eight years as diocesan on San Francisco's Nob Hill must be accounted successful. The Diocese of California is so named because it was the first diocese established in that state (California has, in fact, three other dioceses—Northern California, Los Angeles, and San Joaquin) and the territory for which Bishop Pike was responsible consists essentially of San Francisco and several immediately adjacent counties. Even noting that the state of California itself was in process of unusual growth during this same period, the growth of his diocese under Bishop Pike's leadership, when compared with that of other dioceses, was outstanding.

According to the *Episcopal Church Annual*, between 1958 and 1965 the Diocese of California moved from 112 parishes and organized missions to 124, from a membership of 66,817 to 83,486, from a clergy of 175 to 188, and from the celebration of 775 marriages to 1,055. Oddly, during the same interval burials, to use a grimmer test, *declined* from 1,701 to 1,583, an evidence, perhaps, of the liveliness the tireless bishop imparted to his flock.[25]

Applying that most crass and convenient of standards: the

income of the diocese for its own and national church purposes increased from $390,000 in 1958 to $892,000 in 1964.[26] (Income appears to have "peaked" in the latter year, and increments have been marginal ever since, which has led to something of a financial crisis for Pike's successor, the Right Reverend C. Kilmer Myers.) That diocesan income should have more than doubled in six years is the more remarkable when it is considered that during Bishop Pike's incumbency the diocese shifted from an assessment (taxation) method of collecting from its parishes to a system of voluntary contributions. (Given the predicament now confronting Bishop Myers, Pike thinks that shift was probably a mistake.) Even when he was himself embroiled in controversy Bishop Pike never had any great difficulty raising funds for national and diocesan programs.

Symbolic, perhaps, of Pike's reign as diocesan was the completion, under his direction, of Grace Cathedral on San Francisco's Nob Hill, the first of the three non-parochial Episcopal cathedrals in America—the others are in Washington where Pike was ordained and in New York where he was dean—to be completed. A Gothic structure, it had stood since 1928 with a half-finished nave because funds were denied to the then Bishop of California, Edward Lande Parsons, a man of great social conscience active in the American Civil Liberties Union and many other liberal causes. The depression also interfered with raising building funds.

Notable in the now completed cathedral are the stained glass windows. Bishop Parsons is remembered in one. Albert Einstein and John Glenn ("secular saints" Bishop Pike calls them) are included in a series of celerestory windows marking various breakthroughs in knowledge and endeavor—Thurgood Marshall being another. In a "theological reform" window may be found the late Paul Tillich, the late Martin Buber (both friends of Bishop Pike), and Father Karl Rahner, S.J., the distinguished German theologian. In a window devoted to church reform and ecumenism there is a panel that embraces the late Pope John XXIII, the 99th Archbishop of Canterbury, Dr. Geoffrey Francis Fisher—who preached in the cathedral at Bishop Pike's invitation at a service of intercession for Vatican Council II on the eve of its opening— and the former Presiding Bishop of the Episcopal Church, Arthur

Lichtenberger. Situation ethics even finds a place in yet another window: contrasted with St. Paul instructing the slave Philemon to return to his master is an image of the Quaker John Woolman, moving spirit in the abolition of slavery in the British Empire.

In December of 1960 on the opening day of the quadrennial convention of the National Council of Churches USA, which was held in San Francisco, Bishop Pike invited as guest preacher in Grace Cathedral for the Sunday morning service the Reverend Doctor Eugene Carson Blake, then Stated Clerk of the Presbyterian Church USA and now General Secretary of the World Council of Churches.[27] Dr. Blake set forth in that sermon a major plan for church unity that was to lead in April of 1962 to the formation of the Consultation on Church Unity (COCU), a group of leaders of Protestant denominations—initially four and eventually ten denominations were represented—which has formulated plans that would result ultimately in merging those denominations into one institution, called, by its critics, a "superchurch."

In an unusual brief "aftersermon" on that occasion, and in a subsequent press conference, Bishop Pike gave, as he has put it, "the first Amen" to Dr. Blake's proposals. For this reason, the plan is sometimes referred to as "the Blake-Pike proposals," but the Bishop himself is always careful to give full credit to Dr. Blake. On Friday morning of the following week leaders of the four denominations then involved participated in an exceptional eucharistic service in Grace Cathedral presided over by the Right Reverend Leslie Newbiggin.[28] These ecumenical events, far-reaching in their implications, stand as one of the highlights of Bishop Pike's episcopacy.

The Evolution of Candor

Every year during Lent for some years Bishop Pike has undertaken a week of noonday preaching at St. Thomas Church, New York, a fashionable parish on Fifth Avenue. In 1962, responding to the uproar occasioned by the Georgia heresy charges some months earlier, the Bishop preached on doctrine, somewhat defensively, attempting to demonstrate that his theological views did fall within the bounds of Anglican orthodoxy.

In the congregation one noon was Eugene Exman of Harper's who was moved, after the service, to suggest to Bishop Pike that he write a book on doctrine. The proposal appealed, and during the summer of 1962, which he spent in Wellfleet on Cape Cod, the Bishop began to write under the working title "I Believe," a book that would in the end provoke more controversy than it was intended, initially, to dispel.[29]

As he then conceived it, the book was to consist, after an introductory chapter on the nature of belief, of a series of chapters taking particular doctrines as set forth in the Creeds. Each chapter was to subdivide into three parts: What?—meaning what did the doctrine mean; Why?—meaning why should it be believed; and So What?—meaning what are the implications of the doctrine for daily living, for ethics. In Wellfleet that summer the Bishop wrote several chapters following that scheme, but when he got back in the fall to his duties in San Francisco he found he could not go on, and he put it aside.

During the spring of 1963 the Anglican Bishop of Woolwich, John A. T. Robinson, sent Bishop Pike an advance copy of his book *Honest to God*, which had an impact on Bishop Pike comparable to that it was to have on many others after it became, on both sides of the Atlantic, a runaway best-seller.[30] Bishop Pike puts it this way:

I admired his courage; I felt he was getting somehow closer to the point. And it gave me the courage to throw away all the chapters I had written except the one on belief, and to write an entirely different kind of book, which is quite iconoclastic.

In other words, by then, I really had moved on further, even beyond the place where I was, and I decided not to try to come out smelling like a rose on orthodoxy.

The working title "I Believe" was also jettisoned, and the book became *A Time for Christian Candor*.

For the summer of 1963 Bishop Pike accepted charge of the Church of Saint Michael and All Angels (San Miguel y Todas Los Angeles) in Cuernavaca, Mexico, an English-speaking congregation that jointly shared the church with a Mexican congregation. During that summer he returned to his book, now *A Time for*

Christian Candor, which he organized under three new categories: "Creed," "Code," and "Cult." In the writing there emerged for the first time an assertion of a position basic to all of his subsequent work, namely that there is but one absolute—God—and all doctrinal formulations are relative and historically conditioned—as well as all ethical codes, all forms of church polity, all liturgical customs and forms, including all sacraments.

During the previous winter, before reading Robinson's *Honest to God*, and while reflecting upon the impasse he had reached in his own work, Bishop Pike experienced an insight that seems to have affected him after the fashion of a conversion. It came to him that: "God is not arbitrary, and does not make particular decisions." That insight underlies and informs all of the iconoclastic and so-called "reductionist" theology of *A Time for Christian Candor*. The point itself is specifically and carefully developed in Chapter VII of that book under the title "God and the Particular."[31]

Another winter passed in the course of which the book took shape, and in the summer of 1964, correcting page proofs, the Bishop found himself in residence, preaching and celebrating high mass weekly at Trinity Church, Wall Street, New York. He was, he has said, "preaching chapters of the book," and within a few weeks the usually sparse Sunday attendance at Trinity Church grew until the congregations taxed the full capacity of that edifice. Coverage of his sermons in the press, particularly in *The New York Times* was extensive, culminating in his concluding sermon which dealt with the doctrine of the Trinity. The Bishop was plunged into yet another storm of controversy.

In his discussion of the Trinity (in *of all places* Trinity Church) Bishop Pike for the first time publicly characterized the doctrine as "excess baggage." (In his book, more cautious, he is content to suggest that it might be "a heavy piece of luggage.")[32] It is fair to say that no single utterance of the Bishop, before or since, has attracted such intense and widespread hostility from all manner of conservative churchmen. That bulwark of Anglo-Catholic "high church" conservatism, the American Church Union, publicly excoriated the Bishop and demanded that the church do something about him, and, in general, as Pike puts it, "the flak increased."[33]

A Time for Christian Candor, which was published by Harper & Row in November of 1964, does not, except with respect to the doctrine of the Trinity (which it pretty much discards), appear actually to warrant the reputation for extreme theological radicalism which it has acquired. The other creedal doctrines—even the Virgin Birth—would seem to have survived some searching negative scrutiny sufficiently intact to satisfy the requirements, at least technically, of theological orthodoxy. Even the apparent rejection of the trinitarian formula loses some of its "scandalous" properties when read in the context of the Bishop's thoughtful and often respectful attempt to make some sense out of it.[34]

It was in *A Time for Christian Candor*, also, that Pike first invoked II Corinthians 4:7, a text he has made crucial to much of his work ever since: "But we have this treasure in earthen vessels, that the excellency of the power may be of God, and not of us." Equating the "earthen vessels" with—among other things—the doctrinal formulations of the Creeds, he seeks to distinguish the "vessels" or "doctrines" from the "treasure" or "truth" which they were designed to contain. But, for all that his pilgrimage for candor had brought him to this distinction, he nonetheless, as his concluding "Chapter XI: An Apologia for Earthen Vessels" makes very plain, continued to have a concern—even an affection—*for* those earthen vessels, and is at some pains to preserve them wherever he can. The doctrine of the Trinity alone seems, as of this point in Bishop Pike's thinking, to have dropped out altogether.[35]

The Convention in St. Louis

The 61st General Convention of the Protestant Episcopal Church USA—and, in a sense the last, in that the convention accepted an amendment offered by the Bishop of South Florida that the word "Protestant" be expunged from the name of the church—opened in Kiel Auditorium, St. Louis, on October 12, 1964.[36]

The opening was overshadowed, so far as the news media were concerned, by two extra-conventional events.

The day preceding, honoring a longstanding invitation of the

Bishop of Missouri, George Leslie Cadigan, Bishop Pike had preached at both the 9:00 A.M. and the 11:00 A.M. services in St. Louis' Christ Church Cathedral. The earlier service proving to be a corporate communion service for the Episcopal Society for Cultural and Racial Unity, the Bishop preached on race relations. In that sermon he remarked that Southern bishops had, on occasion, deposed priests for little sins involving but a few people, but had never deposed anyone for the large sin of racism involving many people. That statement was to occupy an executive session of the House of Bishops called for the following day by the Bishop of South Florida.

At the later service the Bishop strongly reiterated his doctrinal position, describing the Trinity as an "irrelevancy" and calling for an end to "outdated, incomprehensible, and nonessential doctrinal statements, traditions and codes." Before a packed congregation that included many standees, he said:

The fact is we are in the midst of a theological revolution.

Many of us feel that it is urgent that we rethink and restate the unchanging gospel in terms which are relevant to our day and to the people we would have hear it; not hesitating to abandon or reinterpret concepts, words, images, and myths developed in past centuries when men were operating under different world views and different philosophical structures.

The Apostles achieved the highest percentage of church growth in history though innocent of the niceties of the fifth century doctrine of the Trinity. Who would say that they were not Christian?[37]

Bishop Cadigan, who had audited both sermons from his episcopal throne, expressed to the press praise and appreciation for what Bishop Pike had said. The Bishop of West Missouri, Edward Randolph Welles, was not, however, similarly captivated, and issued a statement suggesting that Pike was a "publicity seeker" with a "deep-rooted martyr complex" who might be "thirsting" for a heresy trial.[38] The latter sermon was also to suffer the examination of an executive session of the House of Bishops, again at the call of the Bishop of South Florida. Bishop Pike, some thought, had thrown down a gauntlet, and Bishop Louttit, for one, was not disposed to let it lie.

Meanwhile, an Episcopal layman from New York City, mindful of the presidential campaign then drawing towards its close, arrived in St. Louis armed with a statement that denounced the Republican candidates for President and Vice President, Senator Barry Goldwater of Arizona and Congressman William Miller of New York, for their alleged "transparent exploitation of racism among white citizens." The Stringfellow Statement, as it came to be called, bore the signatures of some 800 Episcopal clergy and laity, including many who were delegates to the General Convention, not least among them twelve of the bishops, including the Bishop of California, James A. Pike.[39]

The statement was released to the press, after having been apparently reproduced on mimeograph machines in the convention press room, and it created something of a national furor. Senator Goldwater was understandably especially distressed since he is himself an Episcopalian. Although the statement carefully defined itself as an action only of its signatories and not of the General Convention, the press sometimes neglected to report this, and it was widely construed as an official position of the Episcopal Church. This incident also was to occupy both the House of Bishops and the House of Deputies during the next several days, particularly the latter's Committee on National and International Problems.

These matters, and some others, were subjects for a series of executive sessions of the bishops throughout the week. Such discussions not being on the public record they can be recovered only from the recollections of bishops who were present, but any resolutions issuing from those discussions are recorded in the journal of the convention.[40]

In one such session Bishop Louttit alleged that Bishop Pike in his early sermon in the cathedral had asserted that no Southern bishop would depose a man for racism; he demanded that Pike apologize to the House for this statement. Bishop Pike pointed out that he had said only that no Southern bishop *had* deposed a man for racism. He asked any bishop who had to so signify, and receiving no response declined to apologize. The bishops were not disposed to pursue the matter.

In the closed session Bishop Welles of West Missouri read to the House his statement to the press responding to Bishop Pike's sermon on doctrine. Bishop Pike replied that he was not aware of desiring a heresy trial, nor was he conscious of seeking publicity, and that as to his unconscious motives he could not say, adhering to St. Paul's precept to judge no man, not even himself. He added that there was but One to whom "all hearts are open, all desires known, and from whom no secrets are hid"—"the Great Psychoanalyst"—who was neither the Bishop of West Missouri nor the Bishop of California.

The bishops, finding themselves in some disarray respecting this issue, resolved to appoint a Special Committee on the Faith of the Church. This committee, duly constituted, was chaired by the Bishop of Michigan, Richard S. M. Emrich, and included the Bishops of Virginia, Northern Indiana, Rochester and the Suffragan Bishop of Long Island. Their task was not an easy one. It was clear that they were to find a formula of words that would effectively disavow Bishop Pike's doctrinal erraticism without invoking the awful specter of heresy charges. Their deliberations, during which Pike at his own request was invited once to proffer his own views, consumed better than a week.

Concurrently, again in executive session, another issue of some delicacy arose. Aware that in connection with the civil rights movement tactics of civil disobedience were proliferating in the land, some bishops, for differing reasons, felt the House should take some position. This matter was ultimately brought to the floor of the House, in open session, in the form of two somewhat conflicting position papers, one entitled "On Civil Disobedience" offered by the Bishop of South Florida, the other entitled "On Christian Obedience" offered by the Bishop of Bethlehem (Pennsylvania), Frederick John Warnecke.[41] After protracted, inconclusive discussion Bishop Louttit moved that both papers be referred to the Special Committee on the Faith of the Church, to which would be added, for this purpose only, the Suffragan Bishop of Massachusetts, John Melville Burgess, then the only Negro in the House assigned within the United States, and the Bishop Coadjutor of Alabama, George Mosley Murray, the latter, presumably, for balance.

On October 21 Bishop Emrich of Michigan, reporting for the special committee, offered to the House two position papers:

Proclamation of the Faith

Whereas recent theological discussion has raised certain questions of good order in the Church, we affirm that the issue before us is not any specific doctrine. It is primarily the way in which the Christian Faith (which is greater than any of us and into which we as individuals grow) is presented to the world.

As Bishops, we are obligated by oath to hold and proclaim that Faith. This House does not have the means of evaluating in detail the manner of each Bishop's or Priest's interpretation of the Faith. Nor do we deny—indeed we affirm—the importance of relating the Christian Faith to the growth of human thought and knowledge, and the part that individuals play in this process.

However, this House is concerned that in the public presentation of the Faith, no Bishop or Priest, either in what he says or in the manner in which he says it, denies the Catholic Faith, or implies that the Church does not mean the truth which it expresses in its worship. For us, the criterion of what constitutes the Christian Faith is the corporate consciousness of the Body guided by the Spirit down the ages, in preference to the necessarily limited views of any man or generation living or dead.

On Christian Obedience

Christian teaching holds that civil authority is given by God to provide order in human society, and that just human law is a reflection of immutable divine law which man did not devise. Under all normal circumstances, therefore, Christians obey the civil law, seeing in it the will of God. Yet it must be recognized that laws exist which deny these eternal and immutable laws. In such circumstances, the Church and its members, faithful to Scripture, reserve the right to obey God rather than man.

Thus, the Church recognizes the right of any persons to urge the repeal of unjust laws by all lawful means, including participation in *peaceful* demonstrations. If and when the means of legal recourse have been exhausted, or are demonstrably inadequate, the Church

recognizes the right of all persons, for reasons of informed conscience, to disobey such laws, so long as such persons
  a) accept the legal penalty for their action,
  b) carry out their protest in a non-violent manner, and
  c) exercise severe restraint in using this privilege of conscience, because of the danger of lawlessness attendant thereon.
Before Christians participate in such actions, they should seek the will of God in prayer and the counsel of their fellow Christians.[42]

Both papers were adopted, and the bishops had spoken with notable prudence on two delicate issues, leaving, however, the question of heresy and the problem of obedience somewhat dangling.

The incident of the Stringfellow statement on racism in the presidential campaign was confronted mainly in the House of Deputies, which after much discussion and confusion accepted a resolution, the bishops concurring, in effect acknowledging that the statement was, in fact, a private action of the signatories, regretting that this had been widely misunderstood, and reaffirming that the Episcopal Church is officially neutral as respects any and all political campaigns. An attempt to censure Stringfellow, who was not a delegate to the convention, failed.[43]

Meanwhile, earlier in the convention, Bishop Pike, distressed by the personal attack on him by his brother from West Missouri, had invited Bishop Welles, after morning Communion, for a private breakfast in his rooms. The two bishops had what seems to have been a harmonious conversation. Pike pointed out that after a certain point publicity is not sought; it simply surrounds a man wherever he goes, whether or not he seeks it. Having long since passed that point, Bishop Pike had done what he could to control the publicity he inevitably did attract. He had, for instance, hired a man in his diocese whose job it was to highlight other news in the diocese and to regulate the bishop's own exposure to the various news media. Bishop Welles accepted this explanation.

The two men then agreed that, in consultation with some other bishops, they would prepare a document for the House which might unruffle feathers and point towards some constructive solution to the doctrinal crisis Bishop Pike had provoked. On October

21 the result of that joint initiative was adopted by the House in the form of a resolution offered by C. Kilmer Myers, Suffragan Bishop of Michigan:

Resolved, That the Presiding Bishop appoint a Theological Committee, composed of members of the House, the purpose of which Committee shall be to engage in continuing dialogue with contemporary theologians; and that this Committee report from time to time to the House of Bishops, in order that this House may be better informed as to the nature of the crisis in the relationship between the language of Theology and that of modern culture.[44]

This action of the House seemed to move in a direction Bishop Pike had long sought to lead it: it appeared that future meetings of the bishops would discuss theology as such. The action prompted another member of the House, on the other hand, to this perplexed inquiry: "You mean we're going to talk about God?"

Two other matters, pertinent here, one sad and one solemn, also seized the bishops during the St. Louis convention. On the opening day, October 12, they received the resignation of their Presiding Bishop, the Most Reverend Arthur Lichtenberger, even then so worn by Parkinson's disease that his moving farewell address had to be read for him by the Bishop Coadjutor of Central New York. Five days later, on October 17, in Christ Church Cathedral the bishops gathered in the strictest privacy to elect the 22nd Presiding Bishop of the Episcopal Church. Prior speculation as to the probable choice—from among six or eight possibilities— gravitated around two men: the Director of the Overseas Department of the Church, the Right Reverend Stephen F. Bayne, Jr. and the Bishop of South Florida, the Right Reverend Henry I. Louttit. The secret balloting was to yield, however, an unexpected result: the Bishop of Texas, the Right Reverend John Elbridge Hines.

Bishop Hines was fated (or elected) to preside over the most divisive controversy the House of Bishops had experienced in more than forty years.

On the closing day of the convention, October 23, the Bishop of West Missouri offered, and the House voted:

Resolved, That the House of Bishops express its hearty appreciation to the Bishop of Michigan for his irenic contributions to our deliberations.[45]

This gesture to Bishop Emrich, despite its unimpersonal grammatical flaw, may have been the only genuinely irenic moment of the convention.

The Intervention of a Poetaster

There is resident in Phoenix, Arizona, a retired septuagenarian Episcopal priest, the Reverend Frank M. Brunton, whose active ministry was spent in South Florida, where he remains canonically resident—meaning he continues under the discipline of the Bishop of South Florida—though he has been licensed to officiate as a priest in Arizona by the Bishop of Arizona, John J. M. Harte.

Father Brunton has found in his retirement a new purpose as self-appointed flagellant and scourge of Bishop Pike, whom he considers a heretic and an enemy of the Christian faith. Father Brunton might be dismissed as an eldering fanatic, were it not that his lucidity seems intact and his fanaticism sometimes whimsical. Be that as it may, Father Brunton has played a rather remarkable role in fanning those flames that not a few other Episcopalians hope may eventually consume the Bishop and all that he represents.

Father Brunton, conceding that he is no poet, nonetheless is persuaded that he is endowed with a gift for rhymed verse. In this pursuit he has been influenced by Samuel Butler, a seventeenth-century English poet noted for *Hudibras,* a satirical attack on Puritanism, parts of which are composed in sophisticated mock-heroic octosyllabic couplets. Father Brunton seems to feel that mockery thus—or rather similarly—purveyed will dispose of Bishop Pike, and for some years he has weekly conveyed a verse to California, widely circulated elsewhere in the church, which takes to task the man he now and then calls "Anti-Christ."

It would serve neither Bishop Pike nor Father Brunton nor the history of English letters to rehearse here the good father's astonishing output of scurrility. An example will more than suffice. It is reproduced precisely as the Bishop received it.

WE'RE SICK OF YOU, BISOP [sic] PIKE.

This news I think you will not like
But you shall have it, bishop pike
For many years the world has heard
Your dissertations and your word
On subjects all—though like as not
The things you say are simply rot
High sounding yes, but meaning dense
And lacking quite in common sense
And nowat last you have your due
The whole world is sick of you.

Your fames's a very shoddy fame
We're wearied of your very name
Your photograph, your noxious face
A crowding good newspaper space
The world is sick as it can be
Of you and of your blasphemy
We're sick up to our necks
With all your heresy and sex
We're patient, but you've burst the dyke [sic]
We're soul sick of you bishop pike.

You make us sick with might and main
For purity's gone down the drain
(You've told us that in College Halls)
We're sick of homosexual balls
We're sick of news that does you list
As pike, the pulpit atheist
We're sick of all you say and do
And most of all, WE'RE SICK OF YOU!

F. M. Brunton[46]
[signature]

If Father Brunton's command of octosyllabics seems weak, his grasp on invective is manifestly secure. It is a measure of his pathological antipathy to the Bishop that on the occasion of the death of the latter's son in 1966, Father Brunton saw fit to dispatch the following "condolence": "Thank God for one less pike."[47]

Bishop Louttit, queried about this priest for whom he bears canonical responsibility, affirmed that Father Brunton's ministry in the Diocese of South Florida had been exceptional in its concern for the poor and its attention to parish necessities. As bishop, he had, he said, many times admonished Father Brunton to desist from the distribution of his "doggerel." Those admonitions having gone unheeded, Bishop Louttit has not felt it appropriate to take any other action respecting "a good and elderly priest."[48]

Early in the summer of 1965 Bishop Pike announced that it was his intention to ordain a deaconess of his diocese, Mrs. Phyllis Edwards, as a perpetual deacon of the Church. This seems to have provoked Father Brunton to move from poetry to action. He went to the Reverend Paul B. Urbano, Rector of All Saints Church, Phoenix, suggesting a petition to the House of Bishops charging Bishop Pike with heresy, and the rector encouraged him to proceed. A petition was drafted, Father Urbano modified it, and Father Brunton, having "more leisure," circulated it among clergy in the Phoenix area. He would, he says, have done the same in Tucson but his leisure did not suffice.

Meanwhile, cautious to conform to the channels of the church, the petitioners sought the blessing of the Bishop of Arizona. In a letter to *The Arizona Republic*, printed August 25, 1965, Father Brunton reports it this way:

Of course, before doing anything else, we had to notify Bishop Harte and get his approval, and he gave it wholeheartedly. As the petition would have to go through his office, we did not ask, or expect his signature. He had to be neutral, but he was good enough to call me "a valiant warrior for the Church Faith," and say he was proud of me. I fear this description was very much exaggerated, but I confess it pleased me very much.[49]

In the end fourteen clergy in the Phoenix area did sign the petition, it was forwarded to Bishop Harte's office, and, disdaining the prudence Bishop Stuart had followed in dealing with the Georgia charges, the Bishop promptly indicated he *would* forward the charges to the House of Bishops. (One of the fourteen signatories to the petition subsequently withdrew his name, and, in a letter of apology to Bishop Pike, said he had signed it without having read it. He added that he was not, anyhow, an Episcopalian, and so "didn't have any right" to sign it.[50])

The petition itself (which may be found in the Appendix) consisted of a conglomeration of accusations, for which no evidence or documentation was provided. Having taken exception to Bishop Pike's announced intention to ordain a deaconess (which did not involve heresy), the petition went on to charge the Bishop with repudiation of the Virgin Birth, denial of the Holy Trinity and the Incarnation, denial of the empty tomb and the bodily Resurrection and Ascension, denial that the Creeds contain articles of faith, and with having failed to celebrate in his cathedral the Feast of the Annunciation. The petitioners, "weary of seeing the sheep dispersed by one of their own shepherds," urgently requested their "fathers in God" to challenge Bishop Pike to repudiate the alleged teachings, and if that should fail, to bring him to trial, and if he were found guilty, to deprive him of his "bishopric."

Bishop Harte received this document on July 28, 1965, and on the following day forwarded it to the Chairman of the Committee on the Dispatch of Business of the House of Bishops, Henry I. Louttit, Bishop of South Florida.

Respecting the charge that Bishop Pike had not celebrated the Feast of the Annunciation in his cathedral, the verger of Grace Cathedral, Mr. Charles Agneau, in a letter of August 18, 1965, to the editor of *The Living Church*, which had covered this bizarre episode comprehensively, protested that, in fact, on the most previous Feast of the Annunciation Grace Cathedral had actually celebrated Holy Communion four times (one a choral eucharist), eighty-one persons having received that sacrament, and additionally morning prayer was sung and evening prayer read, a total of six services, most unusual in any church on a weekday, the Feast having fallen, as it generally does, on a day other than Sunday.[51] Bishop Pike has since remarked that the Feast of the Annunciation was probably not more thoroughly observed on that occasion in any of the other more than 8,000 churches in the Episcopal Church.[52]

The Bishop himself issued a lengthy point by point refutation of the Arizona charges. (The full text of his rejoinder appeared in the

October, 1965, edition of *The Churchman,* a liberal monthly journal published out of St. Petersburg, Florida.) He denied each charge, pointing frequently to *A Time for Christian Candor* to demonstrate that he had, in fact, said something quite different from what he was accused of saying. As to the Trinity, for example, he noted that he had claimed only that the classical formulation of that doctrine was "unintelligible and misleading to men of our day." He added: "I affirm of God all that has been affirmed of the 'three Persons.'" His statement concluded: "I have spoken and written openly; I stand on the record."[53]

The House of Bishops, in special session, convened in Glacier Park, Montana, on September 7, 1965, for a three day meeting that to the dismay of some of the bishops was, once again, overshadowed by the Bishop of California.

Glacier National Park being the home of the Blackfeet Indians, the Bishop of South Virginia, speaking for the Committee on Hospitality, at the closing banquet in East Glacier Lodge, began his expressions of appreciation this way:

Our song of thanks and honor is lifted to our hosts and their squaws of "The land of Shining Mountains, where the skies are bluer, the handclasp firmer, and the smile broader," and no one would exchange it for a small green grave elsewhere—with apologies to each chief, brave, and squaw of the Blackfeet who ever lived, does live, or shall live on reservation or in trading post or village.[54]

The meaning may be elusive, but the intent is clearly gracious, an indication that bishops are typically gracious towards the world even though they are sometimes less than gracious among themselves.

On the first day of the meeting the Bishop of Bethlehem, rising to a point of personal privilege, requested that the House restrain the practice of executive sessions, arguing that open discussions generally redound to the greater benefit of the Church at large. In this statement Bishop Warnecke reflected a concern of a number of bishops that the Chairman of the Committee on the Dispatch of Business, Bishop Louttit, at whose call the executive sessions in St. Louis had been held, was attempting to conceal unpleasant discussion from the public. As chairman of that committee Bishop Louttit also had responsibility to report to the press on what happened in executive sessions, an office some of the bishops, including Bishop Pike, felt he had used to "slant" what had happened in a direction that conformed to *his* position. In any event, the point raised by Bishop Warnecke does seem to have introduced a measure of the restraint he proposed.[55]

Responding to the resolution adopted in St. Louis, the Presiding Bishop had, just prior to the meeting in Glacier Park, appointed a Theological Committee, chaired by Bishop Emrich, and including Bishops Dun, Bayne, Sherman, Klein and Pike. It was to this committee that the House promptly referred the Arizona charges. Bishop Pike was "excused," and Bishop Dun being absent, Bishop Creighton temporarily sat on the committee.[56]

Bishop Emrich denied repeated requests by Bishop Pike that he be allowed to answer the charges before the committee, and only after the committee had completed its report was he summoned before it.

On the evening of September 8 the Bishop found himself in a small, dingy room in the basement of East Glacier Lodge, a room illuminated by one naked light bulb dangling from a cord in the ceiling. Bishop Creighton did not attend, but the other bishops were seated in a row "stone-faced and very solemn." There were no attempts to exchange the customary greetings, and without delay Bishop Emrich directed that Bishop Pike read the report.

The first four paragraphs, which, as things turned out, were to constitute, with minor modification, the whole report as received by the House and voted, in effect set aside the Arizona charges, affirmed the value of theological inquiry, and distinguished the teachings of any one person from those of the Church as an official body. Bishop Pike had no difficulty accepting those paragraphs. Then, however, as he puts it: "I came to the 'but.' Looking back, I see that the first part of the report was very plus towards me but would not have been had it not gone on to condemn me. It's like telling you you're a wonderful, wonderful fellow *but* . . . you have B.O." He read the balance of the report, which has never been made public, with mounting incredulity.

In it, as he recalls, he was accused of "self-aggrandizement" and "publicity-seeking" and of "unilateral teaching and action." The Bishop interrupted his reading frequently to rebut such charges, and the other bishops listened but proffered no comments and refused to enter into a discussion. After each such intervention by Bishop Pike the only response came from Bishop Emrich who said repeatedly: "Read on."

Concerning self-aggrandizement and publicity-seeking Bishop Pike repeated the defense he had made against similar charges by Bishop Welles in St. Louis. With respect to unilateral teaching and action he took the position that all changes in thought begin with a unilateral initiative on someone's part, that discussion ensues and eventually—"maybe a hundred years later"—an official body takes a definitive position. He attempted to discuss specifically the Arizona charges but the bishops were not interested. He told them that in respect to doctrinal issues he had in his room the draft manuscript of a new book—*What Is This Treasure*—which explored his views very thoroughly, but the bishops were not interested in that either, and the sole comment came from Bishop Emrich: "What—*another* book?"

Finally, when he had finished reading a lengthy excoriation of himself, Bishop Emrich asked if he had any changes to suggest. He replied that his objections were not to the style, but rather to the content, which he considered personally obnoxious and a reflection on his integrity. He told the committee that, should it present the report, he would have no choice but to oppose it from the floor and to hope others would do the same. Abruptly, and without any amenities, the confrontation ended, and Bishop Pike repaired to the rooms of the Bishop of Pennsylvania, Robert Lionne De Witt.

Other bishops friendly to Pike's cause gathered, and there was conversation about various parliamentary procedures that might be followed to amend, table, defeat, or otherwise prevent the House from taking action on the report. It was decided that two of the bishops—Craine of Indianapolis and Mosley of Delaware—would confer the following morning with Bishop Emrich in an effort to persuade him of the unwisdom of presenting the report, especially in light of Bishop Warnecke's earlier remonstrance against actions taken in closed sessions, and also because it seemed likely that the report would not find acceptance in the House.

That conference, which ultimately included Bishop Pike, arrived at a compromise. The committee would report only the first four paragraphs of its statement, and Bishop Pike would make a brief response of reassurance to the House. Bishop Emrich, obviously in distrust of his brother from California, insisted that after he had read the committee report—but before he moved its adoption—Bishop Pike would have to read his statement. That procedure prevailed, and on the afternoon of September 9 the committee report was read, Bishop Pike responded, the House voted affirmatively, and there was great acclamation and relief. (The committee's report and Bishop Pike's response may be found in the Appendix.)

Concluding his remarks, which had been prepared with the assistance of Bishop Craine, Bishop Pike reaffirmed his "loyalty to the Doctrine, Discipline, and Worship of the Episcopal Church." He has since regretted having done so, considering that it was, in fact, a denigration of himself—"like," he has said, "an immigrant taking the oath of citizenship a second time because someone raised a question about his belonging to left-wing political groups."

The Bishop shared the general relief of the House, and had "a very good feeling about what had taken place," until, some months later, on a plane from London to Israel, it occurred to him that nothing in fact had been settled, that the harmony achieved was more artificial than real, and, that in any event, Father Brunton's charges had neither been heard, nor answered.

Father Brunton, meanwhile, had not even a temporary "good feeling" about what had transpired in Glacier Park. Shortly after the meeting ended he issued yet another bit of doggerel condemning all of the bishops for apostasy because they had failed to cast into outer darkness his principal subject of calumny. (Father Brunton has more recently mellowed, and allows that only 80 percent of the bishops are apostate.)

Bishop Pike has a somewhat variant view of the glacial events in Montana those strange few days in September of 1965: "My jaw got in the way of somebody's fist, and therefore I am the one to blame for the assault."

The Case of the Reverend Mrs. Phyllis Edwards

Sprightly though matronly, Mrs. Phyllis Edwards, widowed mother of four grown children, and a grandmother, having decided in her 40's to devote herself to the service of others, attended theological school, and having graduated became a deaconess of the Episcopal Church, first in the Diocese of Olympia and subsequently in the Diocese of California.

Her service has been distinguished for its adherence to the primary functions of deaconesses in teaching and social work, tasks she has undertaken mainly in the Mission District of San Francisco. An activist, she participated (with the Suffragan Bishop of California, George Richard Millard) in the celebrated march out of Selma, during the racial disorders there, and, later, joined in the picketing of the Crown Zellerbach Corporation's San Francisco offices in relation to that company's alleged discriminatory policies in Bogalusa, Louisiana.

Mrs. Edwards' conscientious dedication to her work, and her singular devotion to racial justice, won her the especial esteem of Bishop Pike and of Bishop Millard. Consequently, in the summer of 1965 Bishop Pike announced his intention to ordain her to the ministry as a perpetual deacon.

This announcement touched off another storm of controversy, not least a part of which was the decision of Father Brunton to inaugurate his charges of heresy, disposed of—or not disposed of—as has been indicated, during the episode at Glacier Park.

Underlying the controversy over Mrs. Edwards lay the whole question of the role of women in the church. This is an ancient (and somewhat frivolous) issue within the churches which has, nonetheless, created more authentic distress than most heresies or alleged heresies. In the General Convention in St. Louis in 1964, for example, the House of Deputies, after many caucuses in smoke-filled rooms, and despite stirring pleas from the retiring Presiding Bishop, Arthur Lichtenberger, voted, narrowly, the clergy heavily favorable, the laity slightly negative, *not* to permit women to serve as deputies to future General Conventions.[57] This matter, no doubt, will arise in the next convention, and perhaps thereafter, and eventually women will be granted status as deputies, but how long the women's suffrage movement of half a century ago will take to overcome the entrenched masculinity of the church, no one can confidently predict. The mills of the institutional church grind, if not finely, with exceeding and deliberate lack of speed.

The specific question of the role of women in the *ministry* is more exasperating and delicate. In the Episcopal Church there are three orders of ministry for men: in descending rank of authority, bishop, priest and deacon. Women desiring ministerial credentials could, until 1964, be "set apart" as deaconesses and as ministers but they could not be "ordained" as ministers, and so were not equivalent to deacons. (Women could not, for example, assist, as deacons do, in the distribution of Holy Communion.) In effect, deaconesses constituted a fourth order of ministry "apart" from the male orders.

(Objection to full ministry for women seems to be directed not so much to their possible service as deacons, but rather to the logical projection of such a concession: if a woman may serve as a deacon, then why not as a priest, and indeed why not as a bishop? While there may be truth in Bishop Pike's observation that some Episcopal congregations consist of "twelve old ladies of both sexes," the clergy generally, and bishops emphatically, recoil in horror at the prospect of a fully female bishop.)

In the convention in St. Louis in 1964 the situation of women in the ministry was rather startlingly altered. On a motion of the Bishop of Florida, and without debate, the House of Bishops voted—the Bishop of California was absent at the vote, being as he says "bugged by other matters"—to eliminate the requirement of celibacy for deaconesses, *and* to change in the applicable canon law the word "appointed" as deaconess to "ordered" as deaconess. The House of Deputies concurred, without dissent.[58]

It was as a direct consequence of this action that Bishop Pike made his announcement that he would ordain Mrs. Phyllis Edwards. He argued (as a canon lawyer of considerable authority) that the word "ordered" could mean nothing else than what it means in the case of deacons: *ordination to full ministry.*

Given that the Bishop was only implementing a decision the convention had duly voted, the uproar his announcement touched off is curious. The Bishop of Quincy, acting as then President of The American Church Union, urgently requested that Pike defer the contemplated ordination until after the meeting in Glacier Park, and, bowing to this and other pressure from within his diocese, Bishop Pike agreed to do so.

At Glacier Park a special committee on deaconesses brought to the floor of the House an opinion that the action in St. Louis had not given deaconesses a "new status" but had merely clarified "a status that was already theirs." There followed a protracted discussion in which Bishop Pike played a prominent part. In the end the House voted, in effect, that deaconesses were to be ordained but would be excluded from distributing "the Elements of the Holy Communion." (The House also voted that when a deaconess is ordered she "receives an indelible character," which is more, Bishop Pike has said, "than I think I've got.") Finally, the House adopted a specific liturgy for use in the ordination of women as deaconesses.[59]

One week later, on September 13, 1965, Bishop Pike, using the service the House had prescribed, invested Mrs. Edwards with ministerial status in a ceremony in Grace Cathedral, San Francisco. She became, thereby, the first woman "recognized" to be a full minister as well as a deaconess of the Episcopal Church.[60] (A number of other Christian denominations have long permitted women in the ministry.)

The future of women in the ministry is an issue that continues to occupy the bishops, but it seems settled that the Diocese of California will be served "with indelible character" for the balance of her ministry by the Reverend Mrs. Phyllis Edwards.

The Baptism of Luci Baines Johnson

"If there is one thing my daughter has learned here, it is the spirit of independence," President Johnson told her graduating class of the National Cathedral (Episcopal) School for Girls in Washington, D.C., in June of 1965.[61] A few weeks later, on her eighteenth birthday, July 2, Luci Baines Johnson, by her own request, was received into the Roman Catholic Church and rebaptized in St. Matthew's Cathedral by Father James Montgomery.

On Sunday, July 4, Independence Day, Bishop Pike preached vigorously against the action of the Roman Catholic priest in reenacting her baptism which had, the Bishop argued, already been validly performed in the Episcopal Church. He called it a "direct slap" at his church, and "a deliberate act denigrating another branch of Christendom." He characterized it as "sacrilegious" in that it was an empty rite without sacramental effect and therefore an abuse of the valid sacrament.

Praising Miss Johnson for her "American independence in making her own religious choice," the Bishop—who in 1960 had co-authored a tract called *A Roman Catholic in the White House?* —nonetheless demanded apologies from the President's daughter, the officiating priest and the Roman Catholic hierarchy for what he deemed "an injury to what have been most promising relationships between the churches." He noted that he had himself been baptized a Roman Catholic and had not, when received into the Episcopal Church, suffered any rebaptism.[62]

Miss Johnson declined public comment, indicating only that she regarded her decision as a "personal matter."[63] Father Montgomery indicated that he had chosen to perform the rite, without consulting the hierarchy, because it had been Miss Johnson's personal wish and he respected that.[64]

A number of Roman Catholic priests expressed agreement with Bishop Pike, notably the Reverend Thomas Stransky, an American Paulist Father then in Rome on the staff of the Vatican Secretariat for Promoting Christian Unity, who said Episcopalians "are perfectly justified in feeling as they do" because Father Montgomery had "followed what is a bad practice in the United States . . . despite clear rulings to the contrary by the Holy Office."[65]

Many Episcopal clergy—including the Bishop of Milwaukee, Donald H. V. Hallock—supported the position Bishop Pike had taken, though some felt his statement had been too strongly worded. Bishop Hallock said Roman Catholic law on the matter was clear, and the problem seemed to be how to find a way of "making individual priests abide by it."[66]

President Johnson made no statement—publicly—on the matter.

The Bishop Takes a Sabbatical

During the summer of 1965, despite these other events, Bishop Pike had completed the "penultimate" draft of a new book on doctrine—*What Is This Treasure*—which had led him deeper into study and reflection upon contemporary trends in theology. Increasingly, he found his diocesan responsibilities precluded the opportunity for theological investigation he desired, and in August he asked, and his Standing Committee granted, a six months' sabbatical leave of absence to commence September 15.

For this period of study he took up residence in Carlton Court, Cambridge, England, with his elder son and namesake, James, Jr., who enrolled for a semester at Cambridge College. This enabled the Bishop to consult the distinguished theological faculty and library of Cambridge University, and also to meet often for conversation with the Bishop of Woolwich, John A. T. Robinson. That this proved to be a fertile experience for the Bishop is evidenced by the numerous citations and footnotes from recent scholarly theological work which found their way into the final text of *What Is This Treasure*.

Halcyon though this interval in a busy life seems to have been, it suffered a number of dramatic interruptions.

Under an official policy adopted by the World Congress of the Anglican Communion the various dioceses throughout the world had agreed to subscribe to what is cumbersomely called Mutual Responsibility and Interdependence (MRI).[67] In essence, the plan calls for two dioceses to adopt each other and work together for mutual benefit. The Diocese of California and the Diocese of Matabeleland, Rhodesia, became, under MRI, "companion" dioceses, and, in 1964 the Bishop of Matabeleland, Kenneth J. F. Skelton, had officially visited Bishop Pike in San Franciso to consider their mutual task. Finding himself in England Bishop Pike accepted an invitation to return that visit, and in December of 1965 he flew from London to Salisbury, the capital of Rhodesia.

He spent most of a day in Salisbury's diocesan house conferring with Bishop Skelton and the Bishop of Mashonaland, the other diocese in Rhodesia, guardedly, because of a fear that the rooms might be "bugged" by the rebel apartheid regime of Prime Minister Ian Smith. The schedule then called for Bishops Skelton and Pike to proceed to the former's see city, Bulawayo, and the two drove by taxi to the airport. There, Bishop Pike was taken under guard and held, incommunicado, for over three hours.

It developed that the Bishop's visit to Rhodesia had been

preceded by letters from Father Frank Brunton of Arizona, one a letter to Prime Minister Smith and the other an open letter to the Salisbury press. The letters were particularly scurrilous, even for Father Brunton, but the pertinent accusation, so far as the Rhodesian government was concerned, was that Bishop Pike was "a notorious racial agitator."[68] On the incredible basis of this charge the Bishop was ordered out of Rhodesia. Bishop Skelton obtained a lawyer, but the authorities denied him access to the client. A request for appeal was also denied, although the so-called Minister of Law and Order was physically present. The Bishop was denied the right to select his destination, and his bags were ordered checked through to London. Once the plane left Salisbury arrangements were made for the Bishop to land in Nairobi, Kenya, where he himself found and removed his bags from the plane's storage compartment.

(Although Bishop Pike had written Bishop Harte some months earlier requesting action be taken against Father Brunton, Bishop Harte has never done so. Following the episode in Rhodesia both Bishop Pike and his chaplain, the Reverend David Baar, wrote Bishop Louttit demanding canonical proceedings against Father Brunton for having placed both Bishops Pike and Skelton in jeopardy. Bishop Louttit declined to take any action.)[69]

Subsequently, in mid-January of 1966, Bishop Pike returned to Africa for a Synod of Central Africa meeting held in Malawi, where he was able to carry on extensive and open dialogue with his brother bishop and other Rhodesian clergy, black and white, and he also visited Tanzania, Kenya, Zambia, and other new nations.

In early December of 1965 Bishop Pike also made a brief trip to West Berlin in his capacity as technical advisor to the Chief of Chaplains, United States Air Force, and while there journeyed into East Berlin to see for himself conditions beyond the Wall, and to meet with clergy and laity to discuss the situation of the Church in East Germany. Once again, conversations were guarded, because of the possibility of "bugging," and some discussions were held in the streets to diminish that possibility, but the Bishop was not ejected from the country. He has since said that fascism of the right and fascism of the left cannot be distinguished from the real evil: totalitarianism.[70]

During the Christmas holidays Bishop Pike and his son visited the Holy Land, a pilgrimage he recalls with evident exhilaration, and a time, he has said, of great closeness and shared joy between the senior and the junior Jim Pikes. Together the two visited many holy places, and the Bishop especially recalls his awe and wonder at the ancient, ruined fortress city of Masada. On Christmas Eve he completed, in Nazareth, the manuscript of *What Is This Treasure*. His visit to Israel also deepened and enriched a growing fascination he had developed with the Dead Sea scrolls and the scholarly work being carried on with respect to those extraordinary archeological "finds." The visit had been, for him, a creative, nourishing joy.

Deeply concerned about what he had seen and experienced in Africa, and filled, perhaps, with an exuberance from the holidays in Israel, Bishop Pike decided, although his sabbatical did not expire until March 15, that he would return to San Francisco, briefly, in early February, specifically to report on the situation in their companion diocese to his own diocesan convention which would then be in annual session. Jim, Jr. was returning, too, to be on hand for the second semester at San Francisco State College, but, having several days to spare, he took a plane first to New York City where he planned to visit friends.

On the evening of February 4, 1966, the Bishop of California, "glad to be home," addressed for over an hour the opening session of the 116th Annual Convention of the Episcopal Diocese of California. His address was an eloquent recital of his experiences in Africa and in Germany and in Israel and a moving invocation for the diocese to come to the aid of its sister in Rhodesia. He spoke from the text: "But woe to the inhabitants of the earth . . . , for the devil is come down among you having great wrath, for he knoweth that he hath but a short time" (Revelations 12: 12b).[71]

The devil, meanwhile, had already struck, and nearer to home than the Bishop knew.

The Death of the Bishop's Son

Immediately upon leaving the platform following his address Bishop Pike was informed that Jim, Jr. had earlier that day shot himself to death in a hotel in midtown Manhattan.

The young man had been 20 years of age.

Jim and Esther Pike and their three surviving children—another son and two daughters—were plunged into shock and grief. The Bishop's celebrity insured that their loss was spread across front pages and television screens.

In a statement for the news media Bishop Pike said that he could not explain what had happened, that it seemed a senseless thing, and that it was incomprehensible to the family.

Messages of condolence and sympathy poured in from all over the world, including that from Father Brunton mentioned earlier and not to be repeated here.

Having buried his son and passed a period of bereavement with his family, Bishop Pike returned to Cambridge.

The Incident at O'Hare

The Most Reverend John Elbridge Hines, Presiding Bishop, happening to pass through San Francisco on his way to visitations in the Pacific while Bishop Pike was in the seclusion of mourning, telephoned his brother bishop, and having offered appropriate commiseration, informed him that a new controversy had arisen about his public ministry.

There had appeared in a February issue of *Look* magazine an article ("Search for a Space-Age God") discussing a number of "new" theologians but with a heavy emphasis, pictorially and in the text, on Bishop Pike. The author, Christopher Wren, had spent considerable time with the Bishop both at Yale, where Pike had passed a week as Chubb Fellow, and in Cambridge, and the *Look* piece is a compact but journalistically responsible account of the Bishop's thinking at that time.[72]

In the article some of the Bishop's positions already discussed in these pages were rehearsed, and additionally other provocative remarks were attributed to him, notably that he had denied the Resurrection of Jesus and had "jettisoned" several other creedal affirmations. It was further stated that he had been "acquitted" of heresy charges in Glacier Park, and had tried but "failed" to have a woman ordained. One of the Bishop's most famous remarks also first found print in that article: "The Moslems offer one God and three wives; we offer three Gods and one wife." (This statement is often cited as evidence of Pike's alleged vulgarity, but we take exception to it only because Moslems, in fact, offer four wives, and so the parity collapses and with it the joke.)

Bishop Hines reported, then, that many bishops were exercised by what had appeared in Look. Pike told him he had already written a brief letter to the editors of the magazine denying he had denied the Resurrection. (That letter appeared subsequently in Look with a concession by the editors that they had erred.)[73] Bishop Hines reported he was writing also to the editors pointing out—which was certainly true—that since Bishop Pike had not been on trial at Glacier Park he could not have been "acquitted" of heresy charges. (That letter never did appear in Look.)

The Presiding Bishop was not persuaded that these actions would satisfactorily dispel the concern of other bishops, and he suggested that, following Bishop Pike's return from Cambridge—that is, after March 15—he would convene the episcopal presidents of the church's nine provinces for the purpose of having Bishop Pike speak to their concerns.

(The Episcopal Church, for administrative reasons, divides its various dioceses regionally into nine provinces, each of which has a president, generally the senior bishop of the province. Presidents of provinces have virtually no functions other than to preside over occasional provincial gatherings. Latterly, the presidents have often been called metropolitans, that being the practice in similar jurisdictions elsewhere in the Anglican Communion, and since Bishop Hines prefers to call them metropolitans they shall be so designated henceforth here.)

Bishop Pike readily agreed to this proposal, and added that, since copies of *What Is This Treasure* would shortly be available, he would see that Bishop Hines and the metropolitans received copies prior to the confrontation, believing that the book itself would relieve them of some of their anxieties.

Upon his return to Cambridge Bishop Pike found in his flat a wire from the secretary to the Presiding Bishop advising that the metropolitans would convene on March 5 in O'Hare Inn at Chicago's O'Hare International Airport, and that it was hoped Bishop Pike would be present. He at once telephoned transatlantically the PB's secretary (bishops commonly refer to the Presiding

Bishop as the "PB") pointing out that the meeting was to have occurred after his return from Cambridge. She replied that the PB had left her instructions to find a date most convenient for the metropolitans and that March 5 proved to be it. (There had been no attempt to determine its convenience for Bishop Pike.)

Bishop Hines then being, as his secretary put it, "somewhere in the Pacific" and so unavailable, and no other dates following March 15 being suitable for a sufficiency of metropolitans, Bishop Pike flew round-trip from London to Chicago to London in 24 hours in order to meet the wishes of the Presiding Bishop and the convenience of his metropolitan brethren.

Upon arrival in O'Hare Inn, very weary and in need of rest, the Bishop had some difficulty locating the others, finally came upon several, including the PB, whom he joined for lunch, during which nothing substantial was discussed, although he recalls that the food was not "too bad" and the atmosphere "reasonably convivial."

After lunch, Bishop Hines indicated that he and the metropolitans would repair to a room to deliberate the problem under consideration, and Bishop Pike should go to his own room and await their summons. Having waited, as requested, about one hour and a half, the Bishop became apprehensive that the others had forgotten he was there, or had departed without bothering with him, or perhaps had misplaced his room number, but, just as he was going to take some initiative of his own, the summons came and he joined the others for a discussion remarkable even in the annals of episcopal conversation.

Bishop Hines opened the matter—speaking, Bishop Pike has said, for what was obviously by that time "a group-mind"—with a question: had the Bishop of California in what he had been doing and saying concerned himself with the effect this had on the little people? (The issue of the little people—presumably the ordinary churchgoing faithful—has frequently been raised by bishops who are critical of Bishop Pike's public comments. Thus, on another occasion, a bishop said to him: "Look, Jim, we know what you've been saying is true, but you can't tell the little people all that.")

Bishop Pike responded that, on the one hand, truth was truth and could not be made different for big people and little people, and, on the other hand, he didn't think the little people were all that little anyway. He pointed out that, as a result of education and mass communications and other modern phenomena, the little people were getting less little all the time, and knew, in fact, much more than some big people thought. He implied that *he* thought the little people would grow even bigger if the already big people would be more candid with them.

Metropolitan Gray, the Bishop of Connecticut, changed the subject by bringing up a complex matter involving a priest of the Diocese of California then serving the Church of Scotland in St. Gile's Cathedral, Edinburgh. This question is so technical and ecclesiastical and remote, that, especially since it had nothing to do with the *Look* article (or the little people), it will not be explored here. Bishop Gray then turned to the Reverend Mrs. Phyllis Edwards, claiming that Bishop Pike had ordained her in violation of the decisions taken at Glacier Park. After much discussion it was accepted that in that service of recognition Bishop Pike had, in fact, complied with the prescriptions the bishops had determined were proper.

Bishop Gray, however, was dissatisfied and introduced a news photograph which he alleged depicted Mrs. Edwards distributing the Holy Communion in clear violation of the Glacier ruling. Bishop Pike, having studied the photograph, pointed out that, while Mrs. Edwards was indeed holding the chalice in her hands, she was also on her knees, hardly a posture one would expect of a minister *distributing* the wine. Mrs. Edwards, he said, was actually *receiving* Holy Communion. (Bishop Gray's confusion about this probably derived from the fact that although almost no Episcopal clergy hand the chalice to a communicant when distributing the wine, Bishop Pike does. He conforms, in this practice, to the *Book of Common Prayer*, which says it should be so administered, and he has also said that he "trusts the faithful not to spill it.")[74]

The other issues raised by the *Look* piece were also talked over in what Bishop Pike remembers as a fairly amicable way, the only evident hostility coming from Metropolitan Gray. Bishop Hines suggested that Bishop Pike's clarifications on various points be incorporated into a letter to the *Look* editors. Bishop Pike pointed out that it was rather late to expect the magazine to run such a letter, and that it would anyway be too lengthy for such a use.

Nonetheless, he agreed to do it, and promised to send a copy to the Presiding Bishop, who in turn promised to reproduce it and send copies to every member of the House of Bishops.

Arriving back in Cambridge, more bewildered even than he was exhausted, the Bishop promptly wrote and on March 8 sent to *Look* (with a copy to the PB), a six-page, single-spaced letter which thoroughly discussed all the issues posed at O'Hare.[75] In it he reiterated that he had not denied Jesus' Resurrection, explained that he had not "failed" to ordain a woman (the bishops having ruled at Glacier Park that she was *already* ordained), said that the word "jettisoned" was not in his vocabulary though it *could* fairly describe his position on certain doctrines, endorsed Bishop Hines' earlier letter on the question of his having been "acquitted" at Glacier Park, and explored in great detail Metropolitan Gray's preoccupation with the priest serving in Scotland.

The letter, as predicted, was not printed in the magazine, and Bishop Hines, while he did send copies to the metropolitans, failed to send copies to the other members of the House of Bishops. The metropolitans having already heard face-to-face Bishop Pike's clarifications, the letter itself would seem to have been pretty much a six-page exercise in futility.

One week later, his sabbatical concluded, Bishop Pike returned to San Francisco and his episcopal responsibilities.

The Worker Priest in the Purple

On March 30, 1966, Harper & Row brought out *What Is This Treasure*—a book the Bishop was later on to refer to rather often as "my latest book of heresies"—and it proved to have a large sale for a book on theology.[76] Unlike *A Time for Christian Candor* its emphasis is upon what *can* be believed rather than what *cannot*. It very plainly reflects the work of a mind in process of quest and examination, and as such may be called transitional.

That process of quest and examination had, in fact, been fostered and accelerated during the Bishop's sabbatical both in Cambridge and in Israel. His return to diocesan routine became for him, therefore, a burden and an interference with the habits of reflection and research he had cultivated abroad. Even before his return he had given thought to the desirability of resigning in order to devote himself more fully to his theological concerns.

He found, however, when he got back, that there were many problems in the diocese, some in consequence of his own positions, and he decided, for the time being, to defer a decision about his own future plans, and he plunged with characteristic vigor into setting diocesan affairs in order.

For one thing, the annual solicitation from "friends" of the cathedral was in jeopardy because the large financial interests involved took exception to participation of the Bishop and others of the diocesan hierarchy in a variety of social controversies in California. The Bishop had, for example, sometime earlier issued a strong pastoral letter opposing Proposition 14, a referendum in the state that had the effect of repealing that state's open housing policy.[77] The diocese was also about to involve itself in community action programs in racially troubled Oakland. (The Bishop as Chairman of the California Committee of the U.S. Civil Rights Commission, was shortly to conduct a series of public forums in Oakland airing the grievances of local citizens.) The diocese had also been involved, one way or another, in the Selma march, in picketing companies alleged to be practicing discrimination, in supporting strikes by migrant grape-pickers and others who were alleged to suffer exploitation.

It should be pointed out, however, that the Bishop himself was not personally involved in all of these activities, and indeed was out of the country when some of them took place. He is rather more conservative on social questions than his reputation would suggest. Bishop Pike is, for example, generally against demonstrations, except as a last resort, and seldom joins them. He has expressed his theory of civil disobedience along these lines: against a bad law which cannot otherwise be changed, Yes; against a company (or other institution) which will not obey a good law, No. It is the Bishop's view, in other words, that civil disobedience is only proper when a bad law is involved, and it is improper when the issue is non-compliance with a good law. So long as a good law is involved it is obligatory, in his view, to respect that law by obedience to other laws. Nonetheless, he took the position, while diocesan bishop, that his clergy had the right peacefully to protest, whether or not he himself agreed with their protest or their tactic, and, on occasion, he arranged for legal counsel for clergy of his diocese who were arrested in a demonstration of which he did not approve. He resisted any and all efforts to have clergy disciplined or removed on account of participation in peaceful demonstrations.

To cite another example of the Bishop's conservative inclinations: he opposed, along with Senator Everett McKinley Dirksen, the first Supreme Court decision against prayer in the public schools. Later, however, after the second such decision, and after discussing the issue on national television with William F. Buckley, Jr., he reversed his opinion and now supports both decisions. Having testified before the Senate Judiciary Committee in favor of Senator Dirksen's proposed constitutional amendment to overturn those decisions, the Bishop, his flexibility intact, would now be prepared to testify against it. The essence of Bishop Pike's approach is that true conservatism is always ready to change its mind where change alone can conserve a basic value.

In any event, the Bishop met with corporation executives who would affect the outcome of the cathedral fund drive, and told them that he could promise no change in diocesan policy in these matters. (Only one of those magnates raised any question about the Bishop's theological views, and it was Bishop Pike's opinion that theology had little to do with the problem.) Persuaded that the requisite funds could not be fully secured from these sources, the Bishop devoted the next several months to raising them elsewhere, an endeavor in which he was successful.

Meanwhile, there *were* rumblings within certain parishes of the diocese concerning Bishop Pike's alleged heresies, and these rumblings came to a focus in a public statement of clergy and laity in Trinity Episcopal Church, Hayward, California, under the date of April 20, 1966. That statement, in effect, while specifically acknowledging Bishop Pike's sincerity and integrity, asserted that he endangered the "basic truths" of the Church. The statement concluded with a recitation of the Nicene Creed.[78] Bishop Pike responded to this challenge by announcing that he would make an episcopal visitation to Trinity Church, Hayward, on May 9 for the purpose of addressing the concerns of the members of the parish.

(Also on May 9, interestingly, the Supreme Court of California ruled that Proposition 14, which the Bishop's pastoral letter had opposed, was, in fact, unconstitutional.)

A large crowd gathered to hear what proved to be an extended dialogue between the Bishop and the Rector of Trinity Church, the Reverend Graham N. Lesser. It was an inconclusive though spirited confrontation. Father Lesser, for example, asked: "Is Christ God incarnate?" Bishop Pike replied: "The word incarnate is unique to the fourth Gospel; I do not feel bound to that word." At another point Bishop Pike asked: "Whom did Jesus worship?" Father Lesser replied: "God." Bishop Pike said: "So do I." And so it went. No one could claim, however, that the issues had not been ventilated, and the crowd had doubtless been entertained.[79]

(Never one to conceal his opinions, large or small, the Bishop had, two weeks earlier, on April 26, speaking to students at the University of California from the steps of Sproul Hall in Berkeley, and queried as to his view on topless waitresses, said: "We must always be in a position of thanksgiving to God for the beauties of his handiwork.")[80]

On April 15, addressing the closing session of the annual meeting of the National Council on Alcoholism in New York City's Waldorf Astoria Hotel, Bishop Pike commented on two other subjects which had long interested him.[81]

He urged the Church to be less judgmental about alcoholics and more constructive in helping them with their problem. He spoke from some experience. For many years well known in church circles as a man with an astonishing capacity for the dry martini, he had found drinking increasingly a personal problem, and on June 30, 1964, abruptly stopped, joined Alcoholics Anonymous, and involved himself more actively in the diocesan Center for the Rehabilitation of Alcoholics. He has not had a drink since, "not even wine with the Communion." He has also been active in counseling clergy—including bishops—afflicted with that condition.

In the same address he made a similar recommendation to the Church with respect to the problems of homosexuals. "There are," said he, "eighty thousand homosexuals in San Francisco. We can't ignore eighty thousand people." Early in his episcopate Bishop Pike was himself somewhat judgmental on this subject, having deposed from ministry a number of his clergy found to be homosexuals. His attitude has, however, changed, and towards the end of his tenure he encouraged an interdenominational move in the San Francisco area to develop programs of assistance for homosexuals. He has also endorsed in California an effort to pass legislation that would, in effect, remove from penalties of law all sexual activity privately undertaken between consenting adults.

The burden of these and other episcopal duties (coupled with the burden of grief following his son's death) were weighing more heavily upon the Bishop than ever before, and he longed to return to his theological and scholarly pursuits. Seven weeks after he arrived back from Cambridge, on May 9, 1966—the very day of his visitation to Trinity Church, Hayward—Bishop Pike wrote to his Standing Committee and to the Presiding Bishop submitting his resignation as Bishop of California, effective the following September 15.

The Standing Committee accepted his resignation "with deep regret."[82] (The resignation of a bishop requires the consent of his fellow bishops, but this proved no barrier and was swiftly accomplished, in some cases, no doubt, with more joy than regret.)

In his lengthy letter to the Presiding Bishop, Pike summed up the reasons for his decision in this paragraph:

A six months sabbatical, added to some years of studying, writing and communication "on the edges" of one's time, is obviously inadequate to this overall task. Back on the job, I am all the more aware of how difficult it will be for me to continue a dual role of scholar-teacher and administrator-leader. I am not growing any younger and this conflict has in fact been characteristic of me all my adult life in two professions, always keeping me much too busy in terms of legitimate allotment of time for family life, rest and reflection. The attempt to fulfill both roles has put great strains on my physical well-being, leaving me feeling exhausted a good deal of the time. My recent sabbatical provided a "laboratory experiment" as to the state of my health while engaging in only one of the two roles; the fact is that I never felt better in my life. In the seven weeks of being back in the dual role, I'm feeling like I did before and it is evident that my health will not endure my going on this way.

When the resignation became public a week later the Bishop informed the press: "I have discovered I am not twins." He added that during his months in Cambridge: "I experienced the sheer joy of staying with something for more than one disconnected hour."[83]

At the same time, the Bishop disclosed that he had accepted an invitation from Dr. Robert Maynard Hutchins to join the staff of the Center for the Study of Democratic Institutions in Santa Barbara, California. (MIND OVER MITER, headlined the *New York Daily News*.)[84] The center, founded by Dr. Hutchins—Bishop Pike calls him "the Abbot"—is a collection of some twenty scholars and students from many disciplines, who, as its name suggests, bring to bear their various insights upon problems of institutions in a democratic society. Located in a charming if somewhat rundown villa on Eucalyptus Hill outside Santa Barbara, the staff gather once each weekday in late morning for about two hours to consider a problem and discuss it. Otherwise, members are free to pursue their own studies as they see fit. Bishop Pike, the first theologian to be a permanent member of the staff, took up residence near the center in August of 1966.

It should be pointed out—because there has been some confusion about it—that Bishop Pike did not *retire* as a bishop. A bishop *must* retire at age 72, but otherwise *may not* retire before age 68, except for reasons of ill-health or infirmity. Even had he wished to retire—and he did not—Bishop Pike could not have done so. He resigned his *office* as diocesan in California, but he continues as a bishop of the church in good standing.

The proper way to refer to him formally is: the Right Reverend James A. Pike, the Resigned Bishop of California.

Though he did not shed his status as bishop—he has continued to officiate at confirmations and other celebrations upon request—he did shed all income from the church, and now depends for his living entirely upon secular sources, his salary at the center, his writings and lectures—which may explain, in part, the frequency with which he appears in print or on public platforms.

Bishop Pike had become, as he himself puts it, "a worker priest in the purple."

The Months of Transition

While it might have been wiser for the Diocese of California to elect a successor to Bishop Pike fairly quickly, it did not, in fact, do so until September 13, two days before he stepped down, and his successor was not to assume responsibility until January of 1967.

The resultant extended period of uncertainty aggravated some diocesan problems, especially financial problems, and there ensued what amounted to a lull more pronounced than the lull most churches experience during summer months.

Bishop Pike took advantage of this interval of relative inertia to arrange for the resettlement of his family in quarters in San Francisco and to locate for himself an apartment in Santa Barbara and to arrange for the removal there of his papers and books. He also accepted appointments, part time, as Lecturer in Law at the University of California, Berkeley, and as Adjunct Professor in the Graduate Theological Union, Berkeley. His plan, which he has followed, was to spend weekdays—when not traveling—at the center in Santa Barbara, and long weekends in San Francisco, teaching Fridays at Berkeley, confirming in parishes of the diocese Sundays, and relaxing with his family.

During the same summer months he began preliminary work on two new books for Harper & Row. One was to be a case history study of ethical problems approached existentially (the so-called "situation ethics" method) and called *You and the New Morality*, a book which appeared in May, 1967. The other was to be another book on doctrine in which he would attempt to state what he could affirm *working from data*. The latter book, then called "Fewer Beliefs, More Belief," has been published in September, 1967, under a new title—which explains itself—*If This Be Heresy*.[85]

The two areas of research the Bishop contemplated for his work at Santa Barbara were the scholarship emanating from the Dead Sea scrolls, and certain socioeconomic studies of the relationship between church attendance and ethical attitudes and behavior.[86] He used the leisure of that summer to explore preliminarily both of these fields. His visit to Israel had already involved him rather deeply in the scroll material which he began to see was likely in the near future to revolutionize traditional understanding of the Scriptures and, possibly, of the figure of Jesus. "It seemed to me that someone responsible in the churches," he has said, "ought to be getting ready to assess what all this might mean in terms of the future of the Church."

In his penultimate sermon in Grace Cathedral on August 7 he spoke to this concern, basing his remarks on an article on the Dead

Sea scrolls by Professor John Marco Allegro which had appeared in the August, 1966, number of *Harper's* magazine. Among other things the Bishop suggested that scholarship such as Professor Allegro's *might* establish that the historical Jesus did not exist, a remark that caused considerable dismay in some quarters. (It is for this reason that Bishop Pike, hedging his bets, perhaps, has for sometime, in most public references to Jesus, used the expression: "the servant image of Jesus.")

On September 5, 1966 Bishop Pike delivered his farewell sermon as Bishop of California. It was a memorable event exceptionally well captured by J. Campbell Bruce in the September 6th *San Francisco Chronicle,* an account which began:

Bishop James A. Pike said farewell as rector of Grace Cathedral to an overflow throng yesterday, and the great gothic pile reverberated with laughter and at the close many an eye glistened.

This was his last sermon as the rector, a post he had occupied since May of 1958. He will appear in the pulpit again September 13, the day a special diocesan convention will elect his successor.

"That sermon is not supposed to be loaded," he said; i.e., for any particular candidate.

They started filling the church long before the 11 A.M. service, sliding into the 2200 places among the pews, occupying rows of chairs, standing in the aisles.

Bishop Pike mounted the pulpit, sent glances along the transept and down the nave, shook his head and said:

"It was never like this on Christmas or Easter. I think I should have resigned once a month."

Then his eye took in the worshippers bracing their backs against the walls, and he said:

"I'm concerned about these standees. It's difficult enough to endure one of my sermons when you're comfortably seated."

In a rare, if not unprecedented action—the last, perhaps, but certainly not the first in his unpredictable reign as Bishop of California—he suggested that standees move up into the choir loft and chancel, where the clergy sit.

He called for a "minute of soft organ music" to occupy minds while this was going on, but he needn't have, he was distraction enough. In his high jutting pulpit, his arms eloquently beckoning and directing, he seemed an ecclesiastical version of a traffic cop.

"Go ahead," he told a reluctant standee, "you might be sitting in the visiting bishop's seat."[87]

His sermon proper began, as all his sermons lately have, not with the customary Episcopal invocation—"In the name of the Father, and of the Son, and of the Holy Ghost, Amen!"—but, the Trinity having fallen from his episcopal vocabulary: "In the name of God, Amen!" He went on to discuss with great feeling his quest for that which could be conscientiously believed by modern man.

On September 13 the convention of the Diocese of California met to elect a new bishop. There were many candidates but probable choice centered on three, one a conservative and two moderates. The deliberations became deadlocked, until finally, after midnight, Bishop Pike was to announce that the result of 14 hours and 9 ballots had elected a distinct dark horse: the Suffragan Bishop of Michigan, the Right Reverend Chauncey Kilmer Myers.

Bishop Myers not being well known to many of the delegates since no one had expected him to win, Bishop Pike spent some time after the final vote informally describing his successor. (Pike and Myers are old personal friends, having studied together under the late Paul Tillich, and having served as tutors together at General Theological Seminary.) He told them that Bishop Myers was theologically more conservative than he was, but even more socially concerned and active, having spent much of his ministry in urban work, and having been very involved in the struggle for integration.

Bishop Pike's last words to his flock, as diocesan, were: "It will be nice some day to be remembered as that conservative bishop you had here once."

The Conference for Disturbed Clergy

A few days later, at the call of their President (or Metropolitan), Albert R. Stuart, Bishop of Georgia, the Bishops of the Fourth Province, sometimes called Sewanee, and consisting essentially of Southern bishops, assembled for a conference on disturbed clergy. It was the purpose of the meeting to consider with the help of psychiatrists and other specialists two rather vexing questions: how to keep disturbed people out of the clergy, and having failed to do so what to do with them after they get in.

The Bishop of South Florida, Henry I. Louttit, was among the bishops present, and he has said that the discussions somehow brought to his mind the problem of Bishop Pike. Reflecting upon the matter—perhaps bored with some learned presentation—the thought suddenly came to him that the time had come formally to charge Bishop Pike with heresy. He raised his preoccupation with his provincial brethren and discovered, he has said, that his own concern was shared by the others. (Bishop Louttit, on occasion, refers to brother bishops to whom he is personally close as his "buddies in Christ.") The Bishop of Kentucky, Charles Gresham Marmion, was moved to race to his rooms to obtain for inspection by the group a newspaper account of Bishop Pike's farewell sermon. Bishop Louttit recalls that he vented his own dismay thus: "This is the last straw!" All bishops present—some fourth province bishops were unable to attend—agreed that the time had come for the House of Bishops to do something about their troublesome brother from California, lately resigned.[88]

Bishop Louttit undertook to have drawn up specifications of charges of heresy against Bishop Pike, and most of the others concurred with this procedure, although a few had reservations about so drastic an action. Bishop Louttit, in any event, returned to his see in Winter Park, Florida, and proceeded with what he has called "a mandate of the Holy Spirit." Whether or not the fourth-province bishops succeeded in resolving the problem of disturbed clergy, it was apparent that they had discerned among themselves—or in their Santa Barbara colleague—the substance of a disturbance that was soon to proliferate alarmingly.

The Evolution of a Born Fighter

Henry Irving Louttit was born on New Year's Day in 1903, and raised by his parents, both of whom died when he was 14, in Buffalo, New York. Graduated from that city's South Park High

School at age 17, he found himself self-dependent for support and worked his way through Hobart College as a farmhand and construction worker, graduating in 1925 with a Phi Beta Kappa key.

He went to Miami where he worked for a year as a surveyor, discovering, in that capacity, that in all of Florida there was but one beach, and that a remote one, to which Negroes had access, a situation he was later to be instrumental in rectifying. The next year he decided upon the ministry as a vocation and entered Virginia Theological Seminary from which he received his Bachelor of Divinity degree in 1929.

Following his ordination he served churches in Tarpon Springs and Miami, Florida, and then became rector of the Church of the Holy Cross in West Palm Beach. In 1937 he married Amy Moss Cleckler by whom he was to have two sons. Mrs. Louttit was to suffer a serious illness in 1960 and has been totally invalided ever since, a personal tragedy that has been a source of immense grief for the Bishop. The Bishop's devotion to his wife is evident, and the loss of her companionship has left him a lonely man whose only interest, apart from gardening, is his work, which he pursues with an energy and tirelessness paralleled, perhaps, among his episcopal brethren, only by Bishop Pike.

During World War II Henry Louttit served as an Army chaplain with the 31st Division in the Pacific, until, in 1944, having contracted a serious skin infection, he was returned for hospitalization in Thomasville, Georgia, after being awarded a Bronze Star. While still in the hospital he was elected Suffragan Bishop of South Florida, a diocese that covers that state's peninsula area below Ormand Beach and the Crystal River. In 1948 he became Bishop Coadjutor, and in 1951 the 3rd Bishop of South Florida.

Under his leadership the diocese has enjoyed remarkable success, the number of churches having more than doubled and the number of communicants having more than tripled during his long tenure. He has been acutely vigorous in pressing for integration not only of diocesan activities but also within the communities of South Florida in all aspects of public life. He has said that "being a damn Yankee in the South has some handicaps," but whatever the handicaps his stand for racial justice within his diocese has prevailed. He resents the implication of Bishop Pike and other non-Southern bishops that the Episcopal Church in the South has not been responsible in the racial crisis. "It's easy," he has said, "to be for civil rights when you're in a place where it isn't a problem." He also believes that he has done more for Negroes, in his quieter way, than Bishop Pike has done, more publicly.

Liberal on most social issues the Bishop is rigorously conservative when it comes to theology. His position he has summed up this way: "The church is in the same position as it was in the first century. It is a tiny minority facing a hostile, unbelieving and materialistic world. Our task is not to adapt ourselves or the Gospel to that world, but to preach with the hope that some people will be moved by the Holy Spriit to believe it." Bishop Pike's apparent denial of the Holy Spirit especially incenses Bishop Louttit for whom the Holy Spirit is "a daily comfort and companion."[89]

Preach that Gospel he does, and with forceful eloquence, reflecting a passionate, unquestioning faith that has won for him the respect and often the devotion of his clergy and flock. An accomplished administrator—his talent for fund raising is the envy of all his brother bishops—Bishop Louttit has played a prominent role in the affairs of the church nationally, and has served for some years as Chairman of the Committee on the Dispatch of Business in the House of Bishops, a position of great influence, affecting as it does what and when and how matters will come before the House. He has also been active in the work of the National Council of Churches USA despite pressures within his diocese to depreciate that institution. In 1964 he was a likely candidate for Presiding Bishop, but because of a deadlocked situation the office went to a compromise choice. An associate has said of him: "The church is his hobby as well as his vocation."[90]

A tiny man, he has the presence of one accustomed to deference, though not greatly desirous of it, and the genial manners of a Southern Yankee. Fond of a good joke or a choice piece of ecclesiastical gossip, his blue eyes have an almost perpetual twinkle, and his joy in conversation and camaraderie is infectious. An ascetic in his churchmanship the Bishop commonly retires at 9:00 P.M. and rises at 3:00 A.M., when as he puts it: "I get up, make two cups of coffee, have a glass of orange or apple juice and say my morning prayers while the coffee is dripping." Thereupon, he prepares for the day, handling correspondence and writing sermons, making use of a dictaphone.[91]

Bishop Louttit has a reputation not dissimilar from that Bishop Pike formerly enjoyed of a fondness for drink. Some bishops are of the opinion that this may have contributed to the debacle into which the House of Bishops was about to be plunged.

The Bishop himself has more soberly appraised his intervention in the Bishop Pike affair, and few who know him would dispute it: "I am," he has said, "a born fighter."

The Presentment of the Charges

Back in Winter Park, then, Bishop Louttit assigned to two of his clergy the task of preparing as prescribed by canon law precise charges of heresy against the Resigned Bishop of California. Those specifications appear to have been based, in part, upon charges previously brought, that is both the Georgia and the Arizona charges. When the scribes had completed a draft document, it was reviewed and refined by Bishop Louttit's old friend and Suffragan, the Right Reverend William Loftin Hargrave, whose jurisdiction is the vicinity of St. Petersburg, and who is, by training, a lawyer. The resultant presentment (the text of which may be found in the Appendix) was, as Bishop Louttit freely concedes, "sloppily drawn" and "not as I would have done it myself." Nonetheless, it was to stand as the fundament of an extraordinary series of ecclesiastical events.

Meanwhile, before he had himself read the charges, Bishop Louttit made, one evening and far into the night, a series of telephone calls to bishops all over the country soliciting support for the action he contemplated. Astonishingly, given that none of the bishops had seen the charges either, twelve agreed to be signatories. (One, Bishop Mason of Dallas, subsequently withdrew his name, and another, Bishop Sherman of Long Island, later disassociated himself from that portion of the presentment which accused Bishop Pike of "conduct unbecoming a clergyman.") Several of the twelve original signers have since indicated that they signified agreement more by way of pacification of Bishop Louttit than out of genuine assent to his action, but none of these saw fit to repudiate his involvement.

On September 19, 1966, Bishop Pike invaded the Diocese of South Florida and delivered a highly publicized lecture at Florida Presbyterian College in St. Petersburg. It was one of his more witty and irreverent utterances, and the audience, in the main, was delighted. (He described Sunday school, for example, as a "dangerous institution," expressed bemusement with *Playboy* magazine's "recreational view of sex," and opined that "God would have not named himself anything as awful as Jehovah.") The substance of his talk was a reiteration of the theology-in-flux that had been his concern for some time, summed up in his often repeated slogan: *fewer beliefs, more belief.* He also dismissed, as he has many times, the "God is Dead" theologians, putting it this way:

Either He wasn't and isn't or He was and is. They think events in our history have downed the God of the universe. I don't take us that seriously.

The lecture was covered by the *St. Petersburg Times* in a colorful article bylined Marjoe Creamer and entitled "The Gospel by Slingshot."[92]

Whatever delight all of this brought to his audience was not shared in Winter Park where Bishop Louttit was even then bringing his mandated presentment to fruition. The following day, in fact, September 20, 1966, Bishop Louttit sent his presentment (together with a copy of a letter thus dated to Bishop Pike and a covering letter) to all bishops except Bishop Pike. In his cover letter he announced his self-appointment as Chairman of the Committee of Bishops for the Defense of the Faith, and he invited his brethren to join by signing the presentment, making such amendments as they might deem proper.

The letter to Bishop Pike—dated *in his case only,* curiously, September 22—was received by him—together with the presentment—airmail, special delivery, and registered on September 28. The six-day delay in delivery is explicable, in part, because the material was sent to the office of the Bishop of California in San

THE CHRONICLE OF A CONTROVERSY   63

Francisco, and Bishop Pike, having resigned, was then resident in Santa Barbara. Bishop Louttit released the letter and the presentment to the press on September 24, and it was printed in some papers on September 26, but major publicity was accorded the story on September 30. Bishop Pike first learned of the presentment from the press, although most of his fellow bishops had already received it.

In a postscript to his September 20 and/or 22 letter Bishop Louttit protested Bishop Pike's visit to St. Petersburg on the grounds that it violated canon law. Pike should have secured his permission before speaking in his diocese, he claimed, but Bishop Pike responded that the canon cited was not applicable to the situation, and Bishop Louttit later conceded that this was correct. (Louttit's letter inaugurated an exchange of correspondence between the two bishops so strange and pertinent that it may be found in the Appendix.) Bishop Louttit has admitted that he was anxious that his version of the presentment reach the press before Bishop Pike would have a chance to "mess it up."

Reaction in the nation's press was flamboyant, but it was more than matched by the response from within the House of Bishops itself. Telegrams and letters from his brethren poured into Bishop Louttit's Winter Park command post. It soon became apparent that while many bishops were in some sympathy with the purpose of the presentment, most, including some who had agreed to sign the document, were apprehensive about an actual heresy trial.

The Bishop of Ohio, Nelson M. Burroughs, who did not sign, wired from Cleveland on September 30:

THE LAST HERESY TRIAL TOOK PLACE IN THIS CITY AGAINST WILLIAM MONTGOMERY BROWN. WE FEEL NEGATIVE EFFECTS OF SAME TO THIS DAY. I THINK IT GROSSLY UNFAIR TO GIVE REST OF US BUT FOUR DAYS TO BE COUNTED FOR OR AGAINST COMMITTEE. SINCERELY FEEL IRREPARABLE HARM WILL COME TO ENTIRE CHURCH BY THIS ACTION BEFORE CONSULTING EACH OTHER. OBVIOUSLY ALL OF US HAVE VITAL STAKE IN THIS MATTER.[93]

Bishop Burrough's reference to "but four days" stemmed from the fact that Bishop Louttit had indicated his intention to file the presentment with the Presiding Bishop on October 1, an action, if taken, that would automatically and irreversibly have set in motion the ecclesiastical judicial machinery.

Also on September 30 the Bishop of Michigan wired:

BEG YOU TO SEE THAT ACTION IS DEFERRED UNTIL WE CAN ALL TALK TOGETHER. PRUDENCE IS THE WISE APPLICATION OF PRINCIPLES TO CIRCUMSTANCES. YOUR MAIN ASSERTION IS CORRECT. SOMETHING MUST BE DONE BUT BELIEVE YOU MISREAD THE EFFECTS OF SUCH ACTION. BELIEVE WE WOULD LIVE TO REGRET IT. YOU WILL LOSE NOTHING BY WAITING. PLEASE FOR THE SAKE OF THE CHURCH.

JOE EMRICH[94]

It is evident that there had been extensive consultation among the bishops and that a consensus of sorts was taking shape.

On September 29 the patriarchal Retired Bishop of Washington, Angus Dun, both wired and wrote the Bishop of South Florida, and the last paragraph of his letter suggests the direction the consensus was taking:

I am clear that at the October meeting the House of Bishops should make a public statement, which I hope would receive overwhelming support, repudiating many of the public statements of our disturbed and disturbing brother.[95]

Other messages of similar purport came from bishops in all parts of the country and representative of many different factions of the hierarchy. Bishop Louttit had come under concerted and compelling pressure from a broad cross section of his episcopal brethren.

Meanwhile, on September 26, the Presiding Bishop had written Bishop Louttit, and this was the pertinent paragraph:

I hope you will change your mind about final action against Jim Pike. I had hoped that his resignation as the Bishop of California would initiate an era in which his voice would be less frequently heard or when heard less attended to and I really think this will be so, but we have got to give it a chance. I believe the coming of the new Bishop to California will assist in this matter, since there is no question about Kim Myers orthodoxy together with his strong sense of the Church. In my opinion formal action will only serve to produce further cleavage even more so than Jim's testimonials have produced and while we need to have concern about defending the Faith I think we need to have concern about individuals like Jim Pike who have plenty of problems but who also have plenty of talents for which the Church should make adequate provision and room. I am afraid that a significant segment of our population which already regards the Church as sterile and self-protective will have more grist for their mill if proceedings against Jim are indicated. I am not afraid for the Church in either instance but I hope some other means can be worked out by which what you wish to achieve can be achieved and without the spat [sic] of emotions which is bound to be forthcoming. I think I ought to say this to you.[96]

Bishop Hines obviously did not welcome the contemplated presentment, and his letter reflects a pastoral concern for all involved very appropriate to the office he occupies.

On September 29 the Bishop of Delaware, J. Brooke Mosley, a close personal friend of both Bishop Pike and Bishop Louttit, telephoned the latter and appealed to him to yield to the wishes of so many of his brothers. He pointed out that the House of Bishops would convene in Wheeling, West Virginia, in only three weeks time and he asked that action with respect to Bishop Pike be deferred until that meeting. Bishop Louttit replied that he never made hasty decisions, begged leave for time "to say my prayers," and promised a decision within 24 hours.[97]

On September 30 Bishop Louttit sent the following telegram to Bishop Hines and to the signatories to his presentment and to those bishops who had expressed to him their concern:

WILL HOLD PRESENTMENT UNTIL HOUSE OF BISHOPS MEETING.[98]

On the same day he received from the Presiding Bishop this telegram:

COULD YOU PLEASE MEET WITH ME AT MY OFFICE ON MATTER OF PRESENTMENT WITH OTHER INDICATED SIGNERS MONDAY NEXT OCTOBER 3, LUNCH TWELVE NOON. YOUR EXPENSES WILL BE MET. IF SUNDAY NIGHT HOUSING DESIRED CALL MY OFFICE OR MY HOME. VITALLY IMPORTANT.[99]

On October 1 Bishop Louttit replied to the September 26 letter from Bishop Hines. He noted that the heavy mail he had received since announcing the presentment was overwhelmingly favorable to his action, and that his "offhand guess would be that the laity behind the movement run 90 percent, the clergy 95 percent, the bishops probably 90 percent." He added that he had already agreed to defer action until the meeting at Wheeling. His letter concluded:

You know John, I love you and will support you in every way I can. In this particular matter, I must do what I sincerely believe the Holy Spirit is leading me to do.[100]

On October 3 Bishop Louttit did meet in Bishop Hine's New York City office with others who had signed the presentment. The Presiding Bishop reported on a survey he had had taken among leaders in the mass media as to the probable effects of a heresy trial on the image of the Episcopal Church. It was their unanimous opinion, he said, that the consequences would be disastrous. He urged the presenters to withdraw their action and leave it to the House of Bishops in Wheeling to find some other way to deal with the problem posed by Bishop Pike.[101]

Bishop Louttit, supported by the others, refused to agree to withdraw his action, adding that he now had many more signers to whom he felt responsible. He did, however, reiterate that he would not formally file the presentment prior to Wheeling.

On September 29 the Retired Bishop of Central New York, Malcolm Endicott Peabody, had written Bishop Louttit expressing doubt that "the struggle of a trial" would be "helpful to the Church." "Surely," he added, "the counsel of Gamaliel (Acts 5: 38f) is still relevant to such a situation."[102] The text to which Bishop Peabody referred reads: "So in the present case I tell you, keep away from these men and let them alone; for if this plan or this undertaking is of men, it will fail; but if it is of God, you will not be able to overthrow them. You might even be found opposing God!"

It is a text worth pondering, but in the hurly-burly of the weeks to come few bishops were to pay it much heed.

The Appointment of the Dun Committee

One of the more quaint customs Episcopal bishops have is the habit—particularly in conversations among themselves—of referring to one another not by name but rather by diocese. Thus, one can project several of the bishops gathered for tea or cocktails, and in the course of light chatter some such remark as this being made: "I understand that Upper South Carolina and Eau Claire are going to support South Florida in his action against Jim Pike." This somewhat total identification of bishops with their territorial jurisdictions is, no doubt, an index of the seriousness with which they apply themselves to their pastoral responsibilities. Nevertheless, there is something whimsical about the habit when it is considered that the bishops are, in fact, chief pastors to a small minority of the people living within their diocesan territory. One can suppose, for example, that a reference to the Right Reverend Horace W. B. Donegan as "New York" might strike his episcopal cousin, Francis Cardinal Spellman, as presumptuous, the latter having far and away more sheep in *his* (Roman Catholic) flock.

South Florida, then, also on October 3, the day of his conference with Bishop Hines and others in New York City, dispatched yet another telegram, this one to certain bishops who had indicated specifically that they would not sign the presentment:

AM HOLDING PRESENTMENT UNTIL HOUSE OF BISHOPS MEETING. HOW DO YOU EXPLAIN TO THE CONSERVATIVES OF [NAME OF DIOCESE INSERTED] AND HAVE NOT SIGNED PRESENTMENT I DO NOT KNOW. I AM PRAYING TWICE DAILY AS I SAY THE OFFICES THAT THE HOLY SPIRIT WILL HELP YOU.

FAITHFULLY YOURS
HANK[103]

Bishops who received this wire were, for the most part, resentful of its implications, as was perhaps best demonstrated in a letter of October 6 to Bishop Louttit from the Bishop of Nevada, William Godsell Wright, who, after rather graciously suggesting that the telegram "must have been very badly garbled in the transmission," went on to complain:

My perturbation is not over the presentment or of the possibility of Jim Pike being brought to trial but over the way your telegram was transmitted to me. It sounds as though you feel that I am and will be in trouble with the conservatives of Nevada if I have not signed the presentment. It, also, sounds as though your prayers for me are to the intent that the Holy Spirit will guide me to sign the presentment. I appreciate your concern and I do appreciate your prayers but as stated it looks as though an effort is being made to conform to a particular course of action irrespective of what my own feelings in that respect are.[104]

Few bishops appear to have been intimidated by the threat or moved by the intercessions proffered in Bishop Louttit's telegram, but for whatever reasons the number of putative signers of the charges had by now risen to twenty-three and was eventually to reach twenty-eight, according to the Bishop's own estimates.[105]

In Chicago on October 4 the national council of the American Church Union—an organization concerned to preserve Anglican and orthodox traditions in the Episcopal Church—convened in St. James Cathedral. Its president, Chandler W. Sterling, Bishop of Montana, who had agreed to sign the presentment, publicly stated that Bishop Pike had "double-crossed" his fellow bishops. Pike had promised at Glacier Park, Bishop Sterling alleged, to consult more frequently with his brothers before speaking out on doctrinal matters, and he had promised not to ordain a woman, and he had violated both promises. Bishop Sterling also, despite the fact that he endorsed the charges, stated he opposed heresy trials as "anachronistic," and indicated that it was his hope that such a trial could be avoided by a voluntary renunciation of orders on the part of Bishop Pike.[106]

(Bishop Pike had, of course, explained the matter of the Reverend Phyllis Edwards in his letter to *Look*, but since the Presiding Bishop—in what he since has conceded may have been "faulty judgment"—failed, as promised, to circulate the letter to all bishops, Bishop Sterling was, at that time, ignorant of the facts.[107] On the matter of more frequent consultation on doctrinal subjects, Bishop Pike, who recalls making no such promise, has since asked: "What do they expect me to do? Do they mean that every time someone in an audience asks me a question on doctrine I should say I'll have to consult my brother bishops and then send you a letter?")

On October 5 the Association of Episcopal Clergy, an unofficial organization with headquarters in Palo Alto, California, which seeks to assist clergy in various sorts of trouble, convened its board of directors (one of whom is the Reverend Mrs. Phyllis Edwards).

The board unanimously voted to submit a lengthy petition to the House of Bishops which demanded an investigation of Father Frank M. Brunton and his Bishop, Henry I. Louttit, in relation to the proposed presentment against Bishop Pike. The petition also argued that Bishop Pike had been twice before "cleared" of heresy charges and that the action now of Bishop Louttit and others placed him in "double jeopardy." The petition concluded that "reasoned disagreement and charitable refutation of Bishop Pike's theological views, if possible, is infinitely more becoming to the church in the twentieth century than heresy trials."[108]

Bishop Pike, meanwhile, had been astonishingly silent, publicly, during all this furor, but that silence was broken on October 7 when two letters he had written Bishop Louttit, one dated September 28 and the other October 7, were released to the press. (The full texts of these and other letters exchanged, at the time, between the two bishops appear, as has been said, in the Appendix.) In substance, Bishop Pike repudiated the charges, and demanded that Bishop Louttit withdraw certain peripheral accusations "with or without apology, as your own ethic demands."

(Bishop Pike's mail at this time had been, if anything, even heavier than Bishop Louttit's, and was overwhelmingly supportive of his position and antagonistic to the Bishop of South Florida. Typical, for example, of correspondence Bishop Pike received from clergy is a letter dated October 7 from the Reverend Michael Allen, Rector of St. Mark's Church in-the-Bowery, New York City, the first paragraph of which reads:

I saw your statement in response to this crazy heresy business in the paper—and I agree absolutely. You're not on trial alone. Not even is it Jim Pike on trial—but a great many of us who have agreed with you and tried to take the same stands through the years, and I know, very deeply know, that what happens to you is happening to me. And therefore I'm damned sore.[109]

An exhaustive audit of the thousands of letters Bishop Pike received then and over the succeeding several months discloses an amazing number of clergy and laity *of all churches*—and even persons of no church—who have felt a similar identification with the Bishop in his tribulation.)

On October 12 Bishop Pike announced that he had submitted his resignation as Auxiliary Bishop of California, an honorary title conferred upon him by his Standing Committee at the time of his resignation as diocesan in California. He did this, he said, because he wished to "disassociate the diocese and my successor from the disturbing controversies Bishop Louttit has initiated."[110] His resignation was accepted, but he continued as an Honorary Canon of Grace Cathedral, San Francisco, and he also continued to assist, without stipend, in diocesan confirmations. Bishop Louttit, the same day, commented: "That's a step in the right direction. But what we want is for him to resign the episcopate. The common word is unfrocked. I want him to admit that he does not accept the Faith."[111]

(Actually, as Bishop Pike pointed out in one of his letters to Bishop Louttit, a bishop cannot "resign the episcopate." There is no provision in canon law for such an action. A bishop may, of course, be deposed, on charges or by his own request, but he would remain a bishop—a *deposed* bishop. In short, under canon law, a bishop has an "indelible character" similar to that the House of Bishops at Glacier Park decreed for deconesses.)

On October 13 the Right Reverend Horace W. B. Donegan, before his diocesan council, made a statement on the gathering turmoil. He also distributed it to his brother bishops and to his own clergy and released it to the press.[112] Bishop Donegan's remarks were a lucid, temperate, and careful expression of the views of moderate churchmen, and were to have considerable influence on some other bishops. For these reasons, it seems fitting to quote from the statement at some length:

Of all the methods of dealing with Bishop Pike's views, the *very worst* is surely a heresy trial! Whatever the result, the good name of the church will be greatly injured.
Should there be a presentment and trial of Bishop Pike (which I hope and pray will not happen) the harm, the divisiveness and the lasting bitterness that will be inflicted on the Church we love and serve will be inevitable . . .
In the long history of the Anglican Communion there have been times of tension when many people took reprisals on those who disagreed in matters of theology. When John Wesley's followers left us, we com-

monly say, it was because the church did not have sufficient understanding and sympathy. By contrast the Oxford Movement (Pusey, Keble and Newman) as a group was not allowed to leave us. Only individual defections took place . . .

It is my conviction that Bishop Pike is trying to tell the new generation something they don't ordinarily hear but which they desperately need to know, namely that Christianity is relevant and has a solution to their problems—the only solution if we can get people to take it seriously . . .

In so far as Bishop Pike rejects the church's doctrines he is wrong. Nevertheless I sincerely believe he is endeavoring to say in a new way to the new generation that dogmas are not mathematical formulas, but descriptive statements of what is really transcendent mystery which, while it cannot be adequately understood, *can be experienced and lived* . . .

All of us must practice compassion, charity and patience and respect each other's integrity, as each seeks in his own way, to proclaim the relevance of the Christian faith to this new age.

The Bishop of New York, fair and frank about the conduct and views of his former dean, proposed, in effect, a reconciliation, not in the end to prevail, based upon honest differences respectfully and sympathetically endured.

The Bishop of Mississippi, John Maury Allin, approached the problem with similar concern for reconciliation but from a rather startlingly original point of departure. In a letter to Bishop Pike dated October 19, after establishing at great length that the issue, in his opinion, was neither heresy nor free inquiry but rather order in the church, he concluded:

For the sake of the Order and the order within the Order, I beseech you now to terminate your Episcopal function and voluntarily relinquish your Episcopal faculties.

This is an hard and courageous action which I request of you. If justice require of one making such a request the willingness to do personally what is being requested of another, then please accept my word that if it is revealed that the Order would be strengthened and the Mission better served if I, too, resigned, I am prepared to deal with the necessary decision. While I find great satisfaction within the Office of

Bishop, I am convinced there is great service and vocation beyond it. In this light, I make my request of you.[113]

Did Bishop Allin mean that he was prepared to relinquish the episcopacy if Bishop Pike would? All that can be said here is: neither bishop has relinquished the episcopacy (and, as has been said, under canon law, neither can).

On October 18 the Presiding Bishop informed his brethren that he had decided to appoint a special *ad hoc* committee to consider all the issues involved in the controversy and to report its findings to the House of Bishops in Wheeling. Noting that Bishop Louttit had agreed to defer his presentment until that meeting, Bishop Hines wrote:

Any official proceedings should they have been initiated prior to the meeting of the House might well have committed the Church for weal or woe so decisively without the House of Bishops having had the opportunity to confront the issue I felt the result might be appalling.

He indicated that the special committee would be chaired by the Retired Bishop of Washington, Angus Dun, but he did not disclose the names of other members appointed to the committee.[114]

To Bishop Dun had fallen a most unenviable assignment.

The Agitation of a Fraternity

An embarrassing oversight had, meanwhile, been discovered, and on October 19 it became public knowledge that the Court for a Trial of a Bishop lacked a quorum.[115] That Court, under canon law, consists of nine bishops, three of whom retire at each General Convention and are replaced by three others elected by the same convention. At the convention in St. Louis in 1964 the committee assigned to nominate new members for the Court never met and never reported. Meanwhile, one member of the Court had died, and there being left only five bishops on the Court the required quorum of six did not exist and the Court could not function until after the General Convention of 1967 met and elected replacements for the vacancies.

The trial Bishop Louttit contemplated could not, therefore, take place until, at the least, a year later.

The chairman of the 1964 nominating committee, the Bishop of Rhode Island, John Seville Higgins, indicated that no one ever asked him for a report and he had himself forgotten that he had the assignment. Responsibility for the agenda of meetings of the House of Bishops rests with the Committee on the Dispatch of Business, whose chairman is the Bishop of South Florida. Bishop Louttit, however, has denied that he bore sole responsibility for the apparent oversight. "I don't figure out what we do," he has said. "I just make up the time schedule."[116]

Whether or not he had, in fact, figured out what to do about the problem posed by Bishop Pike, he had, by his inadvertence, established a more protracted time schedule, a happenstance that allowed "breathing room" for those bishops inclined towards moderation.

Bishop Dun, meanwhile, was at work on the draft of a statement he would bring to Wheeling for the consideration of his committee. It was a committee remarkable in many ways, not least in the nature of its composition. A call of the roster is in order:

The Right Reverend Angus Dun, Retired Bishop of Washington, venerable, scholarly, aloof and highly respected throughout the Church: he had ordained Pike in 1946 and in 1960 chaired the committee that produced the severe Pastoral Letter on doctrine.

The Right Reverend Stephen Fielding Bayne, Jr., Vice-President of the Executive Council of the Episcopal Church and Director of its Overseas Department, former Bishop of Olympia, former Executive Officer of the Anglican Communion, an accomplished administrator: he was a prominent candidate for Presiding Bishop in 1964.

The Right Reverend Walter Conrad Klein, Bishop of Northern Indiana, former Dean of Nashotah House, a junior member of the House, having been consecrated in 1963, self-effacing and able: he had signed the presentment the committee was to consider.

The Right Reverend Henry Irving Louttit, Bishop of South Florida, and instigator of the charges the committee had been appointed to consider.

The Right Reverend Frederick John Warnecke, Bishop of Bethlehem, genial and composed, liberal on social issues, conventional in theology: he exemplifies moderation.

The Right Reverend J. Brooke Mosley, Bishop of Delaware, gracious and dedicated: he is a close personal friend of Bishop Pike and of Bishop Louttit.

The Right Reverend Jonathan Goodhue Sherman, Bishop of Long Island, erudite theologically and conservative by temperament: he had signed, with reservations, the presentment the committee was to consider.

The Right Reverend Richard Stanley Merrill Emrich, Bishop of Michigan, incumbent since 1948, theologically concerned and authoritarian by disposition: he is chairman of the Theological Committee of the House, established in 1964.

Bishop Hines, who created this committee, has explained that its composition came about this way: he took the Theological Committee, exempting, however, Bishop Pike, and adding Bishop Louttit, representing, as it were, the accusers, and Bishop Mosley, representing, after a fashion, the interests of Bishop Pike.[117] However it came about, the committee plainly included three bishops who had signified support of the presentment by signing it—not least the chief accuser—and only two bishops—Mosley and Warnecke—who might be said to have exhibited any sympathy for Bishop Pike's situation. Most incredible, though, is that, while *including* Bishop Louttit, the Presiding Bishop specifically *excluded* Bishop Pike.

The House of Bishops convened in Wilson Lodge, Oglebay Park, Wheeling, West Virginia, on Sunday October 23, 1966, for the most exacerbated three days of deliberation it had ever known. Bishop Dun's committee gathered on opening day. Their discussions are not on public record but it is known that the draft statement of Bishop Dun was insufficient from Bishop Louttit's point of view and too severe from Bishop Mosley's. Modifications were made in both directions, such that Bishop Louttit believes it was strengthened and Bishop Mosley believes it was softened. (The full text of the statement as received and voted by the House may be found in the Appendix.) Bishop Dun had proposed—as the statement makes plain—and the committee was persuaded, unanimously, that a heresy trial would be rejected, but a harsh censure would be visited upon the Resigned Bishop of California.

Bishop Pike had repeatedly appealed to Bishop Dun and to Bishop Hines that he be allowed to appear before this committee to defend himself, but his appeals fell on deaf ears. No opportunity whatsoever was accorded Bishop Pike to explain to the committee his position with respect to the charges Bishop Louttit had made against him.

More than 140 of the nearly 200 bishops attended the sessions in Wheeling—an extraordinary turn-out—and many, especially from among retired bishops, came, some at risk to their health, out of deep concern about the Bishop Pike affair. Numerous were the conclaves, private tête-à-têtes, coffee conversations and other behind the scenes confrontations. The House of Bishops was sorely divided, profoundly distressed, and often anguished.

One aged and revered bishop, who seldom attends meetings of the House in his retirement, journeyed to Wheeling solely in the hope he might somehow be helpful in healing the wounds the controversy had opened. When the debate had concluded, and the House "for weal or woe" had acted, that elderly bishop recalls having gone to bed more agitated than he had ever been in his life, and, for the first time in his life, he required, he has said, a sleeping pill.[118]

The Dealings at Wheeling

Bishop Emrich's Theological Committee, all this while, had not been wholly inactive.

(About a year earlier, Bishop Emrich, in his capacity as chairman of that committee, having read Ved Mehta's series of articles in *The New Yorker* on "The New Theology," discovered to his horror that one of the leaders of the "God is Dead" movement was Dr. Paul van Buren, an Episcopal priest on the faculty of Temple University, and this seemed so outrageous to the Bishop of Michigan that he wrote the Presiding Bishop, demanding that van Buren be removed from orders. Nothing came of this initiative, however, when Dr. van Buren's chief pastor, Robert Lionne De Witt, Bishop of Pennsylvania, indicated that he certainly would not be party to any such action.[119])

The House of Bishops having instructed its Theological Committee to keep it informed "from time to time" on current trends in theology, Bishop Emrich proposed that some sort of presentation on that subject be included in the agenda at Wheeling. He requested members of his committee to come to Wheeling a day early—on October 22—to perfect such a presentation. Several of the members—among them Bishop Pike "at considerable personal inconvenience"—did so, but they found that the chairman had changed his mind, or perhaps had had his mind changed for him.

There would be no theological presentation at Wheeling, he announced, because the time for it had been preempted by the debate now scheduled concerning the problem of Bishop Pike. The chairman proposed, therefore, that the committee instead address itself to a point raised by the Bishop of Connecticut, Walter Henry Gray, namely, whether or not deacons could properly distribute both elements of the Holy Communion. Bishop Emrich offered a paper learnedly recounting the views on that matter of Justin Martyr and other worthies. Bishop Pike introduced the doctrine of concomitance as developed by St. Thomas Aquinas. After much esoteric deliberation the committee concluded that deacons may indeed distribute both elements, and the House was subsequently to accept a resolution to that effect.[120]

Bishop Pike has since said: "I had a feeling we had come a long way and a day early to discuss something quite secondary, to say the least."

Two weeks before his arrival in Wheeling Bishop Pike had received a letter from the Bishop of West Virginia, Wilburn Camrock Campbell, host bishop on this occasion, specifically "inhibiting" Bishop Pike from preaching before any Episcopal congregation in the Diocese of West Virginia. Bishop Campbell cited as justification for this "gagging" of his brother a provision of canon law authorizing such a procedure with respect to any minister who stands under the "imputation of having elsewhere been guilty" of a variety of offenses.[121] It is debatable whether or not the canon applied to Bishop Pike, since the presentment of charges against him had not, formally, been filed, but he acceded, nonetheless, to the inhibition. Two such engagements in Wheeling were cancelled by those who had issued the invitations. He had not been inhibited from preaching before other auspices, however, and he was to make several hugely attended appearances in Wheeling during the several days he was there.

The House of Bishops officially convened on the afternoon of Sunday, October 23, a day devoted to a series of meditations conducted by the Provost of Coventry Cathedral, England, the Very Reverend H.C.N. Williams. The day was designated a "Quiet Day" but except on the floor it was not without discordance, Bishop Dun and his *Ad Hoc* Committee being engaged in the polishing of the statement that would two days later engender unprecedented episcopal acrimony.

Monday morning, October 24, the House got down to business, but there was to be very little business of note that did not revolve around the Resigned Bishop of California.

His status as a resigned bishop was itself among the first matters to arise, since resigned bishops do not, unless specifically accorded by the House, have a seat, voice, or vote in the House. On a motion of the Bishop of South Florida, the status of Bishop Pike was referred to the Committee on Amendments to the Constitution, and he was meanwhile granted temporarily seat and voice but no vote. The committee was subsequently to sustain, the House concurring, *that* status for the Wheeling meeting *only*.[122] (The chairman of that particular committee, Charles Colcock Jones Carpenter, Bishop of Alabama, an extreme conservative in every way, has an undisguised hostility for Bishop Pike. When he has occasion to speak to Bishop Pike, for example, Bishop Carpenter addresses him invariably not by given name or ecclesiastical title but as "Doctor," a reference, presumably, to the celebrated "white divinity" degree fracas in 1953.)

The House thereupon "validated" the *Ad Hoc* Dun Committee as constituted by the Presiding Bishop. It voted to receive the report of the committee the following evening at 9:00 P.M., but this conflicted with a preaching engagement Bishop Pike had, and, on a motion of the Bishop of West Virginia, the time was changed to 3:00 P.M. the following afternoon.[123]

The Bishop of Michigan moved that the Bishops gather, in the coming year, in their various provinces, together with scholars acquainted with the new theology, and report any findings of interest to his Theological Committee, and the House so voted.[124] The Bishop of South Florida moved that a foundation be established for the purpose of reinterpreting the Gospel and the Faith to each succeeding generation, a motion he was ultimately, after complex maneuvering, to withdraw.[125]

Later in the day Bishop Louttit moved to reconsider the question of how the House would receive the Dun committee report. Bishop Dun rose to speak of the burden placed upon him and his committee in trying to resolve an "interfamiliar" quarrel, and he suggested that the burden might be eased if the House would receive the report in closed session. The Bishop of West Virginia, however, objected to closed sessions which he felt were not wholesome for the Church generally. After prolonged discussion the House decided to have it both ways, and voted to receive the report first in closed session and then in open session.[126]

That evening, there being no notable business on the agenda, a substantial number of bishops repaired to a special commissary the officials had established to circumvent the problem posed by the absence of bars in Wheeling. Nothing could drive from their minds the great issue they would the next day decide, and some bishops found it necessary to brace themselves lavishly for the ordeal. Bishop Pike went off to address Bethany College, a Disciples of Christ institution, from which he was to attract for the next day's debate an enthusiastic claque of supporters.

(Late that evening the Bishop "made the rounds" of a series of episcopal parties in order, he has said, "to get the feel of things," having learned from several years' experience that an astute teetotaler can pick up considerable useful information from such occasions. The "feel" he picked up was not encouraging, and he went to bed pondering what he might do should intolerable action be taken against him.)

Tuesday, October 25, the House convened at 10:00 A.M. and received in person "greetings in the love of our Lord Jesus Christ" from the Bishop of the Roman Catholic Diocese of Wheeling, the Most Reverend Joseph Hodges.[127] This ecumenically auspicious commencement was an improbable introduction to a session that was to end in utter disarray.

Business proceeded routinely for some hours: prayers were expressed for Episcopal chaplains, especially in Viet Nam; deacons were accorded the right to distribute both elements of Holy Communion; seminaries were advised to teach Sign Language, giving "credit for it, just as for Hebrew and Greek"; a Position Paper on "Population, Poverty, and Peace" was adopted; two missionary bishops were elected, and one, then Bishop of the Philippines, addressed the House; and a series of proposed changes in canon law were disposed of in assorted ways.[128]

The Bishop of South Florida interrupted these harmonious and harmless proceedings. He called attention to an article by the Reverend Lester Kinsolving in the *San Francisco Chronicle*, under date of October 21, 1966, pertaining, among other things, to the lack of a quorum in the Court for the Trial of a Bishop. Bishop Louttit, noting the presence of Father Kinsolving in the press gallery, moved that the *San Francisco Chronicle* be notified that the Reverend Lester Kinsolving was not acceptable to the House as an accredited reporter. On a motion of the Bishop of Connecticut, Bishop Louttit's petulant motion was tabled.[129]

(Bishop Pike, meanwhile, having spoken against Bishop Louttit's attempt to evict Father Kinsolving, rushed to the Jesuit College of Wheeling to honor a speaking engagement. He returned just in time for the censure debate, and he was shortly to be followed by many nuns and students from that college who were enthusiastically to support his cause from the galleries that afternoon and evening.)

Finally, somewhat tardy, the House moved into executive session at 3:30 P.M. to receive the report of Bishop Dun's committee. No bishop not on that committee had yet seen the report, and copies were distributed while Bishop Dun read out what has come to be called *the censure* of Bishop Pike. (The full text of that censure may be found in the Appendix.) In substance, it declared that a trial "would not solve the problem presented to the Church by this minister," and it went on through many fustian paragraphs to denounce that minister, not for his theology, which it scarcely mentioned, but for sundry unspecified defects alleged to be discernible in his character, conduct, and utterances both as a pastor and as a man. It was not a document likely to adorn the history of redemptive literature, though it may be admired for a certain magisterial style and felicities of vindictive expression.

At 4:25 P.M. the House moved itself out of closed session into open debate, a process accomplished by permitting the entrance of an armada of newsmen, cameramen, episcopal wives, and such plain folk as could find room in the galleries. The atmosphere was electric, as were the klieg lights, and the bishops were in a state of solemn agitation, seated in rows, one hundred forty or more of them physically present, and arrayed according to seniority, the senior bishops to the fore and the junior to the rear. One hundred forty odd bishops in black clerical attire, their episcopal dignity signified by purple vests, would be a somber spectacle under any circumstances, and the medieval modernity of this peculiar occasion introduced the incongruent atmosphere of an ecclesiastical circus.

Few of the bishops chose to direct their eyes toward their episcopal brother, the Resigned Bishop of California, but he was, when he managed to remain in his seat, the unchallenged center of attention.

The Bishop is for Burning

Bishop Hines, presiding, recognized the Clerk of the Bishops in Council, Thomas Henry Wright, Bishop of East Carolina, who moved that debate be limited to one hour: that Bishop Pike be permitted to speak for ten minutes, the Bishop of South Florida for ten minutes, and all other speakers for three minutes; and that members be allowed to address the House only once, except with the consent of the House. These ground rules were accepted without dissent.[130]

Bishop Dun thereupon rose, and having prayed "that the spirit of wisdom may save us from all false choices," explained that the closed session immediately preceding had been solely for the purpose of acquainting the bishops with the proposed censure, no discussion as to its merits having taken place. He noted that the report of his committee was unanimously endorsed, save that the Bishop of Northern Indiana had been unable to participate in drafting it and so had not joined in its submission. Bishop Dun then read the proposed statement in full and moved its adoption, which was promptly seconded.[131]

The Bishop of Northern Indiana, rising to a point of personal privilege, stated that he had been pastorally detained from joining in the draft of the statement, but having read it he wished to give his assent and approval, and he expressed the hope it would be voted without amendment.[132]

Bishop Hines invited as first speaker the Bishop of Easton, Allen Jerome Miller, who had requested this courtesy on account of his age and ill-health. Bishop Miller is a gentle and scholarly man of abundant theological sophistication, and his diocese, which is in Maryland, being one of the tiniest in the Episcopal Church, having fewer than 10,000 communicants, he may be presumed to have had some leisure for the pursuit of his scholarly interests. He attempted to address himself to an issue he thought central to the controversy before the House, namely the distinction between existential and ontological theology. Bishop Hines, incredibly, ruled him out of order, indeed ruled that *any* discussion of theology was out of order, and the debate would be restricted entirely to the merits of the report before the House. Bishop Miller was silenced.

The Bishop of Massachusetts, Anson Phelps Stokes, Jr., rose to state that having had but one hour to reflect on the document he felt unprepared to speak to it, much less to vote on it, and he hoped some way could be found to defer a vote. Bishop Hines ruled that this also was out of order.

John P. Craine, Bishop of Indianapolis, supported Bishop Stokes, noting that the matter was far too serious for "precipitate action." He moved that the statement be referred back to committee for appropriate amendment. He was ruled out of order, though the Presiding Bishop pointed out that amendments from the floor would be in order. Bishop Craine expressed doubt that responsible amendment could be accomplished from the floor, and moved that the matter be held over until the following morning. He was again ruled out of order.

Bishop Pike rose to protest that there had been insufficient time to consider the document as a whole, but that his impression of it was that he was already under trial by a committee to which he had had no access. Bishop Hines replied that Bishop Pike would have ten minutes to protest later in the debate.

Bishop De Witt of Pennsylvania strenuously objected to the censorious and judgmental character of the statement and moved to delete three paragraphs he considered wholly unacceptable.

Bishop Pike rose to speak—not to the whole question but to the motion of Bishop De Witt. He used the three minutes allowed him for that purpose to answer some of the accusations made against him in the committee report. He supported the motion but stated he would prefer that the whole question be put over until the next day so that he might have time adequately to prepare a response.

William F. Creighton, Bishop of Washington, moved to overrule the chair's decision not to defer the debate one day, and he demanded that the vote on his motion be counted. Bishop Hines was sustained in his ruling by a vote of 89 to 38. The House then voted down Bishop De Witt's motion to delete three paragraphs.[133]

The Suffragan Bishop of Washington, Paul Moore, Jr., took the floor. Acknowledging "the great care and beauty of the statement," he questioned, nonetheless, the propriety of the censure, given that far graver "blasphemies" in some dioceses had gone uncensured. While he would prefer that the statement be set aside, he admitted this seemed unlikely and moved certain deletions, the Bishop of Rochester modifying, but these actions also were voted down.[134]

The Bishop of Newark, Leland Stark, deplored much of the language of the statement but said he would vote for it anyway, though he gave no reason for doing so.[135]

Charles Francis Hall, Bishop of New Hampshire, proposed that the following sentence be added to the statement:

We still trust that his leadership may increase by God's Grace as his years go from strength to strength.

The motion was denied.[136]

The hour allowed for debate was drawing near a close, and Bishop Hines noted that "recognizably" Bishop Pike wanted to have his ten minutes before the matter was closed. Bishop Louttit indicated that he would yield *his* ten minutes, and, in fact, that was the sole contribution he was to make to the debate.

The Bishop of Vermont, Harvey Dean Butterfield, protested the absence of the spirit of Jesus Christ from the deliberations, and very vigorously called for the defeat of the proposed censure.

The Bishop of Alaska, William Jones Gordon, Jr., moved to table the matter—an action that would have delayed indefinitely any action on it—and this was defeated, surprisingly narrowly, 74 to 61.[137]

The stipulated hour had by now expired and the bishops proceeded through 30 minutes of complicated parliamentary disorder that ended with a decision to continue the debate until it had reached a conclusion. The Bishop of West Missouri, Edward Randolph Welles, expressed the sentiments of the House: "I don't want people five years from now to say we didn't give Jim Pike plenty of time." On a motion of the Bishop Coadjutor of Central New York the House adjourned until 9:30 that evening.[138]

"That will give us," Bishop Cole, with a touch of cynicism, remarked, "a chance to eat, drink, and be merry."

An Ecumenical Interlude

Bishop Pike was not feeling particularly merry; he does not drink and, because of a longstanding preaching engagement, he was not even to eat.

Instead, time being extremely limited, he was raced, under police escort, to a Lutheran church in Wheeling for a special service of the American Guild of Organists, an event in which ministers of many denominations participated. Bishop Pike delivered the sermon—on liturgical reform, not on doctrine. The benediction was offered by Roman Catholic Bishop Joseph Hodges, who had that morning, as a representative of the Catholic churches in Wheeling, greeted the House of Bishops.

During these ecumenical ceremonies Bishop Hodges provided to Bishop Pike a crozier, the symbol in both their churches of episcopal authority.

It was an exceptional ecumenical gesture, in the circumstances, by a Roman prelate.[139]

A Night to Remember

At 9:30 P.M. the bishops, merry or otherwise, reconvened to endure several hours of rodomontade verbiage, unique even in their cumulatively vast experience of postprandial rhetoric.

Bishop Hines called upon the "Bishop of Olympia," then corrected himself to "the former Bishop of Olympia" (Bishop Bayne, Vice-President of the Executive Council, had resigned his see in Olympia in 1960). "Gee," said the Presiding Bishop, amidst laughter, "it's nice to dream of the past." Bishop Bayne, a member of the censure committee, was on the platform, seated next to Bishop Dun, because the latter could not hear the debate and needed, as Bishop Bayne put it, "an extra pair of ears."

The former Bishop of Olympia, then, explained that he had requested to be first speaker of the evening in order to respond, for the committee, to two criticisms of its procedures that he had detected in remarks made during the afternoon session. Why had Bishop Louttit, chief accuser, been on the committee, and Bishop Pike, accused, denied a hearing by the committee? Bishop Pike was not heard, Bishop Bayne said, because the committee was not a "kangaroo court" and the accused was not on trial. Bishop Louttit was included in the committee, he said, because any statement developed would require that bishop's concurrence if it was to be successful. Somewhat poignantly, he told the House: "I'm in my twentieth year in this House. I cannot remember a more distasteful moment than this in which we are all engaged." There were not a few inaudible amens.

Bishop Emrich of Michigan rose to support the committee's statement. He began with the accusation that Bishop Pike had not played fair with the House since it last met in Montana. He went on to explore Bishop Pike's theological views, which led Bishop Pike, rising to a point of order, to remind the chair that theology had been excluded from the discussion. Bishop Hines sustained Bishop Pike's objection, and the Bishop of Michigan returned to his prior train of thought, concluding that he supported the censure "with all that is in me."

Bishop Pike rose to a point of personal privilege. Bitterly, he took exception to Bishop Emrich's charge that he had not played fair with the House. In some detail he rehearsed the events that had transpired at Glacier Park and at O'Hare Airport and the letter to *Look* never circulated to all bishops. (Following the Wheeling meetings Bishop Hines did so circulate that letter with a cover note expressing regret that he had not done so earlier.) When Bishop Pike had been heard at some length, the Presiding

Bishop ruled that his remarks were "irrelevant." Bishop Pike reluctantly agreed to reserve further comment until his allotted ten-minute period.

J. Brooke Mosley, Bishop of Delaware, probably Bishop Pike's closest personal friend in the House, spoke in support of the statement. He was not himself, he said, offended by Bishop Pike's utterances, but others were, a heresy trial would be damaging, and the committee, he believed, had concluded a "necessary compromise." The Bishop of Bethlehem, Frederick John Warnecke, joined in this opinion, stressing that the matter was a family question; Bishop Pike, he said, had not observed the "courtesies which are necessary in family life," whereas his brothers had displayed great concern for him "in meeting after meeting after meeting after meeting." There were, he seemed to imply, limits beyond which not even episcopal concern should extend.

The Bishop of New York, Horace W. B. Donegan, rose to endorse, with evident misgivings, the censure of his former dean. (He began by noting that the proposed statement said Bishop Pike "would *dissect* the doctrine of the Trinity from the corpus of Christian truth" [Bishop Donegan's words], and he wondered if this would not align the House with the "God is Dead" theology. Perhaps, he facetiously suggested, *"vivisect"* would have been a better choice of language.) "I have been," he went on, "in this House nineteen years, and nothing that has ever happened has caused me more anguish or soul-searching. Bishop Pike was my very able and loyal dean for six years." With intense emotion he declared:

I shall vote for the statement, but I profoundly regret the charge of irresponsibility. This is an attack on a man's integrity. We have refrained from placing Bishop Pike on trial for his theology. But, brethren, according to my judgment, by this statement we are condemning him without trial at a deeper level of his personal integrity, and I hope the document will be amended at this point.

John Maury Allin, Bishop of Mississippi, requested permission from Bishop Pike to read a letter he had written the latter concerning the issues under discussion.[140] Having read part of the letter, Bishop Allin stated that he believed enough had now been said: "If Bishop Pike hasn't heard us now, he will never hear us."

Whereupon, unexpectedly, the Bishop of Mississippi moved to table the motion. He was promptly voted down.[141]

The Bishop of Virginia, Robert Fisher Gibson, Jr., moved to amend the censure by removing two words from it: "and" (a grammatical consideration, apparently) and "totally" as modifying the word "irresponsible." The amendment carried, and Bishop Pike, though still "irresponsible," was no longer "totally" so.[142]

The Right Reverend Daniel Corrigan, Director of the Home Department of the Executive Council, powerfully condemned the proposed censure for its violation of due process of law. He suggested, his voice trembling with indignation, that the real issue was that the House seemed about to condemn a man "in some deep sense to death." Bishop Corrigan may have made the most insightful contribution the collective wisdom of the episcopacy was to summon to this debate.

Roger Wilson Blanchard, Bishop of Southern Ohio, supported by the Bishop of Southwestern Virginia, William Henry Marmion, offered a substantial amendment that, in effect, softened the censure. This was voted down 78 to 53. The Bishop of Erie, William Crittenden, offered a briefer amendment to the same purpose, and this was defeated by voice vote.[143]

The Bishop of Albany, Allen Webster Brown, supporting the statement, announced that he sensed a need for more of a "redemptive tone" in it, and proposed the addition of the following words:

"and we take this action aware of our common need for redemption, forgiveness, and love."

Bishop Dun, on behalf of his committee, accepted this suggestion, and no vote, therefore, was necessary.[144]

It may seem astonishing how easily redemption, in high places, is achieved.

A Rhapsody in Purple

The bishops had by now exhausted their resources in the matter before them, and finally, just after 11:00 P.M., the Resigned Bishop of California rose to exercise his allotted ten minutes, and he was to demonstrate, in the ensuing fifty minutes, that he had by no means exhausted *his* resources.

"Most Reverend Sir and my Brethren," he began, and the hush in the House was to settle into stillness as he earnestly pleaded his integrity through some eighteen tormented minutes, gently interrupted only then by the subdued Presiding Bishop. To the excoriations heaped upon him in the censure document and in the preceding debate, Bishop Pike was to respond with citations from learned men and saints who had bespoken a more catholic comprehension of what the ministry of Christ should be.

Lamenting that he had had inadequate time to prepare, having first seen the censure statement only some seven hours earlier and having been "rather occupied" ever since, he asked Bishop Corrigan to hold up a large pile of documents he had brought with him to Wheeling—"at the cost of overweight baggage"—and which he meant to offer as part of his defense before the Dun committee. That committee having denied him any hearing at all, and ten minutes being obviously insufficient to enable examination of the material, he would, he indicated, content himself with pointing, at least, to the defense he had not been allowed to make. Noting that the censure report specifically stated that certain "conclusions" had been drawn, Bishop Pike asked upon what data those conclusions were based. "I am part of that data," he said, "and I have not been heard, nor has the data I brought with me been reviewed."

The accusations—"unsubstantiated"—made in the contemplated censure were, the Bishop asserted, "far more serious than any charges contained in the presentment brought by Bishop Louttit, affecting, as they do, my work, my ministry, my professional standing and my personhood." The strains of the long day had, he confided, rendered him "a little inarticulate"—[he may, given the circumstances, be forgiven this forensic excess]—and he would, therefore, say what little he could in the words of *others* who had tried to speak the truth in love.

He began with a quotation from St. Augustine, the purport of which was if someone could not understand what had been written then let him read what he could understand, throwing away, if he chose, the book that offended. The quotation concluded: "If what I have written is not according to the truth, then let him only hold fast to his opinion and refute mine, if that is possible, and let me know of it, too, and impart his knowledge to everyone else whom he can reach. The method I sum up in this sentence is brotherly discussion." The point was well taken, but taken, unfortunately, much too late in the day.

Bishop Pike proceeded to cite some remarks about the Creeds made in 1924 by Angus Dun, that same bishop who had ordained Pike deacon and priest, and had now chaired the committee of censure. Dun had been, in 1924, on the faculty of the Episcopal Theological School in Cambridge, Massachusetts, and his theology had been, in those long gone days, liberal, more liberal, perhaps, than Bishop Pike's was in 1966. The burden of the passage Pike cited was that evangelism in America might—if the Creeds were *literally* offered to "semi-pagan college students"—amount to expressing "the unknown by the unknown." Bishop Dun's interest in creedal reformation does not appear to have survived his distinguished episcopacy.

Finally, Bishop Pike read several excerpts from *Freedom Today*, a book authored by Father Hans Küng, the celebrated Jesuit theologian who played a prominent part in the 2nd Vatican Council.[145] The passages, taken together, are an eloquent summary of Father Küng's vigilant concern for maximum freedom of expression in theology. His tenor is reflected in this paragraph, read by Bishop Pike:

The theologian does not have to crouch nervously over his work trying to sprint in every direction at once. He can hold his head up, and look men in the eyes, as he performs his service. What are needed from him are honesty and integrity, fearlessness and steadfastness, intrepidity and determination. Freedom in theology is a necessary condition for multiplicity in theology.

It must be said, however, that not even Father Küng, for all his manifest intellectual courage, has ever been compelled to stand before one hundred thirty-nine Bishops about to condemn him, in order to defend his *right* to hold his head up. One wonders what Pope John XXIII would have felt had he witnessed the events in

Wilson Lodge, Wheeling, West Virginia, on October 25, the year of our Lord 1966.

Bishop Pike concluded his apologia by addressing himself very directly to the charge of "irresponsibility." (First of all, he admitted with chagrin: "I seem to have lost the watch I borrowed from the Presiding Bishop to time these remarks.") He argued that he had been most vocal of any of the bishops in rejecting the "God is Dead" movement, so much so that one of its proponents, Dr. William Hamilton, had described Pike as "the smoothest representative today for orthodox theology." The Bishop noted that he had relinquished "a very interesting and desirable administrative post" in order to devote his full energies to scholarly research, theological reflection, and writing, a step he thought demonstrated considerable responsibility. He had just begun to discuss what it was that he *could* affirm theologically, when his attention was called to the clock, and, with apologies for exceeding his ten-minute allotment, abruptly he sat down.

The chair called upon Bishop Dun to make any closing comments that might seem fitting, and, wearily and with sadness, the 74-year-old patriarch reviewed the arguments previously made in support of the censure, disavowed any intent on his part to engage in "brutality," and expressed his belief that the committee's statement reflected the "mind of this House." He concluded: "I think I will bear no wounds that cannot heal, and I trust that will be true of Bishop Pike."

Amid respectful applause, Bishop Dun resumed his seat, and the great debate was at an end.

The Bishop of Newark, Leland Stark, on a point of order, objected that Bishop Dun should have the last word and asked that Bishop Pike be given the opportunity of a final statement. Bishop Hines ruled that this would be out of order.

Bishop Cole of Central New York, supported by Bishop Barrett of Rochester, demanded that there should be a roll call vote when the matter was put to the House for decision. After some confusion the chair ruled that out of order also, but indicated it would permit a standing vote which would be counted.

Bishop Hines then asked those in favor of the censure to rise and 104 bishops did so; he asked those opposed to rise and 35 bishops did so. William Crittenden, Bishop of Erie, saying he was so confused he didn't know what he was voting, subsequently changed his vote, and the final tabulation stood at 103 to 36.[146]

(A tabulation of this vote by names of bishops, insofar as it has been possible to reconstruct it, may be found in the Appendix. 22 bishops specifically asked that their names be disassociated from the censure, and their names also may be found in the Appendix.)

Anson Phelps Stokes, Jr., Bishop of Massachusetts, noting that the issues under discussion went far beyond personalities, offered a resolution to establish a council to help "re-think, re-structure and renew the Church for life in the world today"—in effect, a call for a sort of "little Vatican Council." (The full text of the Stokes Resolution—which embodied a proposal Bishop Pike had urged for years—as adopted unanimously by the House the following day may be found in the Appendix.)

The Bishop of Washington, William Creighton, presented to the House a "Minority Statement"—which the chair agreed to receive as "information"—with respect to Bishop Pike, supportive of his position in the controversy. (The full text of that statement with a list of 17 bishops joining in it may be found in the Appendix.)

The business before the House seemed to have been concluded, but the House had not reckoned on the resourcefulness of the Resigned Bishop of California.

Rising to a point of personal privilege, Bishop Pike addressed the chair. Asserting that there "are in circulation rumors, reports, and allegations, affecting my personal and official character," he demanded, under pertinent provisions of canon law, an investigation and "such further steps as may become appropriate." (The full text of Bishop Pike's statement to the chair may be found in the Appendix.)

The House was stunned. The action Bishop Pike had taken could, if it were to proceed through its full potential course, eventuate in the very trial for heresy which the bishops had so agonized to avoid. The censure had prevailed, but Bishop Pike had seized the ball, and where he would run with it only time would tell.

As is required by the canons two bishops joined in Bishop

Pike's formal demand for an investigation: John P. Craine, Bishop of Indianapolis, and Chauncey Kilmer Myers, Suffragan Bishop of Michigan and Bishop-Elect of California.

(Bishop Myers, though already elected to succeed Bishop Pike, did not assume his new post until the following January, and was, in fact, consecrated 6th Bishop of California in Grace Cathedral on January 14, 1967, in an impressive ceremony attended by the ranking Roman Catholic, Greek Orthodox, and Protestant prelates in San Francisco, and many other dignitaries. Bishop Hines attended the service, and Bishop Pike participated, seated for the last time near the episcopal throne he had occupied for eight tumultuous years.)

At 11:55 P.M. on October 25, 1966, the House of Bishops, in a chaos of dismay, and on a motion of the Bishop of South Florida, stood adjourned.

An Anticlimax Ends in Grace

The concluding two days of the Wheeling meetings were decidedly anticlimactic.

Some necessary business was transacted, reports were received, and resolutions were referred into and out of committees. On the morning of October 26 George Leslie Cadigan, Bishop of Missouri, read to the House a thoughtful paper on "The Office of a Bishop" the concluding paragraph of which merits recall:

A Bishop is consecrated in the Church of God to provide humble and courageous leadership for all the people of God. By what he does, and more essentially by what he is, will the evidences of reform and renewal emerge from the cloudy multiplicities and perplexities of our times.[147]

Two social events deserve to be mentioned.

On the evening on October 26 "Jim" Pike and "Hank" Louttit, old "buddies in the Faith" as the latter has put it, had dinner together, on the invitation of the former. Bishop Louttit remembers the occasion with evident pleasure. "I love Jim Pike," he has said; "I'll have dinner with him anytime he wants to."

On the afternoon of October 27, its deliberations over, the

House adjourned the Wheeling meetings, having accepted a resolution from its Committee on Hospitality which concluded:

That we express our appreciation to the Wheeling Steel Co. for its gracious hospitality and warm reception, and to the Pontiac Motor Company and its local dealer, Clarke Pontiac, for their generous provision of automobiles for our convenience, and to the many unknown who have contributed to the pleasure of our stay.[148]

That evening the bishops and their wives assembled, many arriving in Pontiac limousines, for the customary closing banquet and dinner dance.

Just as the dinner was to begin the host bishop, Wilburn Camrock Campbell of West Virginia, fraternally invited the Resigned Bishop of California to say the grace.[148] He has since been criticized by two bishops for the grace he chose, one complaining that it was "un-Christian" and the other that it was "un-trinitarian."[149]

The grace Bishop Pike offered was the same grace uttered at the Last Supper by Jesus of Nazareth.[150]

PART TWO

EXEGESIS OF
A CONTROVERSY

As the Church of Jerusalem, Alexandria, and Antioch, have erred; so also the Church of Rome hath erred, not only in their living and manner of Ceremonies, but also in matters of Faith.

—Article XIX Of the Church
Articles of Religion of the Protestant Episcopal Church[1]

So hath the Church of England.
—The Right Reverend James A. Pike[2]

[1] *The Book of Common Prayer.* The Articles of Religion were established in Convention on September 12, 1801.
[2] When asked to comment on Article XIX by the authors.

first

Dogma, Doctrine and Discipline

AN inherent difficulty in any heresy proceeding is the question of what heresy is. To many churchmen unsophisticated in dogma, doctrine and discipline—be they bishops, clergy or laity—the word heresy might seem to have a connotation which is objective, definitive, and unambiguous, much as a criminal act is set forth, specified and condemned in statutory law by the state. Lawyers are aware, of course, that the criminal law is not as cut and dried as is so generally reputed, but, by comparison, heresy is clothed with such extraordinary vagueness and illusiveness that it is hardly imaginable, were the state to have initial jurisdiction over heresy charges, that any case would ever be tried or any conviction ever obtained because of the want of any norm, definition or yardstick by which commission of the offense could be determined by reasonable men.

It has been very often urged, as it is today by Bishop Pike's accusers, that the Apostles' and the Nicene Creeds are the standard of orthodoxy and, therefore, the measure of heresy, but which or whose interpretation of the Creeds defines orthodoxy? Shall it be that of the literalists or that of those who regard the Creeds stylistically? Are the Creeds to be taken as recitals of historic fact or as symbolic expressions of the truth? Are the Creeds "divinely" ordained or venerable but nonetheless acculturated statements? Do the Creeds represent immutable utterances not to be tampered with or, as some of the major Christian churches have undertaken, are "new" creeds appropriate for adoption and for use with the same dignity previously accorded the ancient Creeds?[1]

What Is Heresy?

Such questions have plagued the Episcopal Church, as well as other churchly bodies, for a long time, especially since the advent of scientism, and of reliance on the scientific method, and later in the controversies evoked by the gradual maturing of biblical criticism. In 1894, in the ferment that, among other things, issued in the heresy trial of the Reverend Algernon Crapsey, the House of Bishops issued a pastoral letter condemning "certain novelties of opinion and expression, which have seemed to us to be subversive of the fundamental verities of Christ's Religion." That letter, after declaring the Virgin Birth indispensable to the true, but sinless, humanity of Christ and while repudiating any teaching that "the Resurrection of our Lord Jesus Christ was a so-called spiritual resurrection," goes on to declare that the "Creeds of the Catholic Church do not represent the contemporaneous thought of any age; they declare eternal truths," and concludes that "grave peril to souls lies in the acceptance of the letter of the Creeds in any other than the plain and definitely historical sense in which they have been interpreted by the consentient voice of the Church in all ages. Fixedness of interpretation is of the essence of the Creeds."[2]

The grave jeopardy to souls, of which the bishops warned, the trial and deposition of the Reverend Algernon Crapsey, and the threatened trials of others, did not in the ensuing years suppress the views that occasioned the 1894 pastoral letter. On the contrary they seem to have flourished and by 1923, when the House of Bishops convened in Dallas, where it was suggested that formal charges be prepared against William Montgomery Brown, the retired Bishop of Arkansas, the bishops were under pressures to clarify the issue of the interpretation of the Creeds and, thus, enunciate a standard.

The Bishop of Georgia moved that a petition from "various laymen" be read to the House which beseeched the bishops, as "our Chief Pastors and Doctors of the Faith" to reaffirm the authority of the Creeds because "it is currently reported to us that it is taught, by some of those set apart by your office and ministry to be pastors and teachers in this Church, that the affirmations of those Creeds are not of equal value or verity; and that some of them—and in particular, at this time, the affirmation that Our Blessed Lord in His entry into our human life was 'conceived by the Holy Ghost' and 'born of the Virgin Mary,' . . . need not be accepted in their obvious sense; but that one may lawfully and honorably remain not only as a member of this Church but as a priest and pastor therein, and continue to affirm in public those Creeds, while yet openly denying, or so qualifying as in effect to deny, the plain and simple meaning of those affirmations."[3]

Perhaps under pain of the admonition of their peers, the bishops unanimously adopted and issued, as a pastoral letter, a report which accused any who "explain away" the creedal statements about the Virgin Birth as referring "to birth in the ordinary way, of two human parents, under perhaps exceptionally holy conditions," of abuse of language, and tersely remarked that objections to the doctrine of the Virgin Birth and to the bodily Resurrection of Christ had, anyway, been "abundantly dealt with by the best scholarship of the day."[4]

Within a year Bishop Brown had suffered an adverse verdict in his trial, which challenged the substance of both the 1894 and the 1923 pastoral letters, as well as the position taken by the court which tried him, which was more evasive than the elemental literalism reflected in the pastorals. After the verdict, Bishop Brown issued a statement, which is worthy of recalling now:

. . . It was not that I wished to force my views upon the church. . . . It was simply that I love the church and the masses whom it should serve. I want the church freed from the handicap of an uncertain literalism, so that it may shed its blessings in every age, according to the best thought of that age.

We have utterly failed to draw from the court a statement of any standard of orthodoxy. But this failure is our greatest triumph, because it was our contention, from the outset, that it could not be done.

We are told only that the doctrine is contained, but not formulated, in the Prayer Book, in the Collects, in the Scriptures. So doubtless it is contained in the Dictionary. . . .

Judged by supernatural literalism, I am a one hundred per cent heretic. By the same standard no bishop of this church is one hundred per cent orthodox. The court of course failed to inform us what degree of deviation from literal orthodoxy is permitted for membership in the House of Bishops. The inference is that one may be very liberal as long as no bishop is shocked thereby.

But every new thought is shocking, and so long as the church assumes to set limits to human thinking it must exhaust its time and energies by hunting heretics, instead of ministering to the needs and aspirations of mankind. . . .

(I)t will have become obvious to everyone whose mind lives in this scientific age, that a charge of heresy can not be sustained. More than that, it will become obvious to everyone that such a charge can not even be stated. And what is obvious to everyone sooner or later must become obvious to theologians.[5]

Bishop Brown's point was already obvious to some theologians at the time, including the Reverend Angus Dun, Assistant Professor of Systematic Divinity at the Episcopal Theological School in Cambridge, who was later to become not just a Chief Pastor and Doctor of the Faith, but a patriarch as Bishop of Washington, who became an ecumenical leader of extraordinary influence and eloquence in the World Council of Churches, who was destined in 1948 to ordain an attorney and legal scholar of brilliant reputation, a former Naval officer, ex-Roman Catholic, and lately converted agnostic to the Episcopal priesthood. The priest ordained by Bishop Dun was James A. Pike, whose censure for his views and conduct as a Bishop was uttered by a committee of which—ironically—the Presiding Bishop had named Angus Dun chairman.

Forty-two years prior to the censure of Bishop Pike, the faculty of the Episcopal Theological School, where Bishop Dun was then a professor, had taken a significant initiative in addressing the bishops, in responding to their pastoral letters, in speaking to the Episcopal Church at large and the other churches generally, as well as to the public, about the issues of orthodoxy and heresy in the context of the culture then contemporary. Seven faculty members of that School published a volume of essays on the history, interpretation, and use of the Creeds which was particularly responsive to the controversy attendant to Bishop Brown and of interest sufficiently widespread to be published by The Macmillan Company.[6] The fourth essay in that book—on "The Virgin Birth and Belief in Christ"—was written by Angus Dun. It admits that the fundamental conviction as to the historicity of the Virgin Birth had been decisively challenged by "the scientific spirit" but argues that this challenge did not subvert (as the bishops supposed back in 1894) the doctrinal value or importance of the creedal formularies or of their dependence upon a literalistic actuality. Bishop Dun's essay is particularly sensitive to the accommodations, apologetically requisite in the times of the articulation of the historic Creeds, from Hebraic to Greek ideas, allusions, and semantics. His essay, in its main import, is a lucid celebration of the ubiquity and universality of the Word of God in Jesus Christ in this history. Bishop Dun was, during this traumatic and confused period in Episcopal history, quite perseverant, along with other colleagues of the Episcopal Theological School faculty, in insisting upon the efficacy of healing churchly divisions by resort to and respect for the (then) modern insights of biblical scholarship.

In a speech, indeed, in Boston, on April 30, 1924, he opposed the sort of simplistic creedal literalism which the "various laymen" had entreated the House of Bishops to embrace and which they did, in fact, if temporarily, embrace in the 1923 pastoral letter. Dun, significantly, in this address, associated the issue of churchly literalism with Judaistic apostasy in the early Church. Said he:

> The practical question is not whether the great classical formulations of faith in Christ contained within our creeds enshrine permanent truths and values, but whether they serve . . . to . . . share or sift faith in Christ in our day. I think we must face the fact that they serve these purposes only with very partial success. . . . For increasing numbers there are clauses where the mind goes blank as the words are repeated, where many honest but non-reflective minds feel a vague uneasiness, where the more youthful and more ambitious minds revolt, where the more middle-aged and indolent minds surrender the effort to think their situations through, and where the more docile minds recognize sacred mystery and working where they cannot understand.
>
> Under these circumstances it cannot be said that it is the creeds which unite us or the creeds which we primarily share. There are at

least certain public indications that it is the creeds that divide us. . . . (T)he basis of our unity and our continuity lies deeper than creeds.[7]

Bishop Dun's reflections on the problem of orthodoxy, and, thus, heresy, and on the standards of each, whether marked by the Creeds or otherwise, soon issued, in 1924, in the remarkable and, apparently unprecedented proposal, in which he was joined by Dean Benjamin Martin Washburn of the Episcopal Theological School, later Bishop of Newark, who died before the Bishop Pike affair reached its present proportions, that the liturgical recitation of the historic Creeds be rendered optional until such time as they might be most carefully scrutinized and, perhaps, put in language more comprehensible to ordinary laity, clergy, and bishops so that they could the more conscientiously be employed.[8]

The Dun-Washburn proposal, coming as it did from two distinguished Anglican scholars, and disputing as it did so directly the complacent assertion of the 1923 Dallas pastoral letter that scholarship had abundantly coped with creedal interpretation, seems to have been a very bold one indeed, particularly so, when the atmosphere of the times is taken into account. Not only was Bishop Brown having his difficulties, but the Right Reverend William Lawrence, Bishop of Massachusetts, had given an address, on the thirtieth anniversary of his consecration, only shortly before the Dallas meeting of the House of Bishops which aroused a great stir and caused him to be accused of "appearing to curry favor with heretics." Bishop Lawrence's address had declared that, while the Creeds had value as statements of common faith, they were not, in his view, to be taken as literal statements of historical facts.[9] How many other bishops of the day shared similar sentiments is difficult to discern, though it is known that the attendance at the meeting of the House in Dallas was only sixty-five of the 140 members, and that some of those present did not vote for the pastoral, though they did not record dissent and the vote was reported as unanimous.[10] In any case, in the context in which it was made, the Dun-Washburn proposal appears a daring, if not actually a defiant, gesture. It certainly went beyond the position which Bishop Brown reiterated in addressing the Court which tried him for heresy:

I believe the whole thing [*The Book of Common Prayer*]. I will venture to say there isn't one Bishop here that believes any more than I do and that takes more delight in the worship from that Prayer Book than I do. I believe it from cover to cover, and the Bible too. . . . I don't reject one supernaturalistic representation of the Bible, . . . of the creed, of the Prayer Book. I interpret it all symbolically.[11]

In the present controversy concerning Bishop Pike, the Dun-Washburn proposal assumes an ironic significance. Nothing in Bishop Pike's writings or other public utterances prior to his censure by adoption of the report drafted by the committee which Bishop Dun chaired approaches the radicality of the 1924 suggestion of optional liturgical recitation of the Creeds, although, since the censure, Bishop Pike has had occasion, in a 1967 Lenten sermon at St. Thomas Church in New York City, to commend the Dun-Washburn proposal. Meanwhile, when this was recalled to him, Bishop Dun, with his characteristic candor, complained that "conveniently or inconveniently I have always had a rotten memory and cannot remember what I said last year, much less what I said in 1924."[12]

The interpretation of the Creeds had, of course, plagued the Episcopal Church at the time of the trial of the Reverend Mr. Crapsey, in 1906. In the immediate aftermath of that event, Professor Alexander V. G. Allen of the Episcopal Theological School published a book entitled *Freedom in the Church*, in which he predicted that the "difficulties waiting upon the creeds and their interpretation are not likely to diminish, rather will they increase, for the question at issue is the freedom of the clergy and laity. . . . We have got into the existing difficulty by abandoning the teaching of the Prayer Book, by seeking to make the Church infallible, by substituting tradition for God's Word, and putting a burden on the creeds which they are not able to carry." Professor Allen discusses the importance of distinguishing what the Creeds chiefly contain and whatever may be "in the way of subordinate statement."[13] He then goes on to make an enchanting suggestion for relief from the problems of creedal interpretation:

. . . There is a provision made in the rubric of the English (prayer) book before all the creeds,—Apostles', Nicene, or Athanasian,—that they be "sung or said." . . . There has never been any authoritative decision as to the significance of their liturgical use, nor is there today any common understanding. If they are sung they pass into the rank of the great hymns, the *Te Deum* and the *Gloria in Excelsis*, where misunderstandings disappear. Recited in their original sense, in every clause, they can no longer be. They have been put to the test of Scripture, as Article VIII (of The Articles of Religion) requires, and the clauses, "He descended into hell" and the "resurrection of the flesh," have not stood the test. But as hymns expressing the faith of the Church of the early centuries, they will retain their dignity and importance . . . which if they become the subject of controversy and business contract they must lose. So long as we have the Word of God containing all things necessary to salvation, the creeds are not indispensable. They might be omitted from the offices of the Church and the Christian faith not be impaired.[14]

By odd coincidence, unaware of Professor Allen's urging of sung Creeds, Bishop Pike had taken virtually the same position in his "Three-Pronged Synthesis" in *The Christian Century* and had made the practice normative in the Diocese of California.[15]

If the irony of the Bishop Pike affair needs compounding, let it also be recorded here that, forty-two years after Bishop Dun and Bishop Washburn advocated the optional liturgical use of the creeds, and fifty-nine years since Professor Allen proposed their omission or their being sung rather than said, in October of 1966, the Bishop of South Forida, Henry I. Louttit, after having accused Bishop Pike of denying the Virgin Birth and the Bodily Resurrection, declared that he had commissioned, arranged for, and would finance a meeting of distinguished theological faculty to redraft a "Chalcedonian statement" of the faith of the Church "in modern American" language.[16] While it appears that no seminary faculty of the Episcopal Church has undertaken any such task or has ever assented, as yet, to do so, at the behest of any bishop, the notion of reform and of the need for contemporaneousness at which the House of Bishops had scoffed in 1894, was at least in this way acknowledged by the very bishop who instigated the formal heresy presentment against Bishop Pike.[17]

If nothing else, the Holy Spirit is persistent.

Orthodoxy or Conformity?

There are those who would pursue the query of what heresy is, if it is capable of definition at all, in quite another fashion, without recourse to creedal literalism, or to any lesser formularies, or even to the substantive realms of dogma and doctrine at all.

Perhaps some would appeal to the Articles of Religion, published in *The Book of Common Prayer*, established in Convention of the Episcopal Church in the United States in 1801, and, in the main, copied *verbatim* from the earlier Articles of the mother Church of England originating in the sixteenth century. If there are such, they would be very scarce. The Articles are far more acculturated, far more denominational, far less lucid and far less authoritative than anyone would regard the Creeds. As one of the present authors has had occasion to write in *The Christian Century*:

> Having examined the Articles of Religion with all faithful diligence, I conclude that they are generally vain, frequently pompous, sometimes vacuous, often uncharitable, occasionally incomprehensible, now and then preposterous, and, most of the time authentically hilarious. . . . I do not know "all Satan's lurking-places," but I am in no doubt that one of them is the Articles of Religion.[18]

Still, there they are, in the posterior of the Prayer Book, seldom read and practically never mentioned in the indoctrination of Anglicans for confirmation or in subsequent teaching and nurture of the people in the congregation. They are, perhaps, a kind of quaint and honored relic, but not a norm of orthodoxy. If they were accorded that dignity, then, as Bishop Brown foresaw, every bishop of Anglicanism could doubtless be defrocked and, just as certainly, there would be no church over which bishops might preside since the corpus of the Episcopal Church would be depleted of both laity and clergy.

Yet, if the Articles are to be properly regarded as a particular episode in the history of a tradition, but not as normative doctrine, where is there any standard of orthodoxy and, thus, any test of heresy?

Many of the bishops, and, it may be assumed, numbers of clergy and laity would still follow the argument of the trial court in the case of Bishop Brown that orthodoxy is framed, but not precisely formulated, in the Prayer Book. On several occasions, in interviews with the press, the accusers of Bishop Pike resorted to exactly that fortress. There are problems attached to such a recourse, however, not the least of which is that no sooner had the trial of Bishop Brown been concluded than the revision of *The Book of Common Prayer* was authorized, a process which not only has its parallels in other branches of the Anglican Communion, but is still under way in the American church. When the Prayer Book, taken as a whole, was asserted, for one example, by Bishop Louttit at Wheeling to constitute the general framework delineating orthodoxy from heresy, the question Bishop Pike raised was how the Prayer Book can be so regarded and utilized when it is in fact being currently revised. And, pressing the question further, Bishop Pike desired to know of Bishop Louttit why, if the Prayer Book is the standard, it requires any revision anyway. Bishop Louttit's reaction was significant: he said that his office as a bishop required that he uphold whatever, from time to time, the Prayer Book "teaches" and that if revisions of the Prayer Book are duly authorized then, however the revisions might vary from the original or other prior Prayer Books, that becomes the norm, though the immediately previous version prevails as the standard until a new variant is authorized.[19]

By such reasoning, manifestly, today's heretic might be yesterday's man of solemn faith, and the orthodox of the day may become tomorrow's heretic.

At stake is whether orthodoxy is a matter of content or authority. What is crucial, in legal terms, is not substance but procedure. It does not matter what is said, but it matters mightily who says it. An interpretation upheld is less significant than whether a particular interpretation has been ecclesiastically sanctioned. It is not so much what a Christian confesses as whether such belief has been duly authorized.

Bishop Brown, as has been cited already, ran afoul, in his heresy trial, of this point of view when the ecclesiastical court before whom he was the defendant refused either to admit testimony of theologians, expert in dogma and in the latitude of Anglican doctrine specifically, or to permit depositions of the other bishops as to their confessional positions. The Reverend Algernon Crapsey encountered the very issue in his trial, and the Reverend Lee Heaton was apparently coerced, under the threat of a trial, to acceding to the same proposition in 1924.[20] Now it has become Bishop Pike's turn to confront this idea that heresy is determined not by dogma but by discipline; not as a matter of an orthodoxy which is explicable and explicated, but rather as an issue of conformity which is demanded and which, if not forthcoming, is to be vindicated by the condemnation of the nonconformist.

This displacement of procedure for substance, this fascination for ecclesiastical discipline instead of theological doctrine, this favor of plenary prerogatives for churchly conventions and assemblies of bishops over (even) "fixedness"—as the 1923 Dallas pastoral put it—in interpretation of Creeds and collects, seems very odd as a brief to which Anglican bishops would retreat. After all, applied, in its ultimate logic, it is an argument for the infallibility of Popes, and, as Professor Allen wrote in 1907, in speaking of Number XX of the Articles of Religion, which has been cited in the introit to this chapter, "The infallibility which the Anglican Church refuses to the ancient historic churches, she does not claim for herself. Infallibility is no longer to be held as a mark of the Church."[21]

Nevertheless, Bishop Louttit's defense to Bishop Pike's interrogation about dogma vs. discipline would find powerful support, and, indeed, evidently has found it, in the minds of many other bishops, and priests and laity as well, and in the precincts of the incumbent ecclesiastical establishment of the Episcopal Church in America. So doctrinally erudite and ecumenically exposed a bishop, for example, as the Right Reverend Stephen F. Bayne, Jr., sometime executive officer of the Anglican Communion, in 1964 a leading prospect for the office of Presiding Bishop, and presently an incumbent Vice President of the Executive Council of the Episcopal Church, appears to encourage this cause. Bishop Bayne, who was a key figure in the committee which designed the censure of Bishop Pike, was called upon to preach on "Dogma and Reality" at Trinity Church, Wall Street, in Advent of 1964. Earlier that year Bishop Pike had been in residence as the summer preacher at Trinity Church and had given a series of sermons on doctrine, including one on the doctrine of the Trinity which had provoked an uproar, which subsequently developed in his book, *A Time for Christian Candor*.

Bishop Bayne noted this in his opening remarks by protesting that his sermons were not an attempt to refute those uttered from the same pulpit so recently by Bishop Pike:

> This is to be a series of three sermons on the doctrine of the Trinity, and there may be those who will at once think of them as some kind of response to Bishop Pike, or to Bishop Robinson, or as some other kind of disputatious enterprise. They are not so. I am a very conventional, catholic Christian, with no ability and no desire to argue with another bishop's way of thinking.[22]

Bishop Bayne then observes that the Church has forgotten the "meaning of her greatest word—'belief'" when belief is mistaken for either conformity or credulity, which he condemns as "two contemptible heresies."[23] Yet, straightway, Bishop Bayne appears to come down on the side of discipline when he defines doctrine and dogma:

> A doctrine is a belief held by people about something or other. A Christian doctrine is a doctrine held by Christians. A Christian dogma is a doctrine which is put forward *with authority—an official teaching*. A catholic dogma is a doctrine put forward with the authority of the whole Christian body. . . . (W)hen one says the Creed one is saying that which has been officially put forward by the Church, that which has been most of the time by most Christians, most everywhere, believed.[24]

Conformity and credulity, evidently, become heresies evoking contempt only when that which is believed lacks the imprimatur of ecclesiastical authorization.

By such a rubric the pastoral letters of bishops or messages of the Lambeth Conference, composed of Anglican bishops from throughout the Communion, would presumably qualify as standards of orthodoxy, though the question is encountered of which pastoral or pronouncement is to be relied upon. Do earlier or the most recent of such instruments prevail? Do the documents of a

Lambeth Conference take precedence over a pastoral letter of the House of Bishops of the American Church? How is erraticism and contradiction among such utterances made, as they are, in different generations and diverse circumstances to be resolved? Does it matter, in terms of the dignity accorded a specific pastoral letter how many bishops may be said to be competent theological scholars? Or, for that matter, how many are aged or infirmed, drunk or sober, high churchmen or low churchmen, Republicans or Democrats, racists or social activists, or present or absent? The steadfast refusal of the ecclesiastical court in the trial of Bishop Brown to enter the question of the standard of orthodoxy, except to say that it lies unformulated in the Prayer Book, is no doubt accounted for by apprehension of confronting just such questions. That seems a shrewd reluctance.

Orthodoxy or Semantics?

Despite what many regard as the unfairness of the trial of Bishop Brown, despite the many juridical errors which the record of the trial discloses (the view of the present authors is the real error was to have a trial at all), behind the reticence of the *Brown* court to enter murky and ambiguous issues such as those mentioned above lies the peculiar ethos of Anglicanism with its disposition to tolerate wide latitude in both belief and practice. That stems from an emphasis in the English Reformation upon individual freedom, as reflected in insistence upon the vernacular in public worship and in access to the Bible, as well as from a realism about the frailties of institutions, as reflected in the acknowledgment of errancy in the ancient churches. And, after all, Anglicanism *is* English in origins and inherits a genius for accommodation and compromise which is at once a great strength and a distinct liability.

It is not unfamiliar to hear Episcopalians speak of themselves as "Prayer Book" Christians but the allusion is to a shared style of life rather than to doctrinal uniformity or consensus in belief.

Within such an ethos, a cogent argument can be made that any heresy proceeding is an aberration or, alternatively, that all Anglicans are heretics if the comity of Anglicanism internally is upset or abandoned. With that in mind, the 1894 Dallas pastoral letter, particularly in view of the facts that somewhat less than half of the bishops were present, that it was drafted and adopted within a few hours, that not all present voted, would have to be counted an anomaly. So would the 1923 pastoral, which was also authorized with great alacrity, in a single day. So would the trials of Howard MacQueary, Algernon Crapsey, or William Montgomery Brown, or the threatened proceeding against Lee W. Heaton, or the controversy about the views of William Lawrence. And so, also, with James A. Pike, one would thus conclude.

One of the complexities of the Bishop Pike affair, however, as has been clarified in the interrogatories submitted to all incumbent bishops by the authors of this book, is that many of the bishops who voted to censure Bishop Pike, in terms so harsh and denigrating that he felt compelled to demand a trial, did so supposing that, thereby, they were upholding the internal civility and reciprocity of Anglicanism, which makes a heresy trial ridiculous. One bishop, after reflecting upon this very problem, altered his vote on the censure from aye to nay.[25]

It may also be argued that heresy proceedings in traditions other than the Anglican are not so complex, that is, that in some of the other great denominations or communions a more definitive confessional position does prevail and a different polity is operative in dealing with deviation from the orthodoxy so defined. Lutherans have the Augsburg Confession, and the canon of Luther's works; the Presbyterians and the Reformed churches look to the Westminster Confession and can appeal to the authority of Calvin's *Institutes of the Christian Religion*. Theoretically, the Methodists have the witness and writings of the Wesley brothers, though, they seem not to be very seriously regarded by most American Methodists to, in the authors' opinion, the extraordinary impoverishment of Methodism in the United States. Christian Scientists—granting the dispute amongst themselves, as well as others, about whether they lie within the precincts of the Christian Church—have Mary Baker Eddy and her norms of orthodoxy. Roman Catholics, of course, have Popes, and now, once again, a college of bishops, and, it sometimes seems, in recent times, more ferment than Anglicanism might ever boast about. By the historic concern of the so-called free churches, everybody believes what they care to anyway, so the issue of heresy, as a constitutional matter, need not arise. Fundamentalists of all sects and persuasions abound in most of these churches, along with a multitude of separatist bodies, and they typically are dogmatically totalitarian.

Anglicanism has no Martin Luther, no John Calvin, no John or Charles Wesley (though they could have had Methodism), no Mary Baker Eddy, no Pope, no Jonathan Edwards but no William Channing either, and no Billy Graham or Oral Roberts or Billy James Hargis.

The Anglican tradition, in other words, is, significantly, generically distinguished from the other divisions of Christendom, in which a premium has been attached to a self-styled orthodoxy. Perhaps the only communities in the whole body of the Church that have a more pragmatic and open-ended stance are some of the Old Catholic and the Eastern Orthodox Churches. As a matter of fact after Bishop Brown had been condemned by a court of the Protestant Episcopal Church as heretic he was offered consecration in the Russian Catholic Church, and he was consecrated in the Old Catholic Church, which found no difficulties permitting his views to be represented within the episcopate. Embarrassingly for the Episcopalians, it should be noted, the Apostolic succession in the episcopacy is not challenged with respect to the Old Catholic Church in the United States in the manner in which it is subject to question in the Anglican Communion.[26] One awaits the outcome of the Bishop Pike affair to know whether, in chief consequence of his being accused as a heretic within Anglicanism, he will end up— as Bishop Brown did—with episcopal credentials less vulnerable than those with which he was consecrated.

The generous spirit of Anglicanism vis à vis dogma and, sometimes, discipline, may however, signify something else altogether. It may point to a facility for accommodation which has neither much to do with dogma nor discipline but, basically, with semantics.

In the midst of the strife in the Episcopal Church in the twenties, for instance, the Archbishops of Canterbury and York jointly appointed a Commission on Christian Doctrine. Composed of twenty-five distinguished ecclesiastics and scholars, the Commission labored for fifteen years considering "the nature and grounds of Christian doctrine with a view to demonstrating the extent of existing agreement within the Church of England and with a view to investigating how far it is possible to remove or diminish existing differences." The Chairman of the Commission, William Temple, then Archbishop of York and subsequently Archbishop of Canterbury, notes in his introduction to the Commission's report that little attention is given in it to "The Anglican formularies and, in particular, the Thirty-Nine Articles. There is much ignorance and much confusion of mind about the Articles. They have not, at any rate from the early seventeenth century onwards, taken in our system the place occupied in the Lutheran system by the Augsburg Confession. . . . They are not a complete confession of faith, but a declaration of the position adopted by the Church of England at a critical moment in relation to the chief controversies of that moment."[27] Speaking of the great creedal affirmations, Archbishop Temple writes:

Here it is inevitable that we should in some measure reproduce the divergences that mark the thought of scholars and theologians of our generation. In view of my own responsibility in the Church I think it right here to affirm that I wholeheartedly accept as historical facts the Birth of our Lord from a Virgin Mother and the Resurrection of His physical body from death and the tomb. . . . But I fully recognise the position of those who sincerely affirm the reality of our Lord's Incarnation without accepting one or both of these two events as actual historical occurrences, regarding the records rather as parables than as history, a presentation of spiritual truth in narrative form.[28]

Archbishop Temple is at pains to emphasize that the Commission's report, published under the title *Doctrine in the Church of England*, which is to this day almost universally used in Anglican seminaries throughout the world, is not intended as a *summa theologiae* for Anglicanism. "The Church of England," he insists, "has no official Philosophy and it certainly was not our desire to provide one for it. There is a need for Christian philosophers, who set out the map of the world as it is seen in the light of Christian faith. But the value of their work depends upon their intellectual freedom and independence. An official philosophy is a *monstrum horrendum.*"[29]

Since, thus, a *summa theologiae* is a *monstrum horrendum*—with what relish Bishop Brown would have invoked that in his defense, now that delight is reserved for Bishop Pike!—the *Doctrine in the Church of England* attempts the more meek task of setting forth the scope of Anglican beliefs and of recognizing the diversity of beliefs held within the broad latitude characteristic of Anglicanism, acknowledging, as William Temple repeatedly emphasizes in his introductory remarks that theological formulation is not a fixed but a dynamic work which constantly suffers the impact of whatever is happening in the life of the world, and so, he commends the report "to God with the prayer that He will render ineffectual whatever in our work is due to our blindness or prejudice."[30]

One concludes from this that Archbishop Temple would be horrified by the use of the Commission's report as a standard of orthodoxy and that the intent of the Commission's work was to so explicate the latitude of doctrine in the Church of England that heresy trials would be both inappropriate and practically inconceivable. And one notes, just as a matter of record, that in England heresy proceedings were not instituted against, for example, the Very Reverend Hewlett Johnson, the Dean of Canterbury, a winner of the Stalin Peace Prize and famed as the "Red Dean," or Bishop Ernest W. Barnes of Birmingham, a self-styled "unitarian" in doctrine, nor have any charges of the sort been brought against Bishop John Robinson, whose views, set forth in *Honest to God*, are more theologically radical than any yet uttered by Bishop Pike.

What is involved, of course, in part, in an enterprise like that undertaken by the Commission on Christian Doctrine appointed in the twenties by Canterbury and York, is a semantic exercise. That is, an attempt is made to find a verbal formulation which is comprehensible to and compatible with varying interpretations of doctrine. This is not to imply that this particular Commission spent nearly fifteen years playing games with words but that the problem of doctrinal definition and dogmatic exposition is one in which semantics are profoundly involved and must be dealt with responsibly in the light of Scripture, tradition, scholarship, contemporary events, and the varieties of understanding and belief prevalent in the Church in a given time. And it is to say that the unity of a churchly communion as empirically diverse as Anglicanism is more dependent upon verbal formulations than upon peculiar interpretations of words or phrases. The importance of the former is its emphasis upon freedom within the tradition, not upon prizing ambiguity for its own sake. It is insistence about the latter which betrays an anxiety about freedom and the exercise of an inquiring intelligence which is at least pathetic and sometimes pathological. Or to put it another way, indeed, to put it in terms of doctrine, the concern in Anglicanism, as evidenced by the Commission report, for semantics capable of bearing various interpretations and versatile connotations is—far from playing with language—an affirmation not merely of the freedom of men's minds but a way of honoring the vitality of the Holy Spirit in this world.

This issue of semantics has arisen in another fashion which is poignantly relevant to the Bishop Pike affair: the authorization of the Church's Teachings Series. The six volumes eventually published all bear an imprimatur that they had been officially sanctioned. One of those books has enjoyed the most widespread circulation of any book, apart from the Prayer Book, in the history of the Episcopal Church in this country. It has recently, in late 1966, been issued in a new edition, along with the rest of the series. It is, as one of the authors here can testify, from having visited innumerable Episcopal clergy, on the guestroom bedstand of every rectory, along with the Prayer Book and worn, redundant issues of *Playboy* magazine. The book, of course, in question is called, brashly perhaps, *The Faith of the Church*. Its authors are James A. Pike and W. Norman Pittenger. Dr. Pittenger, an illustrious professor at the General Theological Seminary in New York when the book was written, has since departed those precincts, it is said, though it is not known from his own lips, grieviously hurt and somewhat disillusioned by and about the Protestant Episcopal Church in the United States. Whatever the case, he has repaired to England, where, one likes to believe, the spirit of William Temple still survives and now and then presides again, to be a lecturer in theology at Cambridge University. The book is not entirely the origination of the two authors. It went through, according to Bishop Pike's recollection, at least ten revisions under the aegis of the committee assembled by the national church to oversee the whole "teaching series." The book itself, following, to some extent in intent though not in style, the precedent of *Doctrine in the Church of England,* tries to describe the range and richness of the Anglican doctrinal inheritance. Bishop Pike recalls that in his collaboration with Dr. Pittenger on the book, he usually found himself taking a more conventional and conservative position, notably in connection with creedal affirmations like that concerning the Virgin Birth. That may have served the purpose of the book well, since it was designed quite self-consciously to set out the boundaries characteristic of Anglican belief, rather than to select and advocate one or another particular interpretation within those borders. In the book, therefore, semantics, again, becomes a prime consideration. While Dr. Pittenger's views are not known, Bishop Pike refers to the book, as has been said, as an exemplary exercise in "smooth orthodoxy."

In calling *The Faith of the Church* an item of "smooth orthodoxy" one surmises that Bishop Pike is not repudiating it, but rather characterizing the book and admitting that his views have suffered some changes in substance as well as nuance in the years since it was first published. Meanwhile, it will surely occur to those who wish to prosecute Bishop Pike as a heretic that one standard of orthodoxy to which they might appeal which has been duly ecclesiastically authorized is this very book. That would seem a final irony in the Bishop Pike affair—if, in effect, his own words were used to condemn him. Yet perhaps the caution will prevail that if *The Faith of the Church* were introduced, in trial, as some supposed weapon against Bishop Pike, a nest of worms would be exposed, and every sort of matter which the *Brown* court was so scrupulous to exclude—like depositions from other bishops or the testimony of theological scholars—would then become admissible in evidence. And, surely, among such admissible material, along with *The Faith of the Church,* would be *Doctrine in the Church of England.* Then the matter would really become comfounded, for William Temple, late Bishop of Manchester, late Archbishop of York, 98th Archbishop of Canterbury and Primate of All England, would become, from his grave, an illustrious witness for the defense. And, then, too, every single incumbent bishop's beliefs, interpretations, and miscellaneous opinions might also be summoned and aired. It would be an illuminating spectacle, no doubt, demonstrating not only the exceptional latitude of the Anglican inheritance, but also the inherent absurdity of heresy trials in a Church in which in truth there is no standard of orthodoxy dogmatically, in terms of discipline, or even semantically.

This is a serious matter I full well know and I pray the guidance of the Holy Spirit for all of us. Obviously, those bishops who are already assigned to the Court for a Trial of a Bishop or the Court of Review of the Trial of a Bishop cannot prejudge the matter and sign the Presentment. You might, however, indicate in general your approval or disapproval of the stand taken by the Committee of Bishops for the Defense of the Faith.

> —The Right Reverend Henry I. Louttit, Bishop of South Florida: in his letter addressed to the Bishops of the Episcopal Church dated September 20, 1966[1]

I suggest that from the beginning the due processes that our church has established by which we may bring persons to account—which are very reliable, very dependable and humane in their depth—have been violated by this whole thing. I do not believe in the competence of this House to hear this matter. We have provided means whereby any three members of this House, who have troubles about any one of our members may say, "This man ought to be investigated." And if the investigation indicates that he is off base, that he should be then further examined and finally brought to trial if this be the case. I believe in this due process, and I do not believe that this man should be subjected to processes that are not provided.

> —The Right Reverend Daniel Corrigan, Director of the Home Department, Protestant Episcopal Church: during the censure debate[2]

---

[1] This letter enclosed a Presentment against Bishop Pike, signed by twelve Bishops and solicited other signatories.

[2] As transcribed, live, by the Canadian Broadcasting Corporation, October 25, 1966, at Wheeling, West Virginia.

second

Heresy and Due Process

THE Bishop Pike affair has a symbolic importance for many persons outside the precincts of contemporary Christendom as well as for multitudes within the Episcopal Church or other churches.

One aspect of the interest of such outsiders is manifestly religious and theological, though not sectarian or dogmatic. The involvement of some who reject—or are rejected by—the traditional churches in protest movements, in experimentation with psychadelic drugs, in "be-ins," represents a quest for meaning and, sometimes, an affirmation of life which is essentially and even profoundly religious. It can be cogently argued that, in comparison to the "hippies," creedal literalists in the churches are a variety of nihilists. No doubt the latter find the former vulgar, just as they do Bishop Pike, but the controversy surrounding Bishop Pike evokes the sympathy and respect of those outside the churches because they can at least recognize in the bishop a Christian, and an ecclesiastic at that, who is living in the present century.

There is another dimension to the public concern with the Bishop Pike affair, however, which, in lawyer's language, is designated by the term "due process of law." In one case in Alabama, which the authorities and citizens of that jurisdiction have not always borne in mind, due process of law is thus defined:

Due process of law implies the right of the person affected thereby to be present before the tribunal which pronounces judgment upon the question of life, liberty or property . . . to be heard . . . and

to have the right of controverting, by proof, every material fact . . .
If any question of fact or liability be conclusively presumed against
him, this is not due process of law.[1]

Put differently and more directly, with respect to Bishop Pike,
due process raises the question of whether or not Bishop Pike had
a fair hearing at Wheeling, or in the events prior to the censure, or
in the subsequent happenings, *and* whether he can or will ever
obtain such, considering what has so far occurred, given the
inherited procedures for heresy trials in the Episcopal Church, and
taking the relevant ecclesiastical and civil precedents into account.

That the man was not treated fairly in the censure episode at
Wheeling is a prominent reaction of certain bishops, many
churchmen, and independent observers. An aroma of appeasement
lingers after the censure. Edward B. Fiske in an article in *The
New York Sunday Times* filed from Wheeling reported, under a
headline "Bishops Finesse the Pike Issue":

By the time the bishops convened . . . the Right [sic] Rev. John E.
Hines, the presiding bishop, had set in motion a plan to bring about
a compromise.[2]

Moreover, the issue of resort to the censure has been attacked as
an avoidance of due process:

What precedent is there in the history of the Church for such action?
What happened to the due processes of the Church? Our canons are
unmistakably clear about the processes of accusation, presentment,
inquiry, defense and trial. . . . (S)uch processes have been basic and
fundamental not only to the life of the Church, but to the entire
tradition of common law.[3]

In the deluge of complaints and compliments which Bishop Hines
received immediately after Wheeling, was this, from a fellow
Texan:

In effect, it seems to me, it was a star chamber proceeding without
benefit of defense, with the verdict submitted for referendum. It
combines the worst features of an oligarchy and a democracy.

I hasten to add that there is no question in my mind of good intent;
I simply feel that the fear of a trial led the House to an indefensible

procedure not worthy of such an august body. Neither Christian nor Anglo-Saxon standards have been met.[4]

Whatever the assessment of the Wheeling censure, it was an action without precedent in the Episcopal Church. Query whether it has prejudiced any possibility of due process for Bishop Pike.

An Inherent Profanity

Every accused person suffers some ignominy, some jeopardy to his person or property, by the mere fact of being accused whether the accusation is ultimately established or not. That is perhaps less so where the charge is a traffic violation or tax evasion or drunkenness (though one bishop was deposed for that in 1844) than in a case in which one is charged with adultery or rape or murder.

Though it is not settled whether heresy is an offense of a civil nature or more similar to a crime, the element of humiliation and the risk to liberty and property obviously attach to accusations of heresy, particularly so if the accused be a bishop. That is amply evidenced in reference to Bishop Pike in the prolonged ridicule to which he has been subjected—most pathetically illustrated by Father Brunton's doggerel—since the time of the Georgia charges. Such denigration gained momentum after the Arizona accusations and the attention accorded them at the Glacier Park meeting of the House of Bishops, and reached depths in the Louttit presentment. The Wheeling censure has, if anything, been the most degrading burden of all since, according to Edward B. Fiske, it "proved to be considerably more harsh and judgmental than the critical but eloquent draft that Bishop Dun brought to Wheeling."[5]

The matter goes beyond the impugning of character or personal integrity, however. For Bishop Pike it has occasioned actual danger of bodily harm when in 1966 he was arrested and detained, and then expelled, from Rhodesia. He has suffered the "inhibition" (an injunction forbidding him from officiating in congregations in a particular diocese) of the Bishop of West Virginia, at the time of the Wheeling meeting, and since then Eric Bloy, the Bishop of Los Angeles, in whose jurisdiction Bishop Pike now resides as a member of The Center for the Study of Democratic Institutions, has in effect done the same although Bishop Bloy has failed to meet the canonical requirements.⁶ At least two other bishops have pronounced him unwelcome in their dioceses even for non-ecclesiastical appearances.⁷

Such restrictions involve more than Bishop Pike's freedom of movement, they deprive him of potential income from honoraria customarily tendered for preaching or officiating and, thus, affect his property rights as well as his personal rights. Where such inhibitions or denunciations also interfere with his activities as a lecturer in public forums unrelated to the Episcopal Church the adverse impact upon his property rights is, most likely, much greater. Whether all this represents a loss which is actionable in the civil courts remains an intriguing question and, as far as can be determined, a novel one. A comparable issue did not arise when Bishop Brown was accused of heresy if only because he was a man of considerable wealth and had already retired. Bishop Pike is not rich, has not retired, nor can he, canonically, retire for a long time. The question of his property rights would become acute if he were to be convicted of heresy, and deposed, since he would then forfeit all sums accumulated in the Church Pension Fund of the Episcopal Church. There are those who naïvely suppose that the penalties for heresy are merely ceremonial; however, the ultimate sanction of theological conformity in the Episcopal Church seems, in fact, to be money.

Procedural Defects in the Bishop Pike Affair

At the opening of the trial of Algernon Crapsey in 1906 a newspaperman present commented: "The sitting of an ecclesiastical court might by a lay person be supposed to be an occasion of much ceremonial dignity. But it was not."⁸ Dr. Crapsey himself pointed out that three of the five members of the court which tried him had been appointed by his chief accuser, his own diocesan bishop, and that a "court so constituted made a fair trial impossible."⁹ None of the members of the court had judicial experience and were, as the Reverend Dr. Crapsey put it, "country clergymen." That seems to have been promptly attested:

When the trial opened and Mr. John Lord O'Brian moved the trial of the defendant on the indictment, the president of the court gazed round the audience and asked, "Does anyone second the motion?"

There was a titter in the courtroom and Mr. O'Brian had to explain to the president that no second was necessary.[10]

These are not heartening omens for Bishop Pike, but they seem to typify heresy proceedings. The trial of Bishop Benjamin T. Onderdonk of New York in 1844 is now authoritatively admitted to have been a plethora of judicial errors. *The Annotated Constitution and Canons of the Protestant Episcopal Church* record, of the *Onderdonk* matter:

The trial proceeded under a canon which was enacted several years after the first offense, and more than two years after the last offense, for which he was tried, was alleged to have been committed.

The presentment was made only fifteen days after the adjournment of the Convention which enacted the canon under which he was tried.

Eight of the nine specifications of the presentment, and six of the seven actually tried, were based entirely upon hearsay testimony.

The affidavits on which the presentment was based were all made before the adjournment of said Convention. . . .

The presenters, and the members of the trial court were members of the Convention which, only a few weeks before the presentment was made, had taken part in the enactment of the canon which constituted the court. Three of his judges were the three bishops who had accused him, only a year before, of holding heretical opinions . . .[11]

At the least, in Bishop Onderdonk's case, if virtually all other elements of due process were lacking, alacrity was not. Reasonable speed in trying an accused person is, of course, part of the *esse* of due process, for the obvious reasons earlier mentioned, namely the inherent jeopardies to which an accused person is subjected in his person and property by circumstance of the allegations against him alone. On that issue, Bishop Pike may find cause to complain of a dishonoring of due process that his predecessor, Bishop Onderdonk, could not have found fault with, whatever his other grievances. On the morning after the censure and Bishop Pike's demand for an official ecclesiastical inquiry which would either exonerate him or eventuate in a trial, the Presiding Bishop called for a cooling-off period, though he also declared he would "move with all deliberate speed" to name the board of inquiry which the law of the Church mandates.¹² Despite written inquiries from Bishop Pike, after Wheeling, as to when such a board would be constituted, and in spite of a verbal assurance to Bishop Pike that the same would be done before the end of 1966, no board was so convened.¹³

The reasons for the procrastination of the Presiding Bishop, who has acquired a notoriety among members of his own staff at the Episcopal Church headquarters in New York City for reluctance to make decisions, have been perhaps best explained by himself, in the transcript made by a reporter at a news conference he conducted on January 14, 1967, in San Francisco, while he was there for the consecration of Bishop Pike's successor as Bishop of California, the Right Reverend C. Kilmer Myers, reproduced here exactly as transcribed:

(*Hines*): I think there is considerable dissatisfaction in the Church with what happened to Bishop Pike, because the House of Bishops did not have the chance to deal with the issues which he raised. Furthermore the whole process brought up questions in some people's minds as to whether he was dealt fairly with. I have been dilly dallying ecumenically, because the Church did not and does not want a process which might issue in a heresy trial. The Church does want clarification. It appears to me that in the light of that, it might be the good part of judgment to create a committee of competent people who will take a look squarely at these problems. (mumbles here) What their findings can contribute to help the resolution of the issues of freedom of expression; how far a man goes; this will be helpful . . .

(*Question* from reporter): Would you personally favor a reconsideration of the censure . . . ?

(*Hines*): I can't answer that question.¹⁴

This dialogue took place two days subsequent to Bishop Hines appointment of the "Bayne Committee"—chartered as another *ad hoc* group, responsible *only* to the Presiding Bishop, not to the House of Bishops or General Convention, to study the permissible limits of public theological exploration by bishops and others.¹⁵ In response to this "creative—indeed historic—step" Bishop Pike has said he was "quite content that the Presiding Bishop delay further . . . the appointment of the first of the bodies [investigating panel] involved in the canonical judicial process" which Bishop Pike required be instituted after the Wheeling censure.[16]

In fact the idea of such a commission was constructed in late December, 1966, during a secret meeting which took place in California, in which tentative peace overtures were made to Bishop Pike, evidently with the knowledge and encouragement of the Presiding Bishop. In principle, the establishment of something like the "Bayne Committee" was agreed to then along with announcement by Bishop Hines of the designation of the commission and Bishop Pike's agreement to forbear to press his canonical and other possible legal remedies for the time being.[17] The question which thereby arises, in specific relation to due process of law, is, of course, the same question asked by the reporter at the January 14, 1967, press conference. The "Bayne Committee" is not the House of Bishops. For the purpose of this analysis, let it be presumed that this committee is utterly diligent and accomplishes its report quickly. Let it also be assumed that its view is maximumly favorable to freedom and legal due process. It is still the case that whatever the "Bayne Committee" says neither neutralizes nor erases the Wheeling censure. Only an action by the House of Bishops which has the *exact* dignity of the censure or else an action of General Convention which has *superior* dignity, can do that. When these authors interviewed Bishop Hines and asked, granted the stated presuppositions, if somehow a "Bayne Committee" report might, conceivably, be rendered which was thence adopted by the House of Bishops or General Convention and which, thus, blotted out the Bishop Pike censure and verily obviated a heresy trial, the Presiding Bishop was more emphatic than he was to that journalist in January, 1967, to whom he had said, "I can't answer that question." Now, he said, flatly: "*No.*"[18]

To be sure, some other bishops, and some other politically powerful personages within the Episcopal Church—including that secret December envoy who went to Bishop Pike in California—are more sanguine than Bishop Hines about the prospects for the "Bayne Committee" but practically anyone can discern that it would an extraordinary event if upwards of 103 Episcopal bishops reversed the Bishop Pike censure and confessed that they had been, in one way or another, ill-informed, personally motivated, racists or rightists, unfair, unduly harsh, prideful and judgmental, foolish, stupid, inept or otherwise mistaken. Yet the only other way that the cloud enveloping Bishop Pike because of the censure can be dissipated is if he tires of the matter, quits his demand for vindication, and is content to compromise in a way which indefinitely impugns his credibility as a Christian and his integrity as a man. If Bishop Pike is both or either of the latter, no report of any deliberation without status *at least equal* to the censure at Wheeling will suffice, whatever somewhat belated hopes for accommodation may breathe in bishops' breasts.

Apart from an astonishing gesture from the House of Bishops, Bishop Pike, and all Episcopalians, must take for granted the prospect of a heresy trial and the invitation to schism it obviously implies. One hopes, and one trusts that everybody shares the hope, that a trial of Bishop Pike would be fair. Such an expectation is, as has been pointed out, not historically justified by the experiences of either Bishop Onderdonk or Dr. Crapsey. Neither are they encouraged by the precedents in the trial of Bishop Brown.

Little, evidently, was inwardly digested from the aforementioned proceedings when the time came to dispose of Bishop Brown, for, as in those earlier cases, his trial is replete with legal errors so outrageous that they would scarcely be tolerated even in a night court in a metropolitan jurisdiction by the secular authorities. Moreover, the parallels already evident, from the perspective of due process and common fairness, between the *Brown* case and the Pike affair are so startling as to breach the boundaries of the absurd.

In the preliminaries of the Bishop Brown trial, for instance, it was discovered that the General Convention of 1919 had failed to elect three judges each to either the Trial Court or the Review Court, as required by canon law, and, later, while the complaint against Bishop Brown was pending, the next Convention attempted to remedy this defect by electing to each of the courts six judges in transparent violation of canonical provisions.[19] In the preliminaries of the Bishop Pike case, after the Louttit presentment had been circulated to all bishops and nationally publicized, it became known that the 1964 General Convention had neglected to fill three vacancies on the Court for the Trial of a Bishop, that in addition another vacancy had been caused by the death of Bishop Brinker, and that the 1967 Convention would thus be confronted with a Trial Court without a quorum to hear any matter or render any decision. To compound the absurdity, as has been previously noted, it is the chief accuser of Bishop Pike, Bishop Henry I. Louttit, who was at the 1964 Convention Chairman in the House of Bishops of the Committee on the Dispatch of Business and, hence, responsible for including the making of the judicial appointments on the agenda of the House of Bishops. This omission came to the attention of Bishop Pike through a reply dated October 15, 1966, addressed to him from the Reverend Alexander M. Rodger, Secretary to the House. *Newsweek* religion editor, Mr. Kenneth Woodward, received a teletype message reporting the same information, ending with a farewell "sounds like fun ahead" from the magazine's San Francisco office on October 19th. The next day, *The New York Times* and the major wire services carried the news. What was not, however, indicated in any publication at that time about this oversight of Bishop Louttit was that on September 23, 1966—promptly after he had dispatched the draft presentment to all bishops and had arranged for its publicity—Bishop Louttit received a memorandum from one of his Suffragan Bishops, the Right Reverend William L. Hargrave, a lawyer by training, cautioning Bishop Louttit that such an error existed. It might be added, for whatever significance it may have, that the Reverend Alexander Rodger, who had given this intelligence to Bishop Pike, has since been relieved as Secretary to the House of Bishops at the specific behest of Bishop Louttit.

There are other similarities between the trial of Bishop Brown and the censure of Bishop Pike. In Brown's case, for instance, the bishop who was President of the court which pronounced the sentence of deposition against him had, early in Brown's priesthood, invited him to become a lecturer at the Episcopal seminary at Gambier, Ohio; in Bishop Pike's situation, the bishop who chaired the committee which proposed his censure had ordained him to the priesthood. It might be supposed that in any proceeding involving formal heresy charges or the imputation of heretical views there would appropriately be a consideration of substantive theology. Not so. Despite repeated attempts by counsel for Bishop Brown to introduce theological scholars as witnesses, to take depositions from bishops, or to enter other evidence relevant to the doctrines of the Episcopal Church, the court barred such; in the Bishop Pike censure debate, the Presiding Bishop consistently ruled that there would be no debate concerning theology. Again, Bishop Brown had been assured by the court that he would have a hearing before the whole House, but the House convened in executive session, Brown was denied the hearing, and was preemptorily condemned; on three occasions Bishop Pike sought to be heard by the *ad hoc* committee which brought in the censure; he was refused, the committee deliberations were conducted entirely in secret and, when the House received the report, it was read once and a resolution was then adopted to limit debate to one hour, allotting, officially, ten minutes at the end to Bishop Pike. In the actual debate, the Presiding Bishop called upon the chairman of the censure committee to say the last word, contravening the procedure adopted. Since the ecclesiastical courts function as both jury and judge, Bishop Brown attempted to examine the members of the court to ascertain whether any should be challenged because of prejudice against him but his request was ignored; three of Bishop Pike's accusers sat upon the committee which drew the censure resolution.

The Anatomy of Expedience

Granted these startling parallels between the *Brown* case and the Bishop Pike affair, the Louttit presentment and the Wheeling censure against Bishop Pike are no mere replay of Bishop Brown's heresy trial. They serve mainly to demonstrate the low estate of due process of law in ecclesiastical institutions. The poor esteem for due process seems particularly poignant in the Episcopal Church because of its historic origins in the Church of England and, thus, special connections with the Anglo-Saxon common law and its venerable concern for fair treatment. Still one might minimize the irregularities in, say, the trial of Bishop Onderdonk because it did take place almost a century and a quarter ago. It becomes more difficult to rationalize the errors in the matter of Bishop Brown, since that happened only forty some years ago. It seems ridiculous to even try to excuse the dishonoring of due process of law in the handling of the Bishop Pike affair.

Let it be emphasized that the issue of whether Bishop Pike has been dealt with fairly by his brother bishops stands on its own merits and is not at all dependent upon whether Bishop Pike is a heretic (assuming that any definitive norm exists by which that could be judged). The present canons—pertinent portions of which are set forth in an Appendix to this book—while not beyond reform are not deficient in any serious regard in furnishing due process to an accused cleric, *if the canonical procedures are in fact followed.* So far, in the matter of Bishop Pike, the canons have been repeatedly flouted and ignored.

The Bishop Louttit presentment, in the first instance, can be criticized as an example of exceptionally inept draftsmanship, and that is a criticism which goes not to literateness but refers to the law, since it is an elementary principle of due process that a charge must be drawn with sufficient clarity and definiteness such that the accused may be thereby informed of the offenses he is alleged to have committed. The Louttit presentment fails this test because of vagueness and because of its reliance, in the specifications it contains, upon hearsay; *e.g.,* in one instance views are attributed to Bishop Pike as reported in a newspaper, *The Arizona Republic!*[20] But this critique of the Louttit charges need not be pursued, since Bishop Louttit himself has admitted that the presentment was a "sloppy" job and at one point prior to Wheeling announced that he was scrapping it and having a new presentment drafted by a team of distinguished lawyers and theologians.

More seriously prejudicial to Bishop Pike are the facts that Bishop Louttit contravened the canons in circulating and soliciting all bishops to become subscribers to his presentment. The canonical requirement is that any three bishops *exercising jurisdiction* may make charges against a fellow bishop for any offenses specified in church law. Not content with the canon, Louttit affixed the names of eleven other bishops and his own to his presentment, although few, if any of these appear to have actually signed the instrument, nor were their purported signatures appropriately verified. Some had not read the presentment, some had not consented to the use of their names, some had been solicited by telephone, and some did not even realize their names were being used until they received the circular mailing to all bishops dated September 20, 1966, when some then repudiated the mistaken or unauthorized use of their names. The solicitation of still further presenters extended to all 192 living bishops, except Bishop Pike, including retired and suffragan bishops, who cannot lawfully join in making a presentment.[21] Bishop Louttit even dispatched his papers to bishops appointed to serve on the ecclesiastical courts (it was doubtless then that his earlier omission to put the appointment of judges on the agenda of the 1964 St. Louis meeting of the House came to his notice) in an attempt to procure their expressions of support though not requesting their signatures. How many bishops, whether canonically permitted to do so or not, did sign the presentment is questionable. News media, relying upon information supplied at various times by Bishop Louttit, reported such various figures as 30, 28, 27, 24, 22, 20, 12. Bishop Louttit's own files indicate the final figure, accounting those who withdrew after their names had been publicized, was 28, of whom 7 were not canonically entitled to sign. The authors' poll of the bishops yielded 37 and 10 respectively. It really does not matter what the precise figures were, except to indicate that Bishop Pike has a good many determined opponents in the House, for one reason or another. What matters more is that the initial committee to investigate such charges, plus the Court for the Trial of a Bishop, plus the Court for the Review of the Trial of a Bishop, plus the House of Bishops itself, sitting as an ultimate ecclesiastical court of appeals, are all composed of bishops who were then being importuned to become accusers in a case which they might also judge. The issue which, obviously, arises—and here much more acutely than in the Bishop Brown trial—is whether Bishop Louttit's dissatisfaction with the canon prescribing only three presenters and his solicitation of *all* the bishops to support his accusations has impaired indefinitely the possibility of a fair hearing for Bishop Pike. The blunder, as well as the mockery of canon law, committed by Bishop Louttit in his zeal to line up his colleagues against Bishop Pike may mean that no courts can now be constituted—least of all the church court of last resort, the House of Bishops itself—competent to try Bishop Pike without gross prejudice.

As if to aggravate the offense, Bishop Louttit took elaborate pains to insure the widest possible publicity about his charges, seeking wire service coverage of them before he had any assurance that either the accused or the Presiding Bishop or any other bishops had written notice thereof. Mass media, as is well known, have created problems for the fair adjudication of criminal cases which did not exist previously and the trend in American decisions about the impact of "trying a case in the newspapers" has been toward increasing restraint upon either counsel unduly influencing juries by leaks to the press and editorialized reporting by the media. Those recent precedents in the secular courts might well raise a comparable issue in the ecclesiastical courts, in view of Bishop Louttit's publicity adventures, should Bishop Pike be tried.[22]

The incipient prejudicial character of Bishop Louttit's conduct in the making, circularizing, and publicizing of the presentment may explain why, the morning after the Wheeling censure, Bishop Louttit "disbanded" his "Committee of Bishops for the Defense of the Faith"—the euphemism he employed to describe the bishops whose signatures he had initially added to his presentment. According to *The Washington Post:*

In an hastily summoned caucus of those bishops who signed or promised to sign Bishop Louttit's proposed presentment . . . the Florida churchman said he would "burn" the names of members of the group, thus presumably concealing from Bishop Pike the identities of those not already known.[23]

Forsooth, that fire was unneeded; they are all identified.

If Bishop Louttit's conduct in the making and publicizing of the heresy charges seems precipitous, uninformed, or inept, that may furnish a further explanation—how the expedient of censuring Bishop Pike in exchange for burning the presentment came to pass. It will be recalled that the Presiding Bishop had written Bishop Louttit on September 24 beseeching his forbearance and that numerous other bishops had pled with Bishop Louttit at least to shelve the charges until Wheeling. On September 30, just as news of the allegations was being published in the nation's press, Bishop Louttit informed various bishops that he would wait, though this decision was not made known in the media until about October 3 and Bishop Pike was not otherwise apprised of it. Meanwhile, preparations for Bishop Pike's censure in lieu of a heresy trial were evidently being perfected at Episcopal Church headquarters in New York City. The idea of the *ad hoc* Committee—which has no canonical standing and in the circumstances can well be interpreted as a circumvention of canonical procedures damaging to a fair hearing for the one publicly accused—was being incubated in anticipation of the secret meeting between the Presiding Bishop and Bishop Louttit and other accusers, in New York, on the third of October.

The agenda of that meeting is apparent from the fact that Bishop Hines had requested a journalist to take the pulse of what public reaction would be to a heresy trial and had received the not surprising report that such a proceeding would make the Episcopal Church look archaic and ridiculous.[24] Whether that expectation was reinforced by awareness of the weaknesses inherent in the Louttit presentment and of the vulnerability attaching to the manner in which the charges had been formulated, subscribed to, circulated, and publicized is not known. In any case the desideratum dominating the October 3 confrontation was how to save the Episcopal Church from becoming the laughing stock of the nation. That little or no attention was given to the issues of due process—of fair treatment for Bishop Pike—is a compelling inference in the circumstances, which does not judge the benign intentions of those present at or privy to the October 3 summit conference but only emphasizes that anxiety about the image of the denomination was controlling.

One wonders if, during the discussions that day, any recollection was suffered by Bishop Hines of the bizarre session of the "metropolitans" with Bishop Pike at O'Hare Airport and of the pledge given there to Bishop Pike that if he wrote a clarifying statement about his controversial *Look* piece Bishop Hines would circulate it to all the bishops. Quite possibly, if that promise had been honored, Bishop Louttit's aggression could not have been staged, and, in any event, the question in October would not have been "How can the Church's image be salvaged?—thus, how can a trial be prevented—thus, how can the accusers be appeased?" However else Henry Louttit could be faulted, he is, as he might say himself, a determined cuss, and that quality in him is respected, and rightly so, by other bishops, and, thus, reduced to its essential vulgarity the issue became "what is Hank's price?"

In such an atmosphere was the censure of Bishop Pike covenanted. If O'Hare was forgotten, certainly Glacier Park was not: in those places, by giving Bishop Pike a hearing of sorts, what could have been sharp rebukes became detentes. At Wheeling it would *have* to be a censure and that—though itself conceived in appeasement—must not be compromised or modified. The practical political necessities, eventually, fell, logically, into place: (1) the *ad hoc* committee is not a judicial body, *ergo* Bishop Pike is not entitled to a hearing, (2) the accusers must be represented on the committee to assure that they concur in the censure so that, thereafter, they are satisfied enough to drop the presentment, (3) consideration of the censure in the House must be limited in time and in content—let the bishops adopt it or reject it, but there must be no postponements, no studied discussion, no theological debate, for *that* would never end, (4) the censure must have the appearance of solemnity, authority, and sober deliberation.

What more auspicious figure to move the censure than Bishop Dun? He ordained Bishop Pike, he was one of the few theological scholars in the House, he is ecumenically respected, he is retired and freed from jurisdictional burdens, he enjoys even yet repute as a social liberal, he loves the Church, he is the patriarchal personage of American Anglicanism, he is old but he is fully alert except for his deafness—which, in this situation might be more advantage than handicap. One can almost hear some bishops saying: "Let's use Angus Dun."

Due Process, Episcopal Style

Not everything went as planned at Wheeling, but with a particular exception—Bishop Pike's own demand for an inquiry and trial after the censure—most things did. Bishop Dun agreed to chair the censure committee. The House voted to limit debate. Bishop Louttit and two others represented the accusers on the committee and were satiated. Bishop Pike was denied any hearing before the matter came to the floor and, there, was restricted to minus twenty minutes. Better yet, all motions for deferral of the matter were successfully disallowed, except for one, that some break be taken in the debate so that everyone could relax, have some drinks, and eat dinner and, thereby, incidentally permit

Bishop Pike to preach a sermon scheduled before the censure was arranged at an ecumenical convention meeting that day in Wheeling. This motion to interrupt the debate for a few hours partially failed in its purposes, since most bishops were entertained for dinner without drinks by the local branch of the United States Steel Corporation, in which legions of Episcopalians plus many parishes, dioceses, and boards of the Episcopal Church have investments.

Still all did not go quite according to scheme when the censure resolution reached the floor of the House. The Bishop of Easton (Maryland), the Right Reverend Allen Jerome Miller—with Angus Dun, one of the few bishops holding credentials as a theological scholar and a venerable figure—was granted a privilege, because of his health and status, of speaking immediately after the Dun censure had been read, without prior opportunity for study, to the assembled bishops. As has been alluded to, he promptly arose to complain that the true issues are theological, not procedural or political and, having himself critically examined Bishop Pike's printed works, he purposed to inform the House that Bishop Pike had erred in separating ontology from existence. From the point of view of enjoining substantive theological discourse among the bishops, Bishop Miller's initial intervention in the debate proved opportune to the Presiding Bishop since it afforded him occasions to twice clarify that theology as such was not on the current agenda. In the remainder of the debate, no other bishop—except Bishop Pike and for a few moments Bishop Emrich—ventured into the realms of doctrine or belief.

In other words, there were pressures present at Wheeling which had not been precisely anticipated previously by those committed to a censure. Another of those influences was the vigor of the accomplices of Bishop Pike. Several of these do not evidently, and certainly do not automatically, agree with everything Bishop Pike utters, some are related to him most ambiguously. Many of them, like Bishop Craine of Indianapolis, Bishop Blanchard of Southern Ohio, Bishop Stokes and one of his Suffragans, Bishop Burgess, of Massachusetts, Bishop Myers, the successor in California to Pike, and others, were principally offended by the radical collapse of due process at Wheeling (rather than about doctrine or dogma or discipline). One bishop who is otherwise critical of Bishop Pike, Bishop Crittenden of Erie (Pa.), after reflecting on this issue, altered his vote on the censure from aye to nay, as has been noted.

Such bishops made more of a disturbance in the censure debate than had been foreseen. They attempted to secure more time to study the matter, they moved to table it, they proposed softening amendments, they asked for a roll call, and when the censure prevailed many of them formally disassociated themselves from it and many subscribed to a minority statement. Nevertheless their resistance to Bishop Pike's censure was strenuous enough to elicit a significant admission, and a kind of apology, to the House from one bishop who had been instrumental in the strategy of censuring Bishop Pike. That came from Bishop Bayne.

Bishop Bayne's move came after the U.S. Steel recess. By then so many queries had been raised about the propriety and validity of the censure maneuver that the Presiding Bishop called upon Bishop Bayne to retrieve the situation. (What follows is a precise and complete reproduction from the debate from the typescript of a recording taped by the Canadian Broadcasting Corporation):

CBC REPORTER: THIS IS THE EVENING SESSION. IT WILL SYNC AND WILD SOUND.

HINES: Hurry up please, find a chair if you can. I'll try to identify where we are at the present time and if you have an appeal from the Chair's opinions please make it. The main motion is the pending one on the floor, namely the adoption of the statement as it has been given by the Chairman of the Committee. There are no uh amendments, no other pending motions at present on the floor. We are still operating under the procedure concerning the limitation on ah speakers both time wise and otherwise, but the Chair would have to rule in order to clarify uh positions that an amendment presents a new pending situation uh so that a person would speak to the amendment once and not jeopardize his once for the main motion. We're in order. I recognize the Bishop of Olympia, unless there is a point of order. Bishop of Olympia, no ah former Bishop of Olympia, Bishop Bayne, excuse me (laughter). Gee it's nice to dream of the past (laughter).

BAYNE: Mr. President I asked for the privilege of speaking first tonight. Um my purpose in being on the platform is not to be ornamental as you gather but to try to be an extra pair of ears for Bishop Dun and it makes it hard for me to enter into the discussions except this way and I wanted to say something, perhaps only personal, but I think bearing on the situation in which we find ourselves. Uh through our discussion this afternoon uh there were two recurring questions which I heard which bear I think on the task of the Committee uh as the committee saw itself. It's needless to say I'm sure that there are no volunteers on this Committee. We were asked by the Presiding Bishop to undertake a certain task, on behalf of the House, to try to frame some way to suggest to the House by which we might avoid the stultifying and corrupting impact of a trial and the way which opened to us and the Committee was to try to frame a statement, a statement not for ourselves or of ourselves but a statement for this House as a whole to adopt if it wishes which perhaps might clarify and limit a situation so full of pain and confusion on every side. I'm perfectly certain that I would speak for all of us on the Committee, I speak certainly for myself, in my opinion, that no two members of the Committee think alike, about Bishop Pike and we were not concerned to write a statement which this House could make which would say what the most of this House would want to say.

Now it's against that background that the two questions I speak of are heard. The first was, why was Bishop Pike not invited to appear before the Committee and a moment's reflection will give you the answer. The ruling was made by the Chairman and unanimously supported by the Committee that if we had set up in business to hold hearings in which Bishop Pike would be invited to come and make his defense, we would be in fact doing precisely what some suspect that we did do, namely to act as a kangaroo court. We were not sitting on the virtues of Bishop Pike. Our task was and we all shared this feeling to frame a statement in which this House could wholeheartedly join and there was no unfairness in the fact that we ah held no hearings and did not attempt the kind of behind the door heresy trial.

And the related question, why was Bishop Louttit included? I can't hope to speak for the (beep, beep) Presiding Bishop who appointed him (beep) or for anyone save myself, but I know what I and I think the rest of the committee felt as I did, glad that we had as a member of the Committee the person chiefly responsible for the crisis in which we find ourselves. No statement which we could draft would possibly be of any usefulness to this House, which did not meet at least the minimum concerns of the person who was the aggressor in the immediate circumstances. Uh I prejudge nothing when I say that it was not Jim Pike who was the uh aggressor and therefore the onus lay on another and it was essential, we felt, as members of the Committee that whatever we drafted should be such as to be broad enough to include the extremes that were involved in the situation. Now I hope that saying that which I know expresses what most of us on the Committee, I think all of us, would feel.

Perhaps I allay some of the questions and doubts that were raised in the House this afternoon. I'm in my twentieth year of membership in this House. I cannot remember a more distasteful moment than this in which we are engaged. I don't flatter myself that I am any more sensitive than anybody else in this House is, but do let us be sure what the task before the Committee was and what the issue is which we must actually face and decide.[25]

Bishop Bayne's remarks hardly require exegesis. They stand as an agile exhibition of doubletalk: in the name of preventing a trial a statement was framed "which would say what the most of this House would want to say." "(I)f we had set up in business to hold hearings . . . we would be in fact doing precisely what some suspect that we did do, namely to act as a kangaroo court." Bishop Louttit was included—but Bishop Pike was excluded—because "whatever we drafted should be such as to be broad enough to include the extremes that were involved in the situation." Bishop Bayne's performance at that moment would distinguish many a secular politician.

In hindsight, some bishops have openly speculated about Bishop Bayne's role in the whole Bishop Pike affair, suspecting him of being a Machiavelli. As one Anglo-Catholic—and generally anti-Pike—bishop has ventured bluntly: "I detect Bayne's fine Italian hand in this."[26]

Bishop Pike's Ploy

The censure done, despite acute fatigue and desperate morale, the House that same night received the Stokes resolution authorizing a "little Vatican Council" for the renewal of the Episcopal Church, a purpose which Bishop Pike, in his own fashion, had long so singularly sought. It is said by some that the Stokes' resolution had originally been intended as a substitute for the censure, but, whatever the case, the rules adopted for debate of the Dun committee report precluded its introduction to accomplish that. Its unanimous passage, the day after the censure, may have served some vicarious purpose.

The "minority report" was next offered by the Bishop of Washington and, following some parliamentary confusion, received as a dissent to the censure in which 22 bishops joined.

It was thereabouts that Bishop Pike invoked the privilege of defending himself against what seemed to him harsh and gratuitous assaults on his character and behavior. He demanded, as is a bishop's right under canon law, that an investigation be made of "rumors, reports, and allegations" affecting his personal and official character citing, in the main, the Louttit presentment and the censure itself as the derogatory information in circulation. As required under the canon, he had obtained the consent of two fellow bishops—Bishop Craine of Indianapolis and Bishop Myers of California in the action.

In effect, Bishop Pike was now causing the Church to institute the very steps of inquiry, hearing, and trial which the censure device had attempted to evade.

Due process might still be vindicated and Bishop Pike might yet have his day in court.

Under canon law, a bishop's demand for an investigation of allegations circulating about himself is the equivalent of a presentment made by three bishops against another. The Presiding Bishop is then mandated to summon from three to seven bishops, a majority of whom must determine whether any of the charges, if proved, would constitute a canonical offense. If the charges stand, a Board of Inquiry, composed of five presbyters and five laymen must be convened. That Board is comparable to a grand jury, hears the accusations and such proof in support of them as may be available, and determines whether there is sufficient ground to proceed with a trial. The result in a trial court is subject to review by an appellate court, both comprised of bishops, and the ultimate appeal is to the House of Bishops as a whole, sitting as a kind of supreme court.

The press, in reporting from Wheeling, described the procedure which Bishop Pike thus initiated as being authorized under an "obscure" canon, but there is in fact nothing obscure about it since it is set forth in the canon concerning presentments. If Henry Louttit read the law before uttering his presentment, or if any other bishops bothered to refer to the canon after Bishop Louttit's action, they could scarcely overlook the provision upon which Bishop Pike relied. Curiously, several bishops, including the Presiding Bishop, have professed not to have been alert to the section. Certainly the Dun committee was aware of it, because Bishop Pike himself, in one of his requests for a hearing before that committee, in a letter to Bishop Dun, specifically cited it.[27] Bishop Mosley, who served on the censure committee, says that his colleagues and he discussed the contingency of Bishop Pike's invoking his legal rights repeatedly. Evidently, their hope was that Bishop Pike would suffer the judgment and humiliation of the censure meekly and in silence. The Presiding Bishop has expressed a similar sentiment. It is equally apparent that the possibility that Bishop Pike would demand an investigation that could lead to a heresy trial neither influenced the *ad hoc* Committee to grant Bishop Pike a hearing nor significantly modified the severity of the censure.

So the censure of James Pike, begotten in the appeasement of the bishop's accusers, yielded only the opposite of what was intended: the likelihood of a heresy trial. For the most stubborn enemies of Bishop Pike, the occasion provoked macabre rejoicing. It moved Father Brunton, of course, to lyrics:

> Have you heard bishop pike's last and final report?
> He's been tried, if you please, by a Kangaroo Court
> And the bishops who made up the same
> Have just about put brother pike in a hearse
> For they've called him a cheat, and a liar, and worse
> And have smirched his immaculate name.
>
> So hearken good people to this latest news
> Jim pike thinks those bishops are just kangaroos
> And it hardly seems right, so one fears
> Nor quite in the proper and true legal style
> That kangaroos should put our friend pike on trial
> But that he should be judged by his peers.

But just who are his peers? so to question you may
Well, I fear they are those who eat thistles and bray
And are too mean for most folks to like
Yes, they're mean and they're mangy, and flea bitten too
And we're perfectly sure they will give his full due
To the great and illustrious pike.

So to help brother pike, and to save him his face
We should put every kangaroo out of his place
And pike's peers fill their places "en masse"
Who will say there's but one way this man we may judge
He is one of ourselves—from that truth we won't budge
He's a perfect unparalleled ass.[28]

One would think this outcome would also be enjoyed by Bishop Louttit. After all, the Louttit camp—in itself a distinct minority of the House of Bishops—had bargained to exchange their accusations for the censure and, now, with Bishop Pike's resort to the law, they had both the censure and an excellent prospect of the heresy trial they originally sought. Bishop Louttit, however, does not impress one as being personally elated, whatever may be said of his fellow accusers. He gives, rather, the impression of disappointment or resignation: his part of the excitement is over, the initiative has passed into other hands, the accusers are no longer the center of attention, and the accused has become more conspicuous than ever.

Bishop Louttit, however, may take heart in the matter since his presentment, with every one of its faults and defects, represents one of the major rumors and reports against which Bishop Pike is to be investigated and, perhaps, tried. The Bishop Pike affair has not ended yet for Bishop Louttit and his cabala.

Associated with the fact that the charges to be examined are those of the Louttit presentment and the reports to be investigated are those of the censure is Father Brunton's vulgar question: Are bishops kangaroos or asses? The procedures mandated by Bishop Pike's invocation of due process mean that at only two given points a heresy trial can be avoided: if the investigating bishops find that the allegations made against Bishop Pike, if proved, do not amount to canonical offenses or, in the next step, if the Board of Inquiry, acting as a grand jury, finds that there is not sufficient basis in either law or fact for a trial. In either case such actions would amount to an official repudiation, by duly constituted bodies, of *both* the Louttit presentment *and* the Dun censure and, thereby, an unequivocal exoneration of Bishop Pike.

It is a delicate dilemma which Wheeling has wrought.

Or, as is mentioned elsewhere, it is the House of Bishops and the churchly institution itself which are the defendants in the Bishop Pike affair, not Bishop Pike.

All this seems, finally, to have dawned on whoever is making the tactical decisions in the national and denominational establishment. It is known and admitted, as has been cited, that, after Wheeling, an emissary was dispatched to Bishop Pike to solicit *his* suggestions about how a heresy trial might still be obviated. Certain and numerous others have protested, discouraged, or tried to inhibit the publication of this book. Placating overtures have been volunteered. The committee, headed by Bishop Bayne, appointed by the Presiding Bishop is at work belatedly, perhaps, in search of compromise. No doubt some have thought that the most convenient solution would be for Bishop Pike to drop dead.

As in all dilemmas, there are really only two ways out: either Pike withdraws, which means, as Bishop Corrigan said, die, or Bishop Pike must be tried for heresy and, thus, either be exonerated or condemned, in aid, in either case, hopefully, of canonical due process.

Beclouding the whole matter are rarely used remedies which Bishop Pike possesses from any of the ecclesiastical proceedings in the secular courts. Such forums are reluctant, generally, to review decisions of church tribunals. Bishop Brown, after his conviction, contemplated appeals to the federal judiciary, but failed to perfect his options, though his petitions for reinstitution as a bishop of the Episcopal Church were pursued until his death, some dozen years or so after he was deposed. Bishop Pike has better grounds, more time, and a stronger case, should he decide to seek relief in either federal or state courts.

Should that eventuate from the Bishop Pike affair, there would be—in America—a classic encounter in the history of the idea of due process of law.

By an unquestioned and large majority, your brothers have suggested strongly that pastoral concerns illumine your pedagogy. Their encouragement to you to develop sensitivity to others and humility toward your apprehension of the truth is falling on deaf ears, judging from the action you have taken as your response to this House's action.

If your response had been that of a penitent who had been brought to an awareness of his errors, there would be others than myself who would feel that the traumatic experience through which *all* of us have passed in the last few days was after all beneficent.

>   —The Right Reverend Clarence R. Haden, Jr., Bishop of Northern California: in a letter to Bishop Pike at Wheeling, West Virginia, October 26, 1966

Why is it that this House has not censured any of the rest of us who have spoken, acted out, and allowed to occur within our dioceses greater blasphemies even than the treatment of items of doctrine less than solemnly? I speak of church doors closed against members of another race, clergy denied backing by their Bishops because of their Christian social views, and the public impugning of the motives of fellow Bishops. Is it only because Bishop Pike due to his peculiar genius in commanding a wide audience is a more public figure than the rest of us?

>   —The Right Reverend Paul Moore, Suffragan Bishop of Washington: during the censure debate[1]

[1] As transcribed, live, by the Canadian Broadcasting Corporation, October 25, 1966, at Wheeling, West Virginia.

third

The Fraternity of Bishops

SUBJECTIVE FACTORS invariably influence and frequently determine the conduct and outcome of legal proceedings and are even more conspicuous in the internal dynamics of an institution like the Episcopal House of Bishops. The question inevitably arises, therefore, of the extent to which issues of politics and psychology enter into the Bishop Pike affair and how much these problems may transcend in significance either matters of doctrine or of due process.

In this respect, of course, the House of Bishops, and the Episcopal Church in general, should not be piously exempt. Episcopalians are, first of all, human beings (if sometimes short of civility) and Episcopal bishops are by definition exemplary Episcopalians. That bishops are, often petty, bitter, weak, inconsistent, compromising, envious, condescending, and, otherwise, utterly human is not a surprise. Decisions and actual behavior disclose ethics and ethics betray motives and so the fuss about Bishop Pike becomes a question of the extent his troubles are accountable in the subjectivities of his peers and of himself.

This is an aspect of the Bishop Pike affair which was raised in the House of Bishops by Paul Moore during the censure debate. Subsequently it has been prominent in the reflections of a good many other bishops. The Bishop of Montana, for example, feels that the fundamental difficulty with Bishop Pike is that he did not conform but remained a "loner" in the House. In furtherance of that view, Bishop Sterling—who presides over both the American

THE FRATERNITY OF BISHOPS   141

Church Union—the traditionally Anglo-Catholic wing of the Episcopal Church—and the Diocese of Montana—found himself, at one and the same time, an exponent of the view that the main reason anyone is elected bishop is to remove troublesome figures by incorporating them into the establishment, a secret admirer of Bishop Pike, a reluctant associate of Bishop Louttit, and a much publicized critic reported to have labeled Bishop Pike a "double-crosser."[1]

The Ethics of Episcopal Fraternity

What caused the Bishop of Montana to employ such strenuous language was a recollection of the Glacier Park detente that Bishop Pike had undertaken there to consult more frequently with other bishops before speaking out and had not honored the promise. Other bishops suffered a similar impression though some who felt that a promise had been made also disclose a virtual presumption that it would not be kept. A few days following the Glacier Park meeting, Bishop Charles Ellsworth Bennison of Western Michigan dispatched a letter to the clergy of his diocese which, after reporting that he felt the House of Bishops had determined that "something should indeed be done to have Bishop Pike reaffirm his loyalty to our doctrine, discipline and worship," contains these revealing sentences:

We feel that we have, at least for the moment, accomplished this. We only hope and pray that the days ahead will establish further our present regard for his [Pike's] sincerity and professed loyalty.[2]

Whether a promise was made and, if so, dishonored, is a matter of subjective interpretations. The fact is that Bishop Pike did reaffirm the so-called oath of conformity at Glacier. Some of his brothers in the House evidently took that as a commitment of silence. As one has written, in explaining his vote to censure Pike, "it seemed to me that he is more concerned for his own image *and for being right* than for the good of the Church," and that ultimately a bishop "must be more concerned for the Faith and the Church than being right."[3] Bishop Pike has a different view and has said that when confronted with a question publicly he is not about to respond by saying he will first write to his brother bishops before he answers.

The further facts, relevant to whether Bishop Pike is guilty of breach of promise, are that he brought to the Glacier Park meeting the manuscript of his as yet unpublished book *What Is This Treasure,* offering it to any and all bishops who might like to consult with him about it. None did. Undismayed, he arranged for copies of the book to be sent, at his expense, to all bishops. He published little else of substance in the year subsequent to Glacier, being much of the time in England and, after resigning his See, beginning his new work at the Santa Barbara Center. Things were, in the meantime, published about him, notably, the *Look* article, which seems to have been the immediate provocation for the secret caucus of the "metropolitans" at O'Hare Field. Prior to that meeting and, indeed, before Pike knew there was to be such a confrontation and quite independently of that occasion, Bishop Pike had written to the editors of *Look* in clarification of certain points in the piece.[4] One upshot of the O'Hare Field episode—speaking of promises—was that Bishop Pike would write a second, longer, clarifying letter to *Look,* which it was taken for granted would not be published, because of its length and because of Bishop Pike's earlier letter, which, however, the Presiding Bishop would then circulate to all the bishops. Bishop Pike kept his promise and wrote the letter to *Look.* It was then circulated by Bishop Hines to just the participants in the O'Hare Field event and it was only after inquiries about the matter from the press at Wheeling, and after the specific request of Bishop Pike on November 4, 1966, that Hines fulfilled his promise and sent copies of the *Look* letter to all the bishops, with apologies for oversight and tardiness, on November 15, 1966. These apologies could scarcely undo the harm suffered by Bishop Pike because of Bishop Hines' omission. The *Look* letter clarified, among other things, the issue of Deaconess Edwards and a number of bishops who did not see the letter have admitted that they voted to censure Pike because of their erroneous impressions about the deaconess matter.

Even if it is assumed that Bishop Pike's reiteration of the oath of conformity at Glacier Park embodied a commitment to silence (though that is a hard assumption to make in view of his full

Glacier Park statement set forth in Appendix I) or, alternatively, even if the assumption carries that somehow the oath of conformity could be construed as a pledge to clear public utterances in advance with fellow bishops (which Bishop Pike disputes but which he, paradoxically, implemented by offering the *Treasure* manuscript for the critique of his colleagues and, later, by his primary initiative in clarification of the *Look* article), the facts remain. The facts bespeak a different question than that of the dark suspicions of the Bishop of Western Michigan or the excited libel that Bishop Pike is a doublecrosser. The facts say that, if promises are honored among bishops, Bishop Pike is rather inappropriately accused of breaking promises.

Still the issue raised about Bihop Pike's personal integrity, especially that of his honoring the Glacier Park detente, *whatever* that meant, cannot be isolated from many other problems affecting the manners and morals of the fraternity of bishops. One bishop, who shall remain anonymous because he is reputed by other bishops to be adept at philandering, admits an hostility to Pike which caused him to vote against confirmation of Pike's election as a bishop back in 1958 since Pike had been once divorced and had remarried.

There are bishops with more pressing concerns, too: any number are bothered that Bishop Pike's writings and sayings bewilder many of their constituents. There are some who speak of him as being "breezy" or "blasé" and who complain of having to pick up "the pieces after Bishop Pike cuts his annual swath around the country."[5]

The Bishop of Honolulu, Harry Kennedy for instance, has an ecclesiastical jurisdiction which roughly follows a comity between British and American Anglicanism founded historically in the retrenchment of Britain as a colonial power and the advent of the American presence in the Pacific, signaled by the Boxer Rebellion. He associates the Bishop Pike affair with the war in Vietnam, which, thus, lies within his care. That is not because of Bishop Pike's somewhat outspoken doubts about the war, but because Bishop Kennedy has people "chaplains and others—[who] speak to me about Bishop Pike, wondering why the bishops have not made some definite pronouncements in the defense of the faith."[6]

One of the authors of this book visited Vietnam in 1966 and found that the Anglican churches there embrace Americans and serve remnants of the British embassy staff but have no practical contact among the indigenous folk of Vietnam.[7] Applications to the Episcopal Church headquarters in New York to remedy this have not been affirmatively received.[8] All the same, if the Episcopal Church's efforts in Vietnam have been principally oriented toward ambassadors and field commanders, to Americans or other foreigners, the Bishop of Honolulu might be enlightened by the sentiments of a priest and chaplain serving in Vietnam:

To Bishop Pike's everlasting credit will be his courageous stand on Christian-social issues with his demand for action in combating evils in this sphere. . . .

I call upon you [the letter was addressed to Bishop Louttit] and your fellow bishops to form a committee for the preservation of Christian love. . . .[9]

In the debate, the Bishop of Vermont, who had written to Bishop Louttit he would not sign the presentment and was "prepared to oppose it as a thoroughly evil thing," echoed the concern of the chaplain in Vietnam, when he declared that "the absence of the spirit of Christ allows us to single out one man to bear the burden of our fear."[10]

One of the things which many bishops fear is that the laity of the Church are confused by inquiry or change, especially in that which is said and done in the sanctuary. Richard Emrich, the Bishop of Michigan, who was mentioned prominently for Presiding Bishop when Arthur Lichtenberger was elected and, again, in 1964 when Bishop Hines succeeded Bishop Lichtenberger, feels that "the public confession of doubt is open to abuse and exhibitionism just as much as the public confession of sin—as the latter was discarded by the Church, so the former should be avoided."[11] Bishop Emrich does not oppose theological inquiry, mind you, but the *public* discussion of theology. In effect, Bishop Emrich says that these are matters above the heads of the ordinary clergy and the common laity and should be reserved for scholars and bishops to cope with in private. True to his convictions, he sought the deposition of one scholar and was an architect of the Bishop Pike censure because public utterances of both were sowing confusion among the "little people" of the Church.

A significant number of the censuring bishops were of a similar mind. The Right Reverend Horace W. B. Donegan, who as Bishop of New York had called James A. Pike to be Dean of the Cathedral of St. John the Divine, wrote:

> I wish Bishop Pike would go more slowly, and gather about him clerical and lay theologians competent to advise him as he seeks to present new, fresh interpretations and applications of our timeless faith. Instead he dashes headlong and alone into the fray and leaves it to chance that the general public will understand his *real* purpose.[12]

Oddly enough, it was Pike, while Dean of New York who created the office of "canon theologian" at the Cathedral, a post occupied during Pike's incumbency by the distinguished Kierkegaardian scholar and historian of Anglicanism, Howard Johnson, but which has been vacant since shortly after Pike left as Dean. No Bishop is now known to have *any* theologian in his official entourage. Still more peculiar is why bishops with concerns like Bishop Emrich and Bishop Donegan joined in the censure at all, in view of Bishop Pike's resignation from his diocesan jurisdiction in May, 1966, specifically in order to devote himself more fully to theological study and reflection.[13]

A possible explanation is the association in the minds of such bishops between Bishop Pike's public sayings and writings and demands upon their time. Bishop Bloy of Los Angeles is very sensitive about this. "Don't forget," he complained to these authors, "he resides in my diocese, and I frequently have to 'explain' Pike to irate lay people."[14] Bishop Bloy enacted his distress about a month before Wheeling by instructing his clergy that prior to inviting Bishop Pike to speak at "a function other than a service of worship," he be notified in order to be able to "intelligently answer any questions which might be raised either by clergy or any layman."[15] Since Wheeling, Bishop Bloy has forbidden an invitation from a parish to Bishop Pike to preach, though his manner of doing so was extra-canonical, as has been noted.[16]

The connection between Bishop Pike and time, within the

House of Bishops itself, also exercises some of Bishop Pike's peers. The Bishop of Bethlehem (Pa.), Frederick Warnecke raised that in the censure debate:

> I simply would note the undue amount of time, the trouble, efforts of all of us, great amount of concern we have been giving to one member of our family in meeting after meeting after meeting.[17]

Bishop Warnecke's pique in the fact that the figure of Bishop Pike has overshadowed the deliberations of the House of Bishops in recent years might be mollified if he recalled two obvious things: (1) bishops other than Bishop Pike instigated heresy charges which a remainder of the bishops themselves chose to dignify by acting upon them and (2) Bishop Pike has become—as was foreseen in the sermon at his consecration—a personification of issues of theological ferment and social conscience and the House can neither deal with such matters while ignoring Bishop Pike nor confront Bishop Pike without coping with those issues.

Meanwhile there is an enormous evidence that the supposedly unsophisticated masses welcome a bishop who addresses the present scene in contemporary idiom and do not wish to endure the condescension of being spared from doubt or confusion. The Hon. Woodrow Seals, a judge of the United States District Court in Southern Texas, in a letter referring to *What Is This Treasure*, affirmed "What I like about this book . . . is that I am able to understand it," an affirmation few laymen could make about the Articles of Religion.[18] A housewife in Phoenix became irate when Bishop Harte, in February, 1967, publicly denounced Bishop Pike as a heretic at the time of an appearance of Bishop Pike at the University there, and wrote to the editor of *The Arizona Republic*:

> The headline in *The Republic* of Feb. 4, "Bishop Harte Calls Pike a Heretic," distressed me for two reasons.
>
> First, because Bishop Harte is my bishop I would like to think that he wouldn't reflect the opinions of so many narrow-minded church people in that he would term Bishop Pike a heretic without first listening thoughtfully to what he has to say.
>
> And secondly, because I cannot understand how Bishop Pike can be termed a heretic if one listened carefully to what he did say . . . particularly to his statement on television.[19]

A priest in Connecticut told his congregation Bishop Pike's "effort can help many to understand better the truth which lies behind the ancient thought and wording of the Creed." A mathematician from Manhattan—enclosing a check "for whatever purposes will aid you most"—has written to Bishop Pike, "I find your concepts and approach make good common sense with, most importantly, credibility, in an area where fantasy so often was and still is common." A gentleman who quit the Church said: "(Y)our interest and actions for the man on the bottom, in the street and in distress are more in line of what Christ meant for us." A priest complained to Bishop Louttit that if Bishop Pike is charged with heresy then what is being taught at Virginia Theological Seminary should also be investigated. Some parents in New York City ponder whether to have their two sons confirmed in a Church that might "consider 'unfrocking' a man such as" Bishop Pike.[20] *The St. Petersburg Times* editorialized: "What Bishop Pike has publicly proclaimed—to eager audiences from St. Petersburg to San Francisco—is an urgency to preserve and revitalize the church, not to destroy it."[21] A minister of the United Church of Christ informed Bishop Louttit:

Although I can understand the ways that some conservative churchmen and theologians might be threatened by Bishop Pike's boldness in speech and writing, countless thousands of us, both inside and outside the Anglican Communion, have been deeply moved and influenced by his insight, courage, and candor.

A communicant of Bishop Louttit's diocese admonished her bishop: "If Bishop Pike is found guilty of heresy, and there is no room for him in the Church, then there certainly is not room for me—and I supect many thousands like me." Another Episcopalian, a psychologist, pointed out to Bishop Louttit, "You, too, are confusing some of us among the faithful laity. The ironic thing is that Bishop Pike is only saying what most churchmen believe at heart. In some ways he is more conservative." A churchwoman in St. Petersburg confessed to Bishop Louttit:

When you speak of the faithful laity in this general way, and do not use specific names, you are speaking for me. Frankly, I do not care to have someone else speak for me on such a personal matter. . . .

Often I parrot our Services with little or no thought to what I am really saying. If Bishop Pike confuses me, I can only say, "Thank you for making me think."[22]

Not all expressions volunteered by churchmen, editorialists and others about the Bishop Pike affair have been pro-Pike. The files of Bishop Louttit yield some letters like this one, from an aged man from Oakland (italics his):

[Pike] *has violated his bishop oaths many, many times!* Convict him *of heresy and* UNFROCK *him!* . . . Do not let Bishop Hines outsmart you! . . . I have . . . prayed that our Episcopal Church could stop the wiles of Satan *once and for all!*

A Los Angeles resident—who may be among the "irate" who so harass Bishop Bloy—sent this admonition to Bishop Pike:

I suppose when you come down to it—you do want "a trial"—but *only* for a wide advertisement, for a big platform, to have an audience for "Pikery" and do the devil's work—on a large scale.

Well Judas did repent and sacrifised [sic] himself to his error—But you? You will continue and compound the errors.[23]

Meanwhile other poetasters besides Father Brunton have been moved to rhymes, including one Kathleen Mohr, of Lakeland, Florida, who dispatched her doggeral to Bishop Hines, Bishop Pike and Bishop Louttit, with a covering letter referring to the latter two bishops as "Tweedledee and Tweedledum." The lady explains that she had stopped contributing to the Church or receiving Holy Communion because of what she felt to be the vacillation of the House of Bishops in dealing with Bishop Pike. (It is noteworthy—on the subject of confused laity—that this one accuses Bishop Pike of being outspoken against the Virgin Birth, in one part of her letter, and later on, in the same letter, alleges that the other bishops have absolved Bishop Pike "of his stated and published disbelief in the Immaculate Conception" apparently under the impression that the Virgin Birth and the Immaculate Conception are the same doctrine. She thus unintentionally buttresses Bishop Pike's claim that the use of uncontemporary doctrinal language often results in lay people mouthing words to which no intelligent meaning or actual comprehension attaches.)

Miss Mohr in her poetry is, of course, consistent in her preoccupation with the means of conception and birth (prurient matter has been omitted):

> For now the Bishop tells us
> That Christ was not divine,
> That means that his conception
> Was just like yours and mine.
>
> He says that good St. Joseph
> Was really Jesus' dad;
> He......The Virgin Mary......
> And sired the little lad.
>
> Now church bells have a hollow sound
> The Creed is rent in twain,
> And Sunday's just another day
> When I hope it doesn't rain.[24]

However, far the most hostile and derogatory reactions from "little people" to Bishop Pike, his ministry, and the controversy there attendant, do not disclose confusion about theology, but, instead, reveal distress about Bishop Pike's social radicalism, a matter to which another chapter is devoted. Let it only be recorded now that the authors of this book audited literally thousands upon thousands of letters, editorials, and related documents—made available to them by the principal parties involved, and that, from this data—as the samples published indicate—the conclusions emerge inescapably that (1) Bishop Pike is enormously appreciated by laymen in the Church, and a general public, for his efforts to *clarify* belief, rather than, as so many bishops have supposed, being regarded as a sower of confusion, (2) the enmity among lay folk against Pike on doctrinal—as distinguished from psychological or political—issues alone is exceedingly meager, and (3) the opposition to Bishop Pike, which is vocal among ordinary people, is substantially unconcerned with theology as such but is very absorbed in maintaining or turning back the *status quo* in every respect, socially, racially, politically, scientifically, educationally, religiously, and possesses an economic influence and a mental temperament to further these aims.

Perchance the anxieties of bishops about money, or the infection of such a pathology, added to the internal problems occasioned by Bishop Pike's energy and celebrity, plus those born of vanity and a fraternity spirit, rather than issues of creed or faith, sponsored Pike's censure and his present jeopardy as an accused heretic.

The Notoriety and Naïveté of Pike

Certainly a large element in Bishop Pike's current difficulties and in the situation he symbolizes to the House of Bishops implicates his unusual notoriety. Whatever they may have elsewhere sometimes been, bishops are not any more generally regarded as much other than vintage figureheads adorning ceremonial events. There is simply nobody to coronate in the United States and bishops are not privy to the councils of the state as a matter of prerogative or function. In America, bishops are more ornamental than perhaps anywhere else in the modern world.[25]

Insofar as that be the case, the especial attention which Bishop Pike receives and which he has enjoyed for years on the American scene is likely to be an annoyance to his brothers having less fame, attention, or influence. The specter of envy has been haunting the Episcopal House of Bishops. A detached observer of Wheeling—a Roman Catholic nun—identified that demon in this way:

It was with urgent regret I realized, too, that the Inquisition is not in the past, continuing its outrage—in God's name. As in our persuasion, so evidently in the Episcopal branch, personal jealousy can be vindicated in the name of "orthodoxy"—or exasperated pietism.[26]

Something that seems to confuse bishops—if not laymen—is the notion that the making of a bishop amounts automatically to public recognition and status. But that is hardly the reality. Who, even within the Episcopal Church, can remember the name of the Presiding Bishop of the Episcopal Church in 1924? At the same time a good many recall the bishop—William Montgomery Brown —whose condemnation as a heretic that Presiding Bishop pronounced.

A few incumbent bishops are mindful of history. Bishop Burroughs of Ohio, for example, still labors under burdens inherited from the trial of Bishop Brown, which was an agenda for the House of Bishops thirteen years after the actual trial.[27] The ghost of Brown may have caused Bishop Burroughs to embrace Bishop Pike, at the Sesquicentennial of Trinity Cathedral in Cleveland, where Bishop Pike preached a few days after Wheeling. Bishop Burroughs made this statement in introducing Bishop Pike to the throng:

To preach the sermon, the Dean and Vestry have brought a Bishop whose name is a household word . . . They have my full support in extending this invitation and I am proud to introduce him as a brother bishop and a dear friend. He is an uncomfortable and disturbing factor in the circles I inhabit. He does not . . . destroy my faith, but he forces me to re-examine my faith and to re-discover its power in the contemporary scene which he seems to understand in clearer terms than I do.[28]

Thus Bishop Burroughs anticipated sentiments of "little people" for, the next day, *The Cleveland Plain Dealer* editorialized:

One of the most exciting and important sermons ever heard in Cleveland was given by Episcopal Bishop James A. Pike . . .

The real significance of the sermon lies in the fact that Bishop Pike is aiming to revive the new generation's lagging interest in religion and to have religion speak in terms modern man can understand.[29]

The immense impact—one might even use the word "success"—of Bishop Pike's visit to Cleveland's Episcopal Cathedral, after the denigrating experience of Wheeling, has been repeated time and again in other places. At St. Thomas Church, Fifth Avenue, New York the same thing happened, during Advent, 1966.[30] It occurred again in Richmond, Virginia, in January, 1967, in consequence of which *The Christian Century* reported:

True, there had been many detractors, but many others had been challenged by what he [Pike] had said, impressed by the fact that he was willing to say it, concerned to dig in and, in the bishop's word, "get with it" while there is yet time and vitality in the church.[31]

Meanwhile, seminarians at the Episcopal Theological School in Cambridge, Massachusetts, protested to Bishop Hines their deep disappointment in "the conspicuous lack of creative and dynamic leadership" in evading "an honest solution" to the theological controversy aroused by Bishop Pike and in deploring "the negligence of the bishops . . . to assume any commitment in areas of social crisis," in particular urban racial violence, black power, the white backlash and the war in Vietnam.[32]

The nub of the matter is, of course, that Bishop Pike, despite being in the Church and a bishop, has notoriety, attracts publicity, much more so than any other living bishop, and through these means, and within such limits, tries to communicate the concerns of the Gospel in the succinct or pithy way allowed by such public media.

That he succeeds in this endeavor is not questioned but, in fact, confirmed by his opponents in the House of Bishops. What may, however, be overlooked by some of his associates in that House is that Bishop Pike's celebrity does not originate in his being a bishop. Perhaps his episcopal status makes him more the subject of attention and more vulnerable to assault, but the truth is that he was a national personage long before he was elected a bishop and his eminence does not derive from his present title.

As a young Washington lawyer he had been spotted as a "comer," and the distinction of his legal scholarship had been confirmed by his appointment as a Sterling Fellow at the Yale Law School and by his publication of a casebook on federal procedure that became a standard law school text. It is not at all difficult to imagine that, if he had not turned to the ordained ministry, he would today be the dean of an influential law school or a high ranking member of the federal judiciary or a United States Senator. (Query whether, if Pike had become a Senator, he would have encountered difficulties with the ethics of *that* club as he has with those of the fraternity of bishops.) But he did become ordained and quickly rose in ecclesiastical rank and came to great celebrity as Dean Pike. New York newsmen used to joke about how the Church had two voices—Spellman's Chancery and Pike's Cathedral—because the public recognition of Dean Pike rivaled that of Cardinal Spellman. As a television personality his became one of a handful of names—along with Graham, Peale, Sheen—known throughout the land. Pike did not become a famous person because he was elected a bishop; rather the contrary is the question: how was one already so notorious ever named a bishop?

There is not the slightest room for doubt that the established fame of Bishop Pike and the publicity attendant to it has been a festering irritant in the bosoms of many of the other bishops for a long time. One of the authors recalls, for example, being invited to deliver a paper (on the nature of the episcopal office) to the Little Rock meeting of the House of Bishops in 1963. Most of the news stories engendered by that meeting had not to do with the deliberations of the House but with Bishop Pike, especially an address which he made at the local Roman Catholic seminary. One bishop, friendly to Bishop Pike, wryly observed at the time: "If they were together in the same room, Jim could upstage Jesus Himself." To which this author's response was: "But Jesus wouldn't care."

Whether Jesus would care or not, the bishops *do*, and they have for quite a while. It is not difficult to understand how the notoriety of Bishop Pike would be construed as a violence to the club spirit of the House, nor how that sentiment would conceal personal jealousy or other hostilities, nor how all that would be rationalized most readily in a charge that Bishop Pike is a publicity-seeker even though Bishop Pike is enough of a celebrity, long since, so that publicity seeks him. The much more curious thing is that Bishop Pike emerges as incredibly naïve about public relations and communication while regarded by so many of his colleagues as adept, and even cunning, in such realms.

Picture Bishop Pike as, on one hand, "a loner" in the House of Bishops, but, at the same time, the center of attention in the House. Those bishops who were not, in truth, envious of Bishop Pike or otherwise viscerally or politically motivated against him, were almost certain to have felt left out. Some have said as much. Bishop Mosley of Delaware, for instance, who voted for censure, expressed it this way:

We are presently expecting him [Pike] for three days of teaching in Delaware and shall try to assure him of our love and appreciation. At the same time we hope to help him hear—really to *hear*, which I don't think he ever has—that the good work he is doing requires patient and sensitive pastoral concern for others and that this need not dilute his freedom to explore. In fact, it would increase it.[33]

Gertrude Behanna, the gifted lay evangelist, a personal friend of Bishop Pike, wrote to him after Wheeling:

This insistent need for the limelight so often dims the worth of much that you might be unveiling and always the limelight is on you, Jim. . . . And this is tiresome. Were it all "cake," it would still be tiresome since too much of anything or anybody is *too much*.[34]

If Bishop Pike for some time was naïve or insensitive about the impact of his notoriety upon his fellow bishops, there are indications that he was becoming aware of it in his initiative in trying to communicate with them about his manuscript of *What Is This Treasure* and in the *Look* episode, as well as in his resignation as a diocesan. Unhappily, by then some of the fraternity had become inconsolable. The Bishop of Missouri, George L. Cadigan, understood this when he replied to Bishop Louttit's circulation of the charges:

I thought that this matter was successfully and happily concluded at Glacier Park.

I can foresee in a presentment nothing but schism, unhappiness and unwholesomeness not only for Jim, but for the Episcopal Church. By putting him out on a limb like this, you are only going to aggravate and ulcerate that which I believe is healing and would sooner, rather than later, have been remedied.[35]

Still, only Bishop Pike's death will console some of his brothers. Bishop Pinckney of Upper South Carolina in a letter which he required to be read in all the congregations of his diocese after the censure, wrote:

I wish to say that Bishop Pike has not been tried for heresy, he is still a Bishop. He is no longer a member of the House of Bishops . . . and speaks only for himself. He likes publicity and as such will constantly be in public view. This we cannot control.[36]

The Presiding Bishop, as has been mentioned, was hoping that Bishop Pike would accede to the censure and, thereby, if not make an act of atonement at least perfect appeasement. Bishop Pike's neighbor, the Bishop of Northern California, wanted Bishop Pike to be an abject penitent.[37] Others saw the censure as so judgmental that it was intolerable for any honorable man to live with. In writing to Bishop Mosley expressing his puzzlement at Bishop Mosley's "part in the events," Bishop William F. Creighton said: "I just cannot believe that you think Jim is totally irresponsible, cheap, vulgar and dishonest, as the report made him out to be. . . . I felt the report left Jim no alternative but to try to clear his name."[38]

The publicity issue has some ironic aspects to it, apart from Bishop Pike. For one thing, the presentment relied heavily upon hearsay garnered from newspapers reporting about Pike, the most unreliable variety of hearsay imaginable given the practice, which Bishop Bennison condemned after the *Look* article, of news media reporting statements "so torn out of context" as to be "distorted sometimes beyond recognition."[39] For another thing, the presenters themselves are vulnerable to a charge of publicity seeking. Bishop Louttit went to much greater effort to insure a maximum national news coverage of his charges than he did to make certain that Bishop Pike received timely service of the allegations. He described quite frankly to these authors his arrangements with the publisher of the *Orlando Sentinel* for the release of the news to the wire services and, after a few days had passed and he had not seen the heresy charges in print, he telephoned the publisher to inquire. "What's happened to my publicity?" On September 29, the publisher wrote to Bishop Louttit confirming that the story had been given to the press services. It broke the next day.

Some of Bishop Pike's opponents are discriminating, however, in their desire for publicity, as witness Bishop Louttit's attempt to have a journalist who had written an article that he did not like barred from covering the Wheeling meeting.[40]

Meanwhile, the first concern of the Presiding Bishop was for publicity—he asked that newsman to make the survey about what a trial would do to the image of the Episcopal Church. A score of other bishops responded to the presentment in the same vein.

Yet the larger irony is that by sidetracking the presentment and censuring Bishop Pike with a vehemence which caused him to insist on an inquiry, the bishops only succeeded in enhancing Bishop Pike's notoriety and giving him an even greater audience than ever before. They may well also have succeeded in creating a new sympathy for Bishop Pike as one who, though not exactly an underdog in the circumstances, has been dealt with unjustly and cruelly by the fraternity of bishops.

Vanity and Vulgarity

The bargain by which Bishop Pike was impugned as a charlatan instead of being accused as a heretic has made vulgarity a central issue in the Bishop Pike affair. There are those who think that Bishop Pike is not vulgar enough. William Hamilton, in a condescending mood, responded to a critique by Bishop Pike of the so-called death of God theology which Hamilton espouses, by saying:

> Jim Pike, always more impressive in what he does than in what he writes, cannot be dull, even when he writes hastily. . . . Jim Pike is one of the authentic disturbers of Israel's peace in our midst, and we need him. . . . Surely those whom the establishment dislikes should be a little less careless in commenting upon one another's work. I still think that Pike is one of the canniest spokesmen for traditional theology that we have around.[41]

These statements, which were published in *Playboy* magazine, were carried further by Hamilton in a letter he sent to Bishop Pike after the censure:

> . . . (G)ood luck, and keep it up, and remember that your even crazier friends can always be useful in your encounters with the right as reminders of where you are not. John Robinson says he loves to use the death of God people in this way to his horrified British observers.[42]

Bishop Pike has probably overlooked the gratuitous sound of Hamilton's sallies; he must be used to such things by now. Recall, for example, the outburst of Bishop Edward Welles of West Missouri at the 1964 General Convention—"One wonders if he [Pike] is not surrendering to a deep-rooted psychological compulsion to become a martyr."[43] Or consider Bishop Vander Horst's view: "Jim Pike in my estimation is a long range slow motion picture of deterioration."⁴⁴ The Right Reverend William W. Horstick of Eau Claire has diagnosed Bishop Pike as "a 'sick' man," a comment which he revealingly couples with an attack upon the so-called Blake-Pike proposal which led to the convening of the Consultation on Church Union, a cause which is anathema to the more exalted Anglo-Catholics like Bishop Horstick.⁴⁵

It might comfort Bishop Pike, incidentally, to remember, in the face of such derogatory remarks as these, the classic response of William Montgomery Brown to bishops who had not only accused him of heresy but defamed him as insane but who proposed that a committee confer with him about these allegations that it made no sense for a committee to meet with a crazy man.⁴⁶

There may be further solace in the fact that some of the same critics who have so slurred him have also attacked the Presiding Bishop's special committee to examine issues raised by the Bishop Pike affair.⁴⁷ Some Arizona clergy, so characteristically zealous as folk from that region tend to be, have taken the Presiding Bishop to task for appointing Bishop Bayne as the chairman of that committee, averring that Bishop Bayne is vulgar:

> Over the years Bishop Stephen Bayne, for all his good works, has developed a reputation amongst many of us for an easy, free-swinging glibness which is no substitute for the broad Catholicism he has often claimed to espouse.⁴⁸

The letter complaining about Bishop Bayne was released, by the way, to the press.

A bishop (for his protection he will not be here identified) who joined in the assault on Bishop Pike with some relish, pondered recently what had happened at Wheeling and speculated about whether a Pandora's box had been opened: "I wonder where it will all end?" he questioned. "I wonder who will be next," he thought. "I'll probably be next," he startled himself. He had a premonition.

A Texas clergyman has perhaps uttered the most definitive word on the issue of vulgarity. He told Bishop Pike:

> The biggest irony came in their putting you down for "cheap vulgarization of great expressions of faith." If I understand aright traditional incarnational theology, we are really dealing with the vulgarization of

God, and *any* expressions of faith are indeed cheap vulgarizations hereafter. At least they have welcomed you to the club. Theirs may be older, but no less cheap because your opinions are new.

If you are indeed guilty of caricaturing "treasured symbols" this was a favorite strategy of the great prophets who wished to expose the idolatries of the people of God. Even Moses broke the stone tablets when he found the people worshiping the golden calf. The lesson that that has for me is that worthwhile earthen vessels are not absolute; and even less absolute for an idolatrous people. But in many ways the problem we have is more related to the third commandment. Theological constructs of an earlier time are *equated* with God—a real blasphemy. At least you have the good grace to sign your name after your constructs and not God's. God bless Jim Pike.[49]

The problems of vulgarity and vanity in the House of Bishops are related to other matters besides what Bishop Pike may have said or what other bishops have said of him. Vanity and vulgarity are related to conduct as well as words. Take into account, for instance, the question whether Bishop Pike lacks pastoral sensibility, as many bishops have felt, not merely vis à vis any of his fellow bishops, but with respect to others as well. While Bishop Louttit claims to have either discarded or seldom replied to letters he received about the charges, Bishop Pike, hiring three secretaries at his own expense, answered the much more considerable volume of mail he received, including some manifestly crank letters. Is that relevant to pastoral concern? Or consider some of the tributes to Bishop Pike as a pastor, received in the midst of the strife at Wheeling and its aftermath. A Harvard student asks Bishop Pike's help on a thesis and the bishop tries to assist him. A housewife in an afterthought to a letter says: "Please forgive me for writing about *our* troubles in such detail." A hospital chaplain affirms: "I think it does far less damage to *people* to talk about theology, to become interested in thinking about my relationship to God." A doctor tells Bishop Louttit: Bishop Pike "possesses a mind as searching as it is warm. Certainly he has, on more than one occasion, sustained and comforted me when Bishops of my own denomination were totally insufficient." A lay reader declares: "I want finally to say that I have personally found in your writings every evidence of 'sensitive pastoral care.' If it had not been for the influence of your books . . . I might well have not involved myself in the organized church to the extent I have." A churchwoman begins a letter: "Dear Jim: I used to consider it rather amusing that I should know a bishop well enough to call him by his first name, and if you had been an ordinary bishop . . . I might have gone on feeling the same way for the rest of my life."[50] Are these testimonials of pastoral care or do they show pastoral indifference?

Perhaps the questioning of Bishop Pike's credentials as a pastor is summed up in its full irony in an incident that took place not long after the censure. The wife of a bishop who had praised the censure, including, presumably, its imputation of pastoral insensitivity, as a "balanced" statement approached Bishop Pike to report she had heard that he would soon be in such and such a city. She hoped that Bishop Pike might visit their son who lived in that place because she and her husband, the bishop, were apprehensive that their son would quit the Church and she felt that Bishop Pike was the person who could "reach" the son and save him for the Church.

AM HOLDING PRESENTMENT UNTIL HOUSE OF BISHOPS MEETING. HOW DO YOU EXPLAIN TO THE CONSERVATIVES OF CENTRAL NEW YORK AND HAVE NOT SIGNED PRESENTMENT I DO NOT KNOW I AM PRAYING TWICE DAILY AS I SAY THE OFFICES THAT THE HOLY SPIRIT WILL HELP YOU.

> —The Right Reverend Henry I. Louttit, Bishop of South Florida: a telegram sent to the Right Reverend Ned Cole, Jr., Bishop Coadjutor of Central New York[1]

It seems incredible that millions of Christians should accept meekly the most profound mysteries of faith which no one comprehends, and yet reject the commandment of love which a child can understand. . . . To admit that there are three persons in God and that Mary is a virgin mother causes the Catholic no inconvenience. But when the pastor says to his people, you must love Negroes, you must treat Latin Americans as equals, you must allow honest men of minority groups to live in your neighborhood and, worst of all, you may not pay starvation wages to defenseless men and women, too many Christians declare that the pastor is taking things too far. He must be a communist. He is way to the left.

> —Archbishop Robert E. Lucey, Roman Catholic Archdiocese of San Antonio, address at the installation of the Most Reverend Vincent M. Harris as Bishop of Beaumont, Texas[2]

[1] Identical wires were dispatched on October 3, 1966, to several Bishops who had not responded to Bishop Louttit's letter of September 20, 1966.
[2] As quoted by the *National Catholic Reporter*, October 12, 1966, p. 1.

fourth

Social Radicalism and Heresy

IN the days of the Inquisition, heresy charges were sometimes used to cover the pursuit, persecution, and condemnation of those whose nonconformity was, in reality, political, social or ideological rather than doctrinal, dogmatic, or theological.

Long before that, as conscientious biblical scholarship has established, the Crucifixion of Jesus Christ—however it may be interpreted theologically—was the means of eliminating a social agitator and disturber of the domestic tranquillity, not just a convenient way of disposing of a blasphemer.

In Anglicanism, the very absence of either an historic confessional consensus or a norm of dogmatic orthodoxy renders inescapable as well as intriguing the question of whether Bishop Pike is now so besieged because of his social radicalism rather than because of his theological utterances.

A similar issue was prominent in the presentment of Bishop Brown for heresy. He had been provocative enough to the conservative mentality of his day when he declared his "conversion" to Darwinism, but his offensiveness was coupled with his espoused admiration of Marxism.[1] Earlier, Algernon Crapsey had styled himself a "rationalist" and a "socialist" which attracted to him an astonishing public following if only for the novelty of his being, simultaneously, a cleric but which did not endear him to his ecclesiastical contemporaries and unquestionably influenced the initiative to defrock him.[2]

Bishop Pike's social views, like his theological positions, are not rigid or thoroughly consistent or particularly systematic. They are open to change, subject to question by both himself and others, dynamic. Bishop Pike is *not* an ideological thinker, in the sense of having some fixed and vested point of view or interest to assert or defend. Nevertheless, Pike's social witness would have to be classified as rather tame, especially noting the lapse of so much time, compared with those of either Crapsey or Brown. Yet, when Bishop Pike speaks out on a particular social problem, there is a precision and coherence, subject though it be to the critique of later intelligence, for which neither Bishop Brown nor the Reverend Dr. Algernon Crapsey could be accredited in their more amorphous convictions.

It may well be that what has now so roused controversy around Bishop Pike is not any substantive radicality in his opinions, whether theological or social (if, biblically speaking, there be any admissible distinction between the two) but, rather, that Bishop Pike's mind remains restlessly, enthusiastically, and abrasively radical: acceptive of challenges, free to listen to other insights, appreciative of new data, inclined to embrace change; questing, inquiring, wondering, possessed of awe. Perhaps what is *so* disturbing and, within the churchly institutions, *so* distracting about Bishop Pike is not any extremity in his utterances but the remarkable candor of his mind. Maybe true social radicalism has to do with such a quality and not mere ideology.

In any event, as in the cases of Brown and Crapsey, the Bishop Pike affair is haunted by the query of whether the central issue is social radicalism or heresy.

A Matter of Malice?

With respect to Bishop Pike, this question is prompted in the first instance by both the identity of some of his most persistent detractors and the conduct of some of his accusers.

Among the former are individuals like Carl McIntire, the renegade Presbyterian radio preacher who has made a career out of attempting to smear and sabotage the World Council of Churches and the National Council of Churches in the U.S.A., and the Rev. Frank M. Brunton who not only admits to fancying himself as something like a reincarnation of the seventeenth century's Samuel Butler but confesses that his only remaining purpose in life is to destroy Bishop Pike by weekly assaulting him with doggerel which is, if frequently funny—in a grotesque sort of fashion, usually venomous, consistently libelous, and betrayingly visceral.[3]

While it must be considered complimentary to Pike to have such adversaries, the mere presence of such figures as these among his opponents is hardly sufficient to establish a significant connection between social stands and heresy charges. The McIntires and the Bruntons within the churches, and their brethren and collaborators in secular precincts, might readily be dismissed as revealing symptoms of maladjustment, irrationality, or radical eccentricity which, however much pastoral sympathy they might desire and need, still does not prove much of anything and certainly does not show that Bishop Pike is attacked as a heretic because he is, in some sense, a social radical.

The more telling evidence of the relationship between Bishop Pike the theological gadfly and Bishop Pike the social critic is in the behavior of some of his accusers within the House of Bishops. Some bishops, for example, who advocated a trial and who ultimately settled for the Wheeling censure, were among those who declined to approve the election of James A. Pike as a bishop in the first place. Of those, some refused consent to the election of Pike to the episcopate because they considered him too much the social radical, and their position on the censure issue in West Virginia seemed to them confirmed, to be specific, because not only had Pike, when Dean, refused the Sewanee degree in "white divinity," but, later, when a bishop, had publicly denounced racism as both heresy and sin at the St. Louis General Convention, and, then, became one of those who was involved in the Selma episode, among other misdemeanors.[4]

A Bishop Without a Cause?

In the initial interview of the present writers with the Bishop of South Florida, at his diocesan offices, on March 8, 1967, at 4:16 P.M., the relevance of Bishop Pike's social positions to the allegations of heresy was promptly and gratuitously mentioned by Bishop Louttit. Nobody actually present at that audience—Bishop Louttit, Towne, or Stringfellow—had opportunity to even light a cigarette before the bishop protested that the heresy charges against Pike were no reprisal for his social witness. No such intimation had been yet in any manner suggested by the interviewers; on the contrary, though the association was not absent altogether from our minds, these authors were, at the moment, still attentive to the decent and requisite amenities of meeting the bishop. *But* this problem of heresy vis à vis social radicalism was, evidently, uppermost and defensively conspicuous in the bishop's conscience and conversation. Indeed, in response to the bishop's ready comments that Bishop Pike was not being accosted because of his social positions, the attempt was made to change the subject, or, at least, to open it less bluntly than had the bishop, by our asking Bishop Louttit to simply recount his own acquaintance with Bishop Pike and, particularly, to indicate those events or utterances or writings which has occasioned and seemed to Bishop Louttit to warrant the heresy presentment.

This opportunity to thus deflect the conversation to more comfortable, or less controversial, matters was either unnoticed or ignored, or else misunderstood by or unwelcome to Bishop Louttit, who, at once plunged headlong into a recounting, from his own recollection and viewpoint, of that fateful encounter of Pike and Louttit in Bishop Donegan's premises in prelude to the 1953 Sewanee incident.

Other witnesses shed light upon the Sewanee matter and the variant versions of it attributable to Bishop Louttit and Bishop Pike. Bishop Pike, as has already been here recounted, felt that he was supporting, by his emphatic and public refusal of an honorary degree from a racially discriminatory and then segregated school owned and operated by the Southern dioceses of the Episcopal Church, those faculty and students who similarly opposed racism at the University of the South. Bishop Louttit, as has been indicated, felt that he, among other trustees of Sewanee, had found a quiet, reasonable, more gradual way to breach some of the racist barriers there. At the same time, however, there is the testimony of a priest who was on the scene in 1953 at Sewanee and became a refugee from the dispute. The Reverend Dr. Robert McNair, Professor of Sociology at San Jose State College, was moved to write to Bishop Louttit, at the time of the presentment against Bishop Pike:

As one of the priests who resigned from Sewanee in 1953 and as having met you most recently when you were visiting Bishop of the Church Divinity School of the Pacific when I was teaching there I am writing you concerning the heresy charges against Bishop Pike. . . . (T)he Church had a magnificent chance to speak at Sewanee (which was before the Supreme Court) and the mealy-mouthed decision that came from the trustees was a forerunner of failure later. Bishop Penick spent the evening at my home after that meeting,—and he was a crushed man. 'Tis true that the press made it look like Sewanee was going to face the challenge but he knew that it was not and so did those of us leaving. So since the present racial matter is the real challenge to the whole doctrine of man and Bishop Pike not only speaks to this but to other doctrinal matters I am not sure as to why you think he is a heretic.

I would like to know why heresy charges have not been made against Bishops Carpenter and Juhan rather than a man who is raising the same issues of importance as did . . . William Temple and Paul Tillich.[5]

It is, of course, a matter of record that the Seminary at Sewanee did not admit a Negro student until the fall of 1954, and that a policy of desegregation for the entire University of the South was only authorized much later, though, meanwhile, the trustees voted to award an honorary doctorate of civil law in 1961 to a notorious segregationist editor, Mr. Thomas Waring of *The Charleston News and Courier.*[6]

None of this is recited here to attribute guile to the Bishop of South Florida. Those who would like to find a villain in the Bishop Pike affair and suppose the villain to be Henry Louttit are mistaken. Scoundrels there are in the House of Bishops but one must look beyond Bishop Louttit to identify them. What is emphasized here, however, is the apparent contradiction between the eagerness of Bishop Louttit to disavow any relationship between the charges against Bishop Pike and his social witness, on

SOCIAL RADICALISM AND HERESY 167

one hand, and the prominence, in Bishop Louttit's own recounting of how the heresy presentment came to be, of the 1953 Sewanee episode.

Confronted with this seeming inconsistency, the authors sought out Bishop Louttit's own social views and his record on public issues since he became the diocesan authority in South Florida in 1951. It is an ambiguous account. During Bishop Louttit's incumbency, the Diocesan Convention has made few pronouncements on civil rights; on the other hand, the principal one that has been made directed the integration of the diocesan youth camp at Avon Park, Florida, an action taken at the first convention following the Supreme Court school desegregation decision. It seems a moral certainty that, if he had chosen to, Bishop Louttit could have malingered indefinitely on this issue.[7]

Born in Buffalo, Bishop Louttit, still characterizing himself as a "Yankee", candidly names some of his episcopal brethren from other Southern dioceses as "racists," but he is very sensitive to any other "Yankee" doing the equivalent. In February, 1956, for example, Bishop Louttit, who has been very prominent in the Florida Council on Human Relations bitterly assailed the Department of Christian Social Relations of the Diocese of New York for its condemnation of civil rights murders in the South as a "reign of terror." Bishop Louttit wrote:

. . . We in the South who are struggling with the problem of racial relation tensions have read with great interest your courageous stand on the matter of the "Till Case" (the murder of the Negro boy Emmett Till in Mississippi) and other unfortunate by-products of racial tension . . . "He who is without sin among you, let him cast the first stone."[8]

Since the department speaks with the approval of the Bishop of New York, Bishop Louttit's sarcasm was really a rebuke to Bishop Horace W. B. Donegan. One speculates whether, somehow, this outburst was incited by remembrance of that famous encounter of Louttit and Donegan and Pike on Cathedral Heights in New York City in January 1953.

There are few integrated congregations in the Diocese of South Florida, and some clergy there complain openly that there has been a great deficiency in hierarchical support for such integration. Still in July 1964, Bishop Louttit issued "a godly admonition and godly judgment"—sanctioned by threat of trial—forbidding any priest from barring Negroes from "baptism, confirmation, worship, receiving the Holy Communion, ordination, marriage, or what have you in any and all of our churches."[9] That same message of Bishop Louttit to his clergy sought their initiative in establishing bi-racial commissions in all communities, in securing equal employment opportunity, and in urging obedience to federal civil rights legislation on the part of reluctant whites. At the same time, the Bishop wrote to all mayors and county commissions in his diocese beseeching their intelligence and cooperation in South Florida's race relations.[10] In his epistle to his clergy, Bishop Louttit was emphatic about the need for "tutorial" remedial education for Negro school children and asked that parochial classrooms and other facilities be made available for such programs; still, his diocese has been heavily engaged in expanding a private school system which, because of high tuitional costs, in effect provides prosperous white churchmen with a way of evading the school integration issue.[11]

If Bishop Louttit's position on racism has been ambivalent, then his conduct with respect to the radical right, which has a substantial bastion in South Florida, can only be described as eccentric. The Bishop received a large volume of mail, immediately following the publicity of his charges against Bishop Pike, most of which he says he did not acknowledge and much of which he declares he threw away. It remains clear, however, from the Louttit files which were placed at the disposition of the present authors to examine, that the heresy presentment against Pike attracted substantial support from the ideological right. "So today I praise the Lord for men such as yourself, and Carl McIntire, Billy James Hargis, and many others," wrote one correspondent from Miami. "Your recent actions are a fine step in the proper direction," said a writer from Pompano Beach, Florida, "but please don't stop there," explaining that the further steps needed include the withdrawal of the Episcopal Church from both the World Council of Churches and the National Council of Churches. Some letters, in much the same vein, are more vituperative, both toward Bishop

SOCIAL RADICALISM AND HERESY 169

Pike and in condemning the World Council and the National Council. Yet if such discordant voices were looking to Bishop Louttit not only to destroy Bishop Pike but to lead the faithful out of the Councils, they were to be disappointed. To one churchman who pleaded that if Bishop Louttit assumed this mantle "the day would be complete" and the Episcopal Church would then "be as brave as the Southern Baptists," the Bishop, in one of his rare replies, advised:

... (Y)ou are wrong about the National Council of Churches. Their General Assembly meets in Miami Beach, December 5th through 9th. Please do go and arrange to see and hear for yourself.

Frequently they do not represent my point of view but Christians must learn to work together.[12]

Heeding his own counsel, Bishop Louttit appeared himself at the Miami meeting and rendered a prayer at one of the sessions.

Since at least 1961 a phalanx of ultra-right groups has been openly active within the Episcopal Church, operating under such names as "Episcopalians for Christ," "The Voice from the Catacombs," "Episcopalians for the Faith," "The Foundation for Christian Theology," "Concerned Citizens of Selma." They, generally, embody a mixture of religious fundamentalism with social and economic views similar to those voiced in the public realm by the John Birch Society, and, indeed, certain observers of their activities and tactics have described them as "Birch-front groups" within the Episcopal Church.[13] The other major denominations have suffered dissention and subversion from comparable internal factions, and *The New York Times* has characterized them as employing "the inflammatory appeal of a Christian Nationalist movement."[14] For years Bishop Pike has been a favorite target of such outfits in the Episcopal Church (as well as outside it) and it is hardly suprising that, when Bishop Louttit formed his "Committee of Bishops for the Defense of the Faith," many Episcopalians from such precincts should flock to embrace him or that at least one bishop publicly identified as a patron of one such cause—"The Foundation for Christian Theology"—would be found among those joining Bishop Louttit's charges against Bishop Pike.[15] What influence these supporters had upon Bishop Louttit is something known only in his secrets, but, it is known that he dispatched the telegram—quoted in full in the prelude to this section—to many bishops who had failed to sign up as accusers of Bishop Pike wondering how they might explain their failure to subscribe to the presentment to the "conservatives" of their dioceses.

Meanwhile, it will be recalled that the poetaster priest from Phoenix, who has been pommeling Bishop Pike almost weekly with his doggerel, Father Frank Brunton, served for many years in the Diocese of South Florida under Bishop Louttit's regime and in his Arizona retirement remains canonically under Bishop Louttit's jurisdiction. Further is cited about Brunton presently, the immediate mention of him refers only to the issue of heresy vis à vis social radicalism as this implicates Bishop Louttit.

That, in Father Brunton's mind, heresy and social views are merged is all too obvious from his doggerel. In, for just a single example of literally scores that could be quoted, an item he wrote in ridicule of Bishop Pike's address at the 1964 commencement of the University of California at Berkeley where Pike had spoken of the world population explosion and birth control, Brunton derides Bishop Pike for playing God:

> Young folk who soon will graduate
> And out into the world will go,
> I, with the voice of God can state
> The things of sex you ought to know . . .

Then for advocating birth control:

> And this I tell each lad and lass
> You learn to practice birth control . . .

And, then, some verses on, Brunton concludes:

> O bishop pike, we'd be relieved
> And give our thanks with heart and soul
> If on the night you were conceived
> Your folk had known of birth control![16]

Bishop Louttit is acutely aware of Father Brunton's relentless pursuit of Bishop Pike over the years, of Father Brunton's boasted role in the Arizona heresy charges of 1965, and of his wide circulation of his attacks within the Diocese of California during Bishop Pike's episcopal jurisdiction there, as well as of Brunton's further publication of them through *The Christian Challenge*, a newsletter subsidized by the aforementioned "Foundation for Christian Theology," upon the advisory committee of which Father Brunton serves.

In one conversation with these authors, Bishop Louttit volunteered his opinion of Father Brunton as a perhaps senile or anyway foolish man, recalled his active ministry in the Diocese of South Florida mainly because of Brunton's exceptionally redundant sermons, and allowed that his own accusations against Bishop Pike had no connection with Father Brunton.

The latter seems, to say the least, dubious. For one thing, Bishop Louttit is still Father Brunton's bishop and there is communication between them from time to time, and it is known that in some instances the subject of their contact has been Bishop Pike. For another, comparison of the Arizona charges, which Brunton boasts he drafted, with the Louttit presentment, which Bishop Louttit admits he did not write, discloses marked similarities in both substance and language. That, of course, might be accounted for by Louttit's draftsmen having examined the prior Brunton document as part of their homework. Still, if such were the case, it would not explain how the presentment ghostwriters—who have not been positively identified though there be well-informed speculation about their names—received possession of certain hearsay items cited in the specification of charges against Bishop Pike. Part of the presentment papers rely upon hearsay from *Look* and *The New York Times Magazine* generally available anywhere; part, however, relies upon hearsay uttered in the September 5, 1966 edition of *The Arizona Republic*, reporting on the farewell sermon of Bishop Pike at Grace Cathedral in San Francisco. This Phoenix newspaper is not readily available in Winter Park, St. Petersburg, or elsewhere in Florida. Moreover, news of Pike's final sermon as Bishop of California was carried in the local press in Florida, as well as in papers in many other parts of the nation. The questions, thus, inescapably arise: Why did Louttit's scriveners copy from a source which they could only have obtained on their own with great inconvenience? Did *someone* in Phoenix furnish them with the Arizona clipping? If so, who would be motivated to do so? Was other information tendered or were any proposals made to accompany the story from *The Arizona Republic?* Alternatively, another line of questions becomes insistent. According to Bishop Louttit, it will be recalled, when the name of Bishop Pike was mentioned in informal conversations at the Fourth Province conference of bishops on disturbed clergy, which took place immediately prior to the Louttit presentment, one bishop there, Charles G. Marmion of Kentucky, fetched a newspaper clipping on Bishop Pike's farewell. Could *that* have been the September 5th item from the Phoenix newspaper? Did Bishop Louttit journey back down to Winter Park with *this* in his pocket and on his mind? Is this how this *particular* version of news, which was elsewhere practically everywhere carried in the secular press, came into the hands of the scribes of the Louttit presentment?

Father Brunton has been asked about whether he had a significant role in the engineering of the Louttit presentment. His response is more cagey than Bishop Louttit's. But perchance pride is larger than caution. Father Brunton was interrogated by the National Broadcasting Company, from its' San Francisco affiliate, about his role in the Louttit charges on October 14, 1966. Said he, evidently claiming credit in the matter for himself:

We knew that to attack him [Pike] would bring the Church into unfavorable publicity and he [Pike] thought he could get away with continuing to do what he wanted and that because no one—people—were afraid of publicity they therefore would say nothing against himself. Ah, *we* had to choose the lesser of two evils. Ah, *we* had to bring charges against Bishop Pike and so charges have been brought.[17]

What is, possibly, more important is that before his initiative against Pike, Bishop Louttit had twice received formal requests that canonical action be taken against Father Brunton.[18] What prompted these petitions was *not*, however, the harassment of Brunton's venomous verses, but letters which Brunton had written to Premier Ian Smith of the rebel white regime in Rhodesia and, apparently, to others there, characterizing Bishop Pike as a racial agitator. The letters manifestly, as has been said, put Bishop Pike's personal safety as well as freedom of movement in grave jeopardy, and, in fact, Pike was arrested, detained and then ejected from Rhodesia. The purpose of Pike's trip to Rhodesia was explicitly ecclesiastical. Under the so-called Mutual Responsibility and Interdependence program of the Anglican Communion, a scheme which had been introduced and endorsed at the world Anglican Congress of 1963 in Canada and which is generally attributed to the inception of the Right Reverend Stephen Bayne, Jr., the Diocese of California and the Diocese of Matabeleland, in Rhodesia, had become "companion dioceses." The Bishop of Matabeleland had invited the Bishop of California to visit his jurisdiction in furtherance of their MRI relationship. Father Brunton's intervention succeeded in sabotaging this instance of MRI in application and in endangering Bishop Pike's person. It is not possible to ascertain what consequences his pernicious meddling may cause the Church he professes to love and uphold to suffer in Matabeleland, at the hands of Ian Smith's police state, especially since the Bishop of Matabeleland, Kenneth J. F. Skelton, who has become the spokesman for the ecumenical and interracial Rhodesian Christian Council, has already much suffered the zealous surveillance of the Smith regime.

Having been fully apprised of this outreach of Father Brunton's campaign to destroy Bishop Pike, Bishop Louttit's response to the applications for canonical remedies to restrain this priest of his seems, to say the least, insipid. To the Reverend David Baar, Chaplain to Bishop Pike, who had called the Rhodesian episode to his official notice, Bishop Louttit indicated that he had entirely missed the point of the complaint, unless it is the case that he deliberately ignored it, for he only addressed the issue of the Brunton doggerel:

Thank you for your letter of January 6. Bishop Pike wrote to me directly from England and I replied to him as he requested me to.

I had to tell him that in good conscience I could not start action against the Rev. Frank M. Brunton although I thoroughly disapprove of his silly and unkind jingles.

Many people have approached me about the possibility of making formal objections to many of Bishop Pike's own statements and I have refused on the grounds that I believe in free speech. I cannot very well pick on an old retired clergyman because he exercises the same privilege.[19]

The last paragraph of Louttit's reply to Barr has a certain poignancy, in relation to Brunton, and also as to the identity of the "many people" who had been approaching Bishop Louttit to urge charges against Bishop Pike. Bishop Louttit is steadfastly vague about who the "many people" might have been, but it is known that the Arizona group, including Father Brunton, who had forwarded heresy charges through Bishop Joseph Harte which became the basis of the dispute at the Glacier Park House of Bishops meeting, felt that the failure of the bishops there to go forward with a trial of Bishop Pike was a proof of the spinelessness and deficient zeal of the House of Bishops. Indeed, Father Brunton, temporarily shifting targets, dedicated scathing verses to this supposed betrayal of the bishops, so that they all suffered a sample of the invective with which he had been assaulting Bishop Pike.

In any case, some months later, having done nothing *against* Father Brunton either because of his interference in Rhodesia or because of his outrageous rhymes, Bishop Louttit did something *for* Father Brunton: he overcame his qualms about free speech and instigated the heresy presentment against Bishop Pike.

Subsequently, as the bishops were assembling in Wheeling, West Virginia, Bishop Louttit, perhaps without realizing it, summed up his own disposition on the issue of social radicalism and heresy more aptly and more pathetically than anyone else would dare. He told the Associated Press:

> I've fought the John Birchers,
> I've fought segregationists and
> I'm willing to fight Jim Pike.[20]

Henry I. Louttit is not a man of malice, but he may be a bishop without a cause.

Bishops with Causes or Causes with Bishops?

The problem of social witness apropos heresy charges is not simply framed in the relationships of Bishop Louttit and Bishop Pike. In truth, the subject cannot be readily exhausted for inevitably it involves all of the bishops, especially those incumbent in jurisdictions, from, as it were, the Presiding Bishop on down. All and each of their respective views, theological and social, are challenged in this controversy focused upon Bishop Pike. It is no exaggeration to point out that the integrity and the fate of *every* episcopacy is on trial, not just Bishop Pike or his most conspicuous accuser, Bishop Louttit.

No doubt some bishops voted one way or another on the censure of Pike supposing that they were doing so either simply for reasons of doctrine or for reasons of social concern (leaving aside those who rationalized their vote on personal, pastoral, psychological, or political grounds rather than on either doctrinal or social views). But can there ever be, in the Christian faith, an absolute separation between theology and social issues? Are not those who conceive that such a dividing wall exists and, hence, advocate that the Church should not be involved in worldly affairs, in fact favoring a peculiar form of involvement—the public witness of silence, the social action of abstension, the option of withdrawal?[21] If the Church, or if a bishop of the Church, does not act in social conflict, does not that omission amount to endorsement of the *status quo*? If the Church, or if the House of Bishops of the Episcopal Church, does not speak out in public controversies, does not that quietism in itself become the voice of the House or the commitment of the Church? Does not the Church, and for that matter every Christian, including every bishop, *always* take a stand on *every* social question, whether intentionally or inadvertently, either advisedly or *in absentia*, sometimes by intervention or sometimes by withdrawal?

To put it all a bit differently, far from being able to isolate theology from social issues and thereby also disengage heresy from social witness, is not the elementary significance of the Incarnation the event of God's militancy in this world which authorizes an involvement unto death of Christians and of the body of the Church in this world? If that be the case for all Christians, does it not manifestly bestow a vocation of leadership upon any who, holding the office, is conscientiously a bishop and not just a shrewd or lucky ecclesiastical politician?

At the Glacier Park meeting, the House of Bishops seemed to

recognize this inescapable connection of theology and ethics when it declared that "many an allegation of heterodoxy against any of us, or our clergy, is in fact a covert attack on legitimate Christian social concern and action."[22] Oddly enough at Wheeling it was the secular press which, editorially, reminded the public, as well as the bishops, of the same truth, though in less delicate language:

> The movement of a group of highly incensed bishops of the Episcopal Church to discredit and unfrock Bishop Pike of California is altogether preposterous in this age and, we fear, at this late date tends to make the Episcopal Church slightly ridiculous. . . .
>
> The . . . inquisition bears every evidence of having been inspired by the resentment which a number of corn pone diocesans feel toward Bishop Pike because of his support, preaching and marching in years past for . . . civil rights . . .
>
> (I)t seems a pity that the Episcopal hierarchy . . . has turned to heresy and forsaken its mint juleps.[23]

Nor are lay people, of all sorts of social and ideological persuasions, generally as insensitive to the conjunction of heresy charges and social witness as some of the more condescending bishops may assume. That fact has already been documented in the deluge of correspondence which Bishop Louttit received from radical right-wingers. It is, in turn, reflected in the much greater volume of mail which Bishop Pike received. One very candid and quite prominent layman from South Carolina, for example, wrote:

> My bishop, John Pinckney, and my cousin, Jack Vander Horst, have followed Henry Louttit, and they will receive the overwhelming support of most of the lay people in their respective dioceses. Unfortunately the political and religious views of most southerners are based today on racism. Any liberalism is regarded as tending to break down racial barriers and *ergo* is evil.[24]

Ralph McGill, the distinguished publisher of *The Atlanta Constitution* and an Episcopalian, in one of his columns at the time of the Arizona charges against Pike, reported that a Selma, Alabama, group "which rather shamefully chose to remain anonymous," calling itself "Concerned Episcopalians," and identified only by a

SOCIAL RADICALISM AND HERESY 177

post office box number, had circulated letters urging support of the Arizona accusations. Wrote McGill:

The Selma group was reportedly led by those Episcopalian communicants who, during the recent troubles at Selma, barred the church door even to white Episcopalians who were observers of, or participants in, the civil rights protest demonstrations. . . .

The source of the attacks against Bishop Pike were too embarrassingly obvious and their motivation too suspect to give the charges any standing or hearing beyond the most casual.[25]

About thirteen months after Ralph McGill wrote these words, the bishops had transcended embarrassment and suspicion so effectually that the Louttit presentment—remarkably similar, as it is, in tone and content to the charges initiated by the Arizona clergy and clandestinely supported by the "Concerned Episcopalians" of Selma—prepared the way for the "casual" censure of Bishop Pike.

The clergy are not indifferent to the intermingling of theology and social conscience. The Executive Director of the Episcopal Metropolitan Mission in Hartford, Connecticut, the Reverend William Penfield, addressed, shortly before Wheeling, a letter to all active bishops of the Episcopal Church, commending to them —as Bishop Peabody had to Bishop Louttit—the Fifth Chapter of *The Book of the Acts of the Apostles*. Therein the admonition of Gamaliel the pharisee to the senate of Israel about how Saint Peter and the other Apostles should be dealt with is to be found, and bears repetition:

So in the present case I tell you, keep away from these men and let them alone; for if this plan or this undertaking is of men, it will fail; but if it is of God, you will not be able to overthrow them. You might even be found opposing God![26]

Penfield's letter expresses the juxtaposition of heresy and social stands in this way:

I am distressed because such action (against Bishop Pike) suggests that deviations from traditional theological definitions formulated centuries ago constitute the major heresies of today. . . . The major heresies of our day include those of silence in the face of racism; aloofness to the demands of social change; a Pelagian attitude towards ecumenical encounters and activity; indifference to, or agreement with, the militaristic thinking and activity associated with a war that is a horrible contradiction to many of our citizens and terribly disturbing to the Christian conscience.[27]

The Reverend William Penfield was not as persuasive as Gamaliel, however, for even the bishops of the diocese in which he serves evidently voted to censure Bishop Pike rather than leave him alone.

Other clergy, particularly those who like the Reverend William Penfield and his colleagues are involved in urban work, have been more explicit. A member of the Experimental Ministry Project in Kansas City, Missouri, told Bishop Louttit that while he didn't know how it is in South Florida, "here in Kansas City, the 'faithful laity' get shook up simply hearing about the equal rights of minority groups, much less . . . doctrinal matters (of which they know little or nothing). . . . In these days of tremendous social concerns—or lack of them—it would seem to some that the Bishop of Alabama is far more a heretic than James Albert Pike ever thought of being."[28] This letter, of the Reverend Richard L. Shacklett, is, of course, reminiscent of the one previously cited of the Sewanee refugee, Professor McNair. It is of some incidental interest that on the question of which bishops *are* racists and therefore *ipso facto* heretics the interviews conducted by the present authors with bishops have redundantly named the same names cited by McNair and Shacklett, along with some additional ones.

Yet in the Wheeling censure debate, as taped in full by the Canadian Broadcasting Corporation, only *one* bishop in the whole House raised this issue of heresy and social views. That bishop was the Right Reverend Paul Moore, Suffragan of Washington. Bishop Moore, it should be noticed, began his own ministry in the abominable slums of Jersey City, in association with C. Kilmer Myers eventually to become Bishop Pike's successor as Bishop of California. Bishop Moore later was Dean of Indianapolis—a hotbed of doctrinal fundamentalism and of the ideological rightwing—and thus went from the fire into the frying pan, and now as a bishop is profoundly involved in social action. Paul Moore heads the Delta Ministry project in Mississippi, has fought for its survival as a program supported through the churches and, though his St.

Paul's–Yale pedigree and ecclesiastical status provide a direct access to the premises, he is more likely to be found picketing the White House than dining with its tenants. That is, of course, why Bishop Moore has been publicly blamed for the depletion of income in his diocese and the delays in completion of the Washington Cathedral since he became Suffragan. Bishop Moore asked his brethren during the debate:

Why is it that the House has not censured any of the rest of us who have spoken, acted out, and allowed to occur within our dioceses greater blasphemies even than the treatment of items of doctrine less than solemnly? I speak of church doors closed against members of another race, clergy denied backing by their bishops because of their Christian social views, and the public impugning of the motives of fellow bishops.[29]

Thus, in the censure debate itself, was the connection of heresy allegations and social radicalism raised, and quickly passed over, though, more privately, it remained upon the minds of some of the bishops, and, then, not only in relation to the racial crisis and civil rights.

After the censure session had been adjourned late on the evening of October 25, Bishop Pike is reported by several of his colleagues to have made a deliberate effort to remain on the scene, to be accessible to any or all who would speak to him, to seek no one out but, at the same time, to hide from none, and to resist the temptation to go off somewhere alone to sulk or sorrow. So available and vulnerable, Bishop Pike was passing down a corridor of the resort premises where the bishops were being accommodated and entertained at Wheeling and, as he passed by, was hailed and beckoned into a suite occupied by the Bishop of Springfield (Ill.) and his spouse. (Other bishops witnessed this scene). She, pointing a finger at Pike, explained: "*We* voted against you because you're for homosexuals!" (The Diocese of Springfield has a long and notorious repute in the Episcopal Church as adventurously "high church" but diligent inquiry has uncovered no other incident of the episcopal office being claimed as vested in both the bishop *and* his wife.) Whatever the ecclesiology of the occasion, a plain admission had been made that the censure was prompted in part, anyway, by social concern and that such had become in the mind(s) or the censuring person(s) persuasive. Before Bishop Pike had opportunity to respond to the first accusation the Bishop of Springfield stirred to comment that "they" were also aware that Bishop Pike advocated incest. Hence a second confession, though from the same episcopal throne, that social issues had primarily influenced the censure vote.

Bishop Pike's response to these simultaneous attacks on two fronts from a practically synonymous source was apt and crisp: "Please make up your mind."

There is a background to this incident, and to how it took place, that, in fairness to the Bishop(s) of Springfield and to Bishop Pike requires mention. Advocacy of incest was, manifestly, imputed to Bishop Pike because he has advocated, repeatedly and publicly, therapeutic abortion in, among other circumstances, cases of incestuous conceptions.[30] Sympathy for homosexuality was alleged against him because he has long been numbered among distinguished lawyers urging the adoption of the American Law Institute recommendations for penal law reform in this area and because he had, while Bishop of California, supported a specific ministry to San Francisco's somewhat sizeable homosexual community.[31] The collapse of human communication which caused an accusation of incest to arise from advocacy of abortion in limited situations or which occasioned the allegation of pro-homosexuality to stem from endorsement of the American Law Institute's proposals for penal law revision has earlier been noted. The immediately significant thing is the indication that this peculiar incident reveals just how heavily social concerns, of many varieties, both well-informed and ill-advised, weighed in the censure of Bishop Pike.

Sometimes it is not any particular social stand that is taken that has become an irritant between Bishop Pike and his peers. Often it is just the fact that Bishop Pike speaks out at all, no matter what he substantively says, that is provocative and engenders hostility among his fellow bishops. That seems to have been a factor, some weeks after Wheeling, in the strenuous public denial by the Bishop of Dallas that he had anything to do with Bishop Pike's appearance in that city at a meeting of an agency of the National

SOCIAL RADICALISM AND HERESY 181

Council of Churches, as well as in Bishop Bloy's restriction previously discussed.³² Moreover, prior to Wheeling, Bishop Louttit himself characterized Bishop Pike's public appearance at the Florida Presbyterian College, which is located within Louttit's diocese but is entirely outside his jurisdiction, as an event which provoked the presentment.

The Bishop of Arizona, John Joseph Meaken Harte, has gone much further than the other bishops just mentioned. At the time of the Arizona clergy charges in 1965, Bishop Pike had received an open invitation to preach at Trinity Cathedral in Phoenix from the Dean, the Very Reverend Elmer Usher. As Dean Usher expressed it: "I'll put my neck on the block if you will accept."³³ Dean Usher renewed his invitation for Bishop Pike to visit Phoenix in February, 1967, and both Arizona State University in that city and the University of Arizona in Tuscon extended lecture engagements to Pike. Bishop Harte rescinded Dean Usher's invitation. Bishop Pike fulfilled his commitments at both universities. It is needless to say that there is blood on the block to which Dean Usher referred.

Not content with that, Bishop Harte seized the occasion of Bishop Pike's addresses at the two universities in Arizona to denounce Bishop Pike publicly as a heretic. In this sentiment, Bishop Harte was echoing Father Brunton, who had written to the editor of *The Arizona Republic*, lamenting the universities' invitations to Bishop Pike and who had by this time concluded that Bishop Pike steps outside of all religions and is a sort of superheretic.

Bishop Harte's excoriation of Bishop Pike in February, 1967, may seem redundant in light of the Wheeling censure, but in fact it reflects a significant dissatisfaction with the readiness, at Wheeling, of the accusers of Bishop Pike to settle for a censure instead of demanding a trial. Among others of the radical right, Carl McIntire has sounded such disappointment.³⁴ No doubt some of the same ilk who so quickly embraced Bishop Louttit when the presentment was first publicized could only now regard him as having failed their cause. Father Brunton and the Reverend Paul Urbano, the prime collaborators in the 1965 accusations against Bishop Pike which Bishop Harte brought with him to the Glacier Park meeting of the House, share this discontent with the mere censure, for they had been seeking a proper burning at the stake. Urbano appears now to be quite discouraged about the crusade to destroy Bishop Pike: "I consider the whole matter a lost cause," he has confided to these authors.[35] Father Brunton, on the other hand, as might have been prognosticated clinically, seems all the more relentless and much more stimulated since now not only Bishop Pike but virtually the whole House of Bishops has betrayed the faith.[36]

Father Brunton's relationship with Bishop Harte, like his relationship with Bishop Louttit, evidently moves in one direction; that is, while he has prodded and plagued these bishops to act against Bishop Pike and has been an incalculable influence upon their hostile actions toward Bishop Pike, neither of them has been significantly influential over Brunton's activities. Certainly neither has curbed Father Brunton, though both have had his singular conduct officially brought to their attention.[37] Both have neglected to act, and, in the case of Bishop Harte, there is evidence that Father Brunton was encouraged, as in Bishop Harte's designation of Father Brunton as "a valiant warrior for the Church Faith," earlier cited. The steadfastness with which both Bishop Louttit and Bishop Harte—especially, perhaps, the latter—have failed to cope with Father Brunton raises the dignity of the question of whether or not, apart from being rather old, retired, and unoccupied and having a reputation as a repetitious preacher, Frank Brunton is a member of the John Birch Society. Here the evidence is conflicting though not unrevealing. In a letter to *The Living Church*, a prestigious unofficial Episcopal magazine, Brunton identified himself as a member.[38] Secular newspapers have carried the same information. *The San Francisco Chronicle*, for one example, ran the following item on October 19, 1966:

> *The Chronicle* has learned that Louttit has utilized the services of an admitted member of the John Birch Society, the Rev. Frank Brunton, of Phoenix, Ariz., who provided part of the written evidence cited by Louttit against Pike.[39]

Whether this news influenced Bishop Louttit's announced purpose to have the presentment against Bishop Pike redrafted by a team of lawyers and seminary professors is not known, though, in fact, the presentment has not been recomposed and since it was cited as among the derogatory reports and rumors in circulation in Bishop Pike's demand for an investigation, the Louttit presentment now cannot be altered or amended.

Despite his letter to *The Living Church,* Father Brunton has been, in other circumstances, more cautious and coy about affiliation with the John Birch Society. He has said, "I do not hold membership in it."[40] He has also declared, "I have much sympathy for the views held by the John Birch Society."[41] He has, meanwhile, been rumored as a pending applicant for membership.

Should he not be a member, it would be odd, for the John Birch Society surely requires zealots such as he. Let the Birchers consider, if they have not already done so, the credentials of Brunton, quoted from his own mouth:

I count it my good fortune I have never seen Bishop Pike. . . .

The San Francisco Chronicle rang me up a week or so ago to tell me that friends of Bishop Pike told them I was his most bitter enemy. I felt like St. George on a white horse. No greater accolade or medal could be given. . . .

I hold him up for ridicule whenever possible. In fact, I feel another rhyme coming along now.[42]

A subsequent rhyme of Father Brunton's, which Birchers might admire, concerned Bishop Harte's public denunciation of Bishop Pike as a heretic during the February 1967 appearances of Bishop Pike in Arizona. It documents Father Brunton's own spirit as well as his association with Bishop Harte perhaps more than it says what it does about Bishop Harte and Bishop Pike as fellow bishops:

> When mighty Caesar fell and died
> Within the Roman Capital
> With fifty daggers in his side
> Which drained his blood, both each and all
> 'Twas said by the historians, then
> He gazed on those who daggers drew
> And saw a friend amongst these men
> Which made him cry, "Et Brute! Tu!"

> So brother pike, whom most men know
> Who [sic] few respect, and fewer like
> Came to this State, not long ago
> The Great Omnicient [sic] bishop pike
> To make the headlines, big and bold
> So all might him on T.V. view
> And spread moth eaten errors old
> To the young folk of A.S.U.
>
> But something shocking happened then
> The Bishop of this Diocese
> Wrote dreadful words unto all men
> Concerning pike, so if you please
> Suggested he made people sick
> Said it was true beyond a doubt
> That pike was a poor heretic
> Who all good folk could wish were out.
>
> Poor pike—his anguish and surprise
> Were surely something sad to see
> To think that unto pike—all wise
> A fellow bishop should set free
> Such words to cause pain, grief and hurt
> It fairly filled our hearts with rue
> As pike in broken tones, did blurt
> "It cannot be!—Et Brute! Tu!"[43]

What Father Brunton utters is, technically, his own responsibility. What Bishop Harte does or omits to do about Father Brunton, as with Bishop Louttit, remands to him. Whether Father Brunton is a member of the Birchers, or an eager applicant, or a sentimental sympathizer or, most pathetically, a reject from the John Birch Society is of small consequence. A damage has been done, not alone to Bishop Pike, but to all bishops. The boast which Father Brunton makes is not vain: he has evidently intimidated both Bishop Harte and Bishop Louttit and, through them—tentatively at Glacier Park, more openly at Wheeling, who knows what comes next?—has extraordinarily influenced other bishops against Bishop Pike.

In such a context it becomes quite secondary whether James A. Pike is, in any rational reference, a heretic or not. What matters more is how to abate the assault, how to halt the scandal which unproved accusation incubates, how to salvage the "image" of the Episcopal Church, how to safeguard bishops from flak, how to appease, as Pilate wondered, those who can only be satiated by an execution. Such were the questions haunting so many of the bishops at Wheeling.

A Problem of Appeasement?

If pressures external to the House of Bishops were vigorous enough to at least win Bishop Pike's censure at Wheeling, it does not represent an unprecedented situation.

Predecessors of the incumbent bishops did much the same in 1844 in the trial of Bishop Benjamin Tredwell Onderdonk of New York for "impurity." Bishop Onderdonk had ordained to the priesthood a man accused of holding certain views which, in those days, were considered to be so advanced as almost to be papalistic. Bishop Onderdonk had been denounced as a heretic by three other bishops because of this, but no formal presentment was ever made. Instead a canon was enacted under which Bishop Onderdonk was tried for alleged offenses affecting his moral character. The canon was an *ex post facto* law, that is, the alleged offenses had occurred before the canon condemning such conduct was adopted. For the incidental enlightenment of some of the Wheeling bishops, let it be recalled that the "impurity" with which Bishop Onderdonk was charged was drunkenness.

The trial of Bishop Brown in 1924, as has been noted already, was heavily influenced by factions outside the House of Bishops which were incensed by Bishop Brown's social views.

Ulterior circumstances have been prominent and relevant in heresy proceedings in other churches, too, in recent times. One distinguished Lutheran theologian, Professor George Forell, has been frank to declare: "All this [the trials of three Wisconsin Lutheran pastors for heresy in 1953] occurred during the heyday of Senator Joseph McCarthy. The people involved in the prosecution were clearly influenced by the McCarthy mentality."[44]

That era has either not yet ended or else it has a renascence. In any case, the mentality is militant.

The workings of that mentality in the churches exerts an awesome power over bishops, causing them constantly to try to pacify the dissidents even though experience argues that appeasement only teases and whets such aggressors. Perhaps, at Wheeling, most bishops thought they were ridding themselves of the Bishop Pike problem by voting for the censure, but, if that was the case, they failed to comprehend that within the Episcopal Church there are persons and factions including at least a few bishops who, among other things, will never be satisfied until Bishop Pike is dead under circumstances in which they can boast that they killed him.

This is an insight which, in the course of the Wheeling debate, Bishop Corrigan alone seems to have suffered.

The issues go beyond Bishop Pike and his personal destiny though they have become personified in him and he has become a conspicuous and immediate target. Some discern, however, that what is at stake is not Bishop Pike but the integrity of the Anglican tradition as such and the survival of the Episcopal Church in that inheritance in the United States. Lester Kinsolving, son of a late Bishop of Arizona, reported in *The Nation* of January 23, 1967:

Coordinator of these Birch-front groups (in the Episcopal Church) is a dynamic and handsome woman, Mrs. Dorothy Faber of Washington, D.C., who edits a periodical called *The Christian Challenge*, published in Michigan. While Mrs. Faber vehemently denies any connection with Robert Welch's organization, her editorial line is remarkably similar, the particular points of attack being Bishop Pike, the National Council of Churches and the church's activity on behalf of civil rights.

. . . (T)he actual existence of an arch-conservative beachhead is evident in the present constituency of the Executive Council [of the Episcopal Church].

. . . Perhaps the most widely known member of the Executive Council is the erstwhile ghost writer, Senate campaign manager and at present historian to Barry Goldwater—Stephen C. Shadegg. . . . (H)e can be formidable indeed when he teams up with other leaders of the conservative block—most notably Charles Crump (of the

Memphis Crumps), Prime Osborn of Florida, and the . . . Coadjutor (heir apparent) Bishop of Alabama, George Murray.

This aggregation has not yet been able to effect a complete coup in Executive Council, but it did manage to pass in 1965 a measure which in effect forbade all clergy on the Episcopal headquarters staff to participate in civil rights demonstrations. . . . (O)nly after receiving vehement protests from such giant dioceses as Massachusetts and California were the liberal and moderate members of Executive Council able to rescind this gag law of the Shadegg-Crump machine.

Although stymied in this particular attempt, the machine has made an impression upon national headquarters staff. The possibility of a right-wing take-over is a critical issue today in hundreds of local Episcopal churches.[45]

Others have sounded similar warnings. In the Diocese of New York, early in 1966, a special conference was convened at the Cathedral of St. John the Divine on the problem of rightist extremism in the Episcopal Church, at which the Reverend Canon Walter Dennis admitted: "I may be nervous, but there *is* the possibility of a coup."[46] *The Witness* magazine, a widely respected but unofficial Episcopal Church periodical, has several times editorialized to the same effect.[47] The Reverend Dr. John Krumm, Rector of New York's prestigious Church of the Ascension on Fifth Avenue and former Chaplain of Columbia University, has put it bluntly. The problem now coming to an abscess in the Episcopal Church, he says, is of a "frightened people, who in the face of world revolutions—notably in minority rights—see their whole world crumbling about them and with it their hope of status and superiority."[48]

To the unwary or complacent, such remarks may sound overanxious or even alarmist, but the evidence is impressive that the ultra-right-white wing has already acquired dominance in certain parishes and dioceses and is steadily gaining power in the Executive Council and in the triennial General Convention of the Episcopal Church. In the Convention, which is the ultimate legislative authority of the Church, wealthy, white rightists have some built-in advantages, since they are more likely to be able to spare the time—about two weeks—and bear the expense of attending. Moreover, since there is not proportional representation, delegates from the smaller hinterland dioceses, especially from the South and the Midwest have greater voting weight than those from the great urban dioceses. Indeed, the Convention, which elects the interim Executive Council and which controls the budget of the national denomination, can not be said to be representative to any serious extent of the actual constituency of the Episcopal Church in America, or of the theological or social views of that constituency. The prevailing polity, nonetheless, makes a rightist, racist, anti-ecumenical, traditionalist *coup d'église* a realistic, and imminent, possibility.

How these folk grasped Bishop Louttit, though he eventually disappointed them, has already been mentioned. There is some information that, 1964, some rich and reactionary Southerners pledged a huge sum in attempting to elect a Southern bishop as Presiding Bishop and had settled upon Bishop Louttit as their candidate. Perchance the increasing power of the radical right caused another prominent aspirant for the office of Presiding Bishop—Stephen Bayne—to disassociate himself in 1964 from the Episcopal Society for Cultural and Racial Unity.[49] Right wing pressures appear to explain the bitter complaint of another bishop —Thomas Augustus Fraser of North Carolina—that he lost a great deal of money for not signing the presentment.

This specter has befuddled, embarrassed or made dilettantes or appeasers of innumerable bishops. Clergy active in civil rights protests have lost their pulpits, been denied licenses, been banished from some dioceses to placate this minority, and commonly the sanction employed against bishops has been withdrawal or reduction of pledges or bequests, or the threat of economic reprisals. On such a scene, Bishop Pike, "incarnating," as Dean Coburn put it in his sermon at Bishop Pike's consecration, a Christian social concern and communicating it with his inexhaustible vigor through the mass media, was bound to seem to many other bishops as more and more expendable.

The Bishop of Indianapolis, John P. Craine, is among those who find themselves ambivalently located—excruciatingly so— because of the Bishop Pike affair. Bishop Craine, it will be remembered, gave his consent and endorsement to Bishop Pike's demand for an ecclesiastical inquiry and trial after the censure at

Wheeling. Yet a few months later, according to *The Indianapolis Star* of January 18, 1967, Craine was to be found consorting with the ultra-right at a banquet in his See city.⁵⁰ The occasion was a meeting of the Foundation for Christian Theology convened to aid the teaching of conservative theology principles. The Right Reverend William R. Moody, the Bishop of Lexington (Kentucky)—who is a member of the Court for the Trial of a Bishop— is the only other bishop known to have participated in this conference.⁵¹ The foundation, which publishes *The Christian Challenge*, condemned, at this gathering, "the introduction of an element of strange and sometimes radical theological thinking into the church in recent years," and decided to publish a book on doctrine written by "leading bishops of the Protestant Episcopal Church."⁵² The foundation's principal intention is to endow chairs in theology in seminaries and to aid candidates for the ministry, thus, presumably, assuring the future indoctrination of Episcopalians in the tenets of "conservative" theology. The same issue of the *Challenge* which publishes a photograph of Bishop Craine with delegates to the Foundation's conference, contains the stereotype rightist attacks upon the National Council of Churches, the *Revised Standard Version* of the Bible, the peace movement, the war on poverty, the Episcopal Society for Cultural and Racial Unity, the Reverend Malcolm Boyd, the use of modern idiom liturgically, the Reverend Adam Clayton Powell, evolution, and the Right Reverend James A. Pike. The question is unavoidable: What is Bishop Craine, who voted against the Pike censure and who went further and subscribed to Bishop Pike's demand for a trial, doing in lending his name and presence to such causes? Maybe he is uninformed, though that seems unlikely, since the general missioner for his own diocese is a prominent figure in the foundation's activities, and the addresses and discussions at the conference, as well as the prospectus of the Foundation, leave no room for doubt that this is an operation dominated by a Birch-like mentality.⁵³ Conceivably, as bishop, he sees his role as one which should remain in touch with all factions within the Church, yet he does not have a reputation in his own diocese, for an example, of undertaking public visitations to anti-war demonstrations sponsored by some of his own clergy. Other explanations can be inferred: historically, the most prominent Episcopalian family in

Indianapolis are the Lillys, whose fortune is the manufacture and sale of drugs. The Lilly family has numerous philanthropies, and the Episcopal Diocese of Indianapolis has been a favored charity for generations. Through the Eli Lilly Endowment Fund some purposes of the Foundation for Christian Theology are now being subsidized.[54] Thus for any bishop of Indianapolis to fail to heed and honor a meeting of this Foundation in his own city could jeopardize the assistance of Eli Lilly for the diocese, particularly so since Eli Lilly, unlike some other members of the Lilly clan, is not a man who could be fairly described as a "liberal," either socially or doctrinally.

Bishop Craine is not the only Episcopal bishop who has found himself on a spot in relation to the Bishop Pike affair and the issues which it personifies. Bishop Donegan, who called Pike to be Dean of the New York Cathedral in 1952, has suffered both abuse and the loss of commitments for the completion of the Cathedral because of his occasional outspokenness on civil rights. Bishop Hines, while incumbent as the Bishop of Texas, in what already appears to have been an apocalyptic episode, found himself fighting an attempt to subvert and "take over" the vestry of Houston's Church of St. John the Divine, by persons identified within the orbit of the John Birch Society.[55]

It is this earlier confrontation between Bishop Hines and the radical right which prompted George Cornell, the religion editor of the Associated Press and an Episcopalian, to characterize Bishop Hines in this way:

Out of a segregated atmosphere he forged his firm stand for racial integration. Amid Bible-belt aspersions, he built his commitment to Christian unity, to free religious inquiry, and to bold involvement in causes of social justice.[56]

Or, as one so-called liberal bishop said, more unkindly, of Hines on the day he was elected Presiding Bishop: "John is the perfect compromise for everybody."[57]

There are signs that the lesson of the Texas encounter with the right wing have not been well remembered by the Presiding Bishop, and a good many other bishops, in the handling of the Bishop Pike affair and in the more profound crisis in the Episcopal Church which Bishop Pike exemplifies. After all, in supplement of innumerable, often hidden, episodes proving the rightist designs upon the whole denomination, there has been now a full dress rehearsal of how to accomplish a *coup d'église*.

The rehearsal has happened in Louisiana. There had developed in that diocese through recent years coincident with the maturing of the civil rights movement a grave unrest among some white Episcopalians about the involvement of the Episcopal Church in the National Council of Churches and of some of the bishops, including Bishop Pike, and other clergy in social witness. The focus of that discontent became the parish of St. Mark's, Shreveport, which determined, in 1964 and subsequently, to withhold portions of the parish budget which "might have gone to these uses," namely the missionary budget of either the diocese or the national Episcopal Church. These budgets have been the funnel through which this denomination gives modest sums to the National Council of Churches. Because of a determination by the 1964 General Convention, it should be noted, funds for *direct* support of the civil rights movement were *not* incorporated in the budget, or any subdivision thereof, authorized for expenditure in the ensuing triennium by the national staff of the Episcopal Church. Instead, a special fund was permitted to which individuals might voluntarily contribute. In other words, not a dime of any money which might have been pledged or collected in St. Mark's, Shreveport, or any other Episcopal parish, would, through the budgetary restrictions adopted at the St. Louis Convention in 1964, have directly financed civil rights advocacy and activity. Nevertheless, St. Mark's persevered.

The rebellion spread to other parishes in Louisiana and by 1966 had become so notorious a "cleavage" that the diocesan convention requested "that the Bishop appoint a committee to attempt to work out a reconciliation of all parties within the Diocese."[58] The same was done in February, 1966, by the Bishop, the Right Reverend Girault Jones, acting in conjunction with the Coadjutor, the Right Reverend Iveson B. Noland. The bishops' committee held four meetings, including one attended by two members of the Executive Council, the Right Reverend George M. Murray, Coadjutor of Alabama and Prime Osborn of Jacksonville, Florida. Meanwhile the vestry of St. Mark's has continued to allow the circulation, in part through the Foundation for Christian Theology, of a scurillous document aimed at justifying their sedition.[59] The report of the bishops' committee was rendered at the 1967 diocesan convention in Shreveport. It announces glad tidings for extremists of the right:

> That our voice, combined with others, is and has been heard, is confirmed in the heartening reports of Bishop Murray and Mr. Osborn, . . . on their own beliefs and activities . . . Consideration by that [the Executive] Council of the Church's problems are in better perspective; staff activities of our National Church and the NCCCA are being monitored more carefully; the authority, direction and guidance of the Presiding Bishop is more fully exercised. The Executive Council of the National Church has officially informed the NCCCA that it is not to speak for or in the name of the Episcopal Church, or its members, unless specifically authorized to do so by the General Convention, The House of Bishops, or the Executive Council. The committee was gratified to hear a report of discussion on this subject at the February 1966 Executive Council meeting . . . (at which) the Presiding Bishop, finally, stated his firm position against the identifying of any specific legislation as being the embodiment of "the" Christian position.[60]

The report urges that the diocesan convention of Louisiana "carefully and deliberately elect its delegates to the General Convention . . . with full recognition of the importance of viewpoints they will represent."[61] Lest this be too euphemistic, the diocesan periodical in Louisiana in its issue prior to the Shreveport convention is specific in admitting that the concern of the bishops' committee on "existing tensions" was "the conservative approach in many matters concerning the Church of today."[62] So effective have economic sanctions been in resolving schism in favor of the radical right in this instance that this has already come to be known in the Episcopal Church as the "Louisiana Purchase."

An Ominous Portent?

Appeasement of the ultra-right-whites in the Episcopal Church is now so widespread, has happened so often in so many ways in so many places, that it is apt to become habitual among bishops. It is not that bishops are themselves rightists or racists—though a few are, and not that bishops are cowards—they don't need to be. It is, rather, that the assaults of Birchers and their ilk within the Church are so relentless and that Episcopal bishops are exceptionally vulnerable partly because of the very nature of the Anglican tradition. Freedom, which is inherent in that tradition: freedom of association, freedom of inquiry, freedom of action—the freedoms which Bishop Pike so poignantly exemplifies—is a weakness which the totalitarian mentality exploits.

To take a homely example, if the ideological right and the white supremists chose to usurp the Southern Baptist denomination (though that might seem a needless enterprise) they must wage their struggle in each and every congregation, one by one. By contrast, because of the difference in polity between Baptists and Anglicans, if the same factions want to subvert the Episcopal Church in the United States all they really have to do is gain a working majority in the Executive Council, an objective which does not necessarily require initially obtaining the majority in the General Convention, much less in the House of Bishops. If they can attain that, they can stymie the whole Church: dismantle its historic ecumenical concern, frustrate its social witness, imprison its prophets, manipulate its wealth, and throttle its bishops.

That is why, of course, the appeasement of such elements by the bishops, both jointly and severally, is so significant. The "Louisiana Purchase" is only the most recent and most grotesque case in point which demonstrates that each attack portends later aggressions and that one appeasement begets no peace but only further appeasements. That is why, manifestly, the Bishop Pike affair assumes an importance larger than the persons involved. Some say that Bishop Pike seeks to be a martyr; it is more likely to be true that his martyrdom has been sought by his enemies and adversaries. He has become and is the symbol of everything that is distressing and provocative to the ultra-right-whites in the Episcopal Church and within the contemporary American churches generally.

If ever there was a doubt about the inextricability of theology and social conscience, and, hence, about the intimacy of heresy charges and social witness, it was answered by the Wheeling censure, whether the bishops there comprehended what they were saying and doing or not.

Pathetically and paradoxically, at Wheeling, two days following the censure, it was Bishop Pike who, rising as a matter of personal privilege, addressed his peers on the war in Vietnam—a subject which had been twice tabled by the other bishops, but which was thus reopened—and, thereby, Bishop Pike also spoke of the vocation of bishops, a matter the House of Bishops had only negatively dealt with in censuring Pike. Said Bishop Pike:

> I have been censured for irresponsibility. It is toward the end of purging myself with those of you who believe that charge (and on larger grounds also I assure you) that I now display a sense of responsibility as to the image of this House and our Church, that I say this:
>
> . . . (I)t cannot fail to be noticed that we can spend much time here on my real or supposed faults and yet are determined to remain silent on the most grievous moral question in which our nation and people are involved, namely the destruction of and burning alive of persons in Vietnam. As a leading cleric in England has said, when the Church talks about "the unchanging moral law," it's apparently always talking about sex, not about war. To keep our image and leadership in proportion, I plead with you that a way may be found to address ourselves at this meeting to this subject which is more important than me.[63]

The plea of Bishop Pike was in fact rejected, as had been any resolution at all about Vietnam, prior to Bishop Pike's statement, deferred. Now a statement was readied quickly and adopted which praised, with respect to that war, "repentence," "compassion," "faith," "justice," and "love," opposed "hate," regretted "anguish," and, in effect, commended the escalation of the war.

What does such an episode mean? Is this action of the bishops a more terrible omen than the "Louisiana Purchase?" In the aftermath of the censure of Bishop Pike, was this repudiation by the bishops of Bishop Pike's Vietnam exhortation in truth an ultimate appeasement?

Is such the ominous, obvious portent of the Bishop Pike affair?

If you did say things about Sacred Things I am sure you did not mean them.

> —From a letter from a laywoman to Bishop Pike, after the censure

This is about the way I prayed for you—"Now look Jesus and Moses, you have to help Bishop Pike. The wolves are after him."

> —From a letter from a second laywoman to Bishop Pike, following the censure

a homily

The Humor of Heresy

THE authors would like to emerge briefly from such anonymity as may be said to have cloaked them.

Shortly after the Wheeling debacle and just prior to the November 8 elections of that year, we came upon a poignant letter to the editor of *Newsday*, a Long Island newspaper. The correspondent complained of numerous headlines reading: "PIKE ACCUSED OF HERESY" and "PIKE CENSURED, ASKS PROBE OF OWN VIEWS." The letter was signed by Congressman Otis G. Pike of Long Island.

Under date of January 17, 1967, we received, in response to an inquiry we had addressed to him about the Bishop Pike affair, the following letter from the Right Reverend Frank Alexander Juhan:

I am returning herewith the questionnaire.

Being the Senior Bishop of the Episcopal Church, retired after more than 40 years as diocesan of the Diocese of Florida, and having been the husband of one woman for more than 55 years, I can more fully appreciate the extent of human agreement and disagreement.[1]

In December of 1966 we spent several days in Santa Barbara interviewing Bishop Pike in connection with this book. On the last day of our visit we stopped by the Bishop's apartments to pay our respects. The conversation turned to liturgics, and the Bishop told us about an ancient biblical formula for making the chrism mixture used for anointing the faithful at the time of confirmation. The substance had, he said, certain psychedelic properties tending to engender slight elation. In his enthusiasm he searched out a sample, crossed each of our foreheads with it, and rejoiced that we did indeed enjoy a slight elation. That his gesture also had a sacramental dimension seemed to have escaped him, but we have not forgotten it.

In March of 1967 we spent some days in Florida interviewing Bishop Louttit for the same purpose. On the last day of that visit we went at noon to hear the Bishop preach in St. Petersburg, a sermon of great vigor and eloquence on, among other things, race relations. Following the service the Bishop and his Suffragan, William Loftin Hargrave, treated us to a most delightful and enjoyable lunch in the St. Petersburg Yacht Club, a segregated premises. The irony of these events seemed to have escaped the Bishops, but it lingers in our memories together with their graciousness.

Early in 1961, just after he had been first charged with heresy by the Georgia clericus, Bishop Pike was preaching in San Francisco at the installation of a new rector for Trinity Church. Suddenly, the church was plunged into darkness. Ushers hastily surrounded the pulpit with tall candles. The Bishop looked slyly at the circle of fire, paused in his sermon, and blurted out: "I thought I was going to get a trial first."[2] Whether or not Bishop Pike ever comes to formal trial, he has known already many years of trials, great and trivial.

There is, we suggest, an element of humor—diabolical and divine—about heresy in the Church of Christ.

This is not the place to spell out Bishop Pike's continuing work as theologian, especially since he has spelled it out himself in his just published *If This Be Heresy*.[3] Oversimplifying, however, we detect that he now professes three affirmations:

(1) A personal God of the universe,
(2) The servant image of Jesus, or the man for others,
(3) The ongoingness and potential continued development of human personality even after death.

Forgive us, bishops one and all, if we profess to discern in these three affirmations a suspicious resemblance to the doctrine of the Trinity.

Appendix

1. The Arizona Charges and the Glacier Park Detente

(*On July 29, 1965, the following petition received from the undernamed clergy of his jurisdiction was forwarded by the Bishop of Arizona, the Right Reverend Joseph M. Harte, to the chairman of the dispatch of business of the House of Bishops, the Right Reverend Henry I. Louttit, Bishop of South Florida, with a request that the matter be placed on the agenda of the meeting of the House at Glacier Park, Montana, September 7–9, 1965.*)

RIGHT REVEREND FATHERS IN GOD:

We, the undersigned clergy of the diocese of Arizona, understand that Bishop Pike of California will bring his plan to ordain women to the Sacred Ministry of the Church before the Bishops assembled at the September conference.

We would consider such action utterly at variance with apostolic custom, Anglican tradition, and practical wisdom. It met with the disapproval of the last Lambeth Conference, and is found in our Church in no part of the world. If it should be allowed, our position as clergy in the Episcopal Church would become, to say the least, difficult.

We therefore respectfully request that Bishop Pike's suggestion be emphatically denied.

We also wish to bring charges against Bishop Pike as follows:

That he has been false to the vows he took at ordination, in which he pledged himself to drive away, as best he could, all erroneous and strange doctrine. Instead, he has actively promoted the same, ignored the authority of the Church, and substituted for it his own opinions. So doing, he has brought grave scandal upon our Communion and given much heaviness of heart to the faithful.

In particular:

Bishop Pike has repudiated our Lord's Virgin Birth. In his own cathedral, we understand, the Feast of the Annunciation is not celebrated.

He has denied the doctrine of the Blessed Trinity and of the Incarnation as the Church has received the same, claiming that Christ was divine as all men are, except that He was peculiarly conscious of His relationship with God (which is the Unitarian position). He also maintains that the Incarnation was not unique in Jesus, but had occurred in other great religious leaders before His time.

He denies the empty tomb and the bodily Resurrection and Ascension.

He denies that the Creeds contain articles of faith at all.

We respectfully submit that, in denying these things, the Bishop of California has denied the Christian religion. A man who denies what he denies may, unquestionably, be a man of high moral character; but a Christian he is not.

We, therefore, the undersigned clergy, to whom the faith of the Church is a precious heritage, weary of seeing the sheep dispersed by one of their own shepherds, urgently request that our fathers in God challenge Bishop Pike on the above-mentioned teachings, and demand that he make public repudiation of them. Should he fail to do so, we request that he be brought to trial and, if found guilty of heresy, deprived of his bishopric.

(*Signed*) The Reverend Messrs. PAUL D. URBANO, ELVIN GALLAGHER, GEORGE J. SMITH, DAN J. GERRARD, THOMAS HOBSON, JOSE VEGA, ARTHUR LEWIS, ROBERT KELLY, RICHARD WESCOTT, GEORGE RAY, THAD HARRIS, GEORGE BILLINGS, REMUS MURAY, AND FRANK M. BRUNTON.*

(*Excerpted from the Minutes of the House of Bishops, East Glacier, Montana, September 7–9, 1965.*)

At pp. 5–6
—Referral of the Arizona charges to Committee

The Chairman of the Committee on the Dispatch of Business submitted the following matters:

A statement from several clergymen of the Diocese of Arizona with regard to the Bishop of California. **Referred to the Theological Committee.** The Chair announced that for this session, the Bishop of California would be excused from sitting on the Theological Committee and that the Bishop of Washington would sit in his place.

At pp. 23–24
—A statement on Bishop Pike

The Bishop of Michigan reported for the Theological Committee, presenting a statement in answer to a letter from several clergymen in the Diocese of Arizona pertaining to the Bishop of California, as follows:

The Bishop of California is not on trial in this House, nor does the present accusation against one of our members have standing among us. The sincerity of his profession of the Catholic faith is not questioned. We do not doubt the integrity which alone makes it possible for him, or any of us, to join in the Church's worship, celebrate its rites, or repeat its formularies.

Nor will we limit the historic, disciplined, liberty of theological inquiry and the necessary devout testing of the vessels of Christian belief. Language

* One signatory later recanted, complaining his signature was deceptively procured. He was Remus Muray, who was not an Episcopal priest at the time.

changes; the concepts which are the furniture of men's minds change; the Faith given in the mighty acts of God does not change. Nor do we doubt that many an allegation of heterodoxy against any of us, or our clergy, is in fact a covert attack on legitimate Christian social concern and action.

It is a good thing responsibly to explore alternative ways of stating our unchanging Faith and to press for amendments in Church Order. We are indebted to many for such pioneering exploration. Continuity and change are both facts of life to be held in fruitful tension.

Because of misunderstandings which so easily occur, we say to those outside and inside the Church that the Church's Faith is expressed in its title deeds—the Scriptures, and the Creeds which guard them—and in the prayers and sacramental acts in the Book of Common Prayer, which express Christ's continuing ministry within the Church. Let no publicity mislead anyone as to the sincerity with which this Church and its people accept the historic Christian Faith and try to live it. An individual may well claim the freedom to think aloud, to discuss, to explore. But when he does, whatever his station, he does so as one member of Christ's Body. Only the whole Body, speaking maturely and corporately, can officially define the Faith it confesses before its Lord. Individual speculations or opinions are just that.

The Bishop of Michigan moved that the House approve this statement.
The motion carried.

The Bishop of Michigan then called upon the Bishop of California to speak to this statement. The Bishop of California responded by reading the following statement in support of the Report of the Theological Committee:

I am deeply moved by the concern of my brothers in this House. Let me take this opportunity to say that certainly I have never had any desire to damage this brotherhood, which is precious to me. All of us are working in difficult times and painful situations, and if my witness has made your task more complicated, I am truly sorry.

I must be faithful to the task to which I believe God has called me—that of seeking to distinguish the earthen vessels from the Treasure, and in the hope of setting forth, with integrity and dedication, more contemporary carriers of the reality of the Catholic Faith. But in this fast-moving world, the communications media are generally able to utilize only brief expressions; and all of us in this House have known the pain of misinterpretation of our words by some hearers and readers, and misunderstanding often by those inside and outside the Church whom we long to serve. I assure you that for my part I shall try always to be responsible in the written and spoken word, in concern for the brotherhood, and in the promotion in today's world of the mission of our Lord Jesus Christ.

No man has authority who is not under it, and I reaffirm my loyalty to the Doctrine, Discipline, and Worship of the Episcopal Church.

The House gave its hearty approval to the statement of the Bishop of California.

II. The Presentment Papers of Bishop Louttit

(*Letter of Transmittal to the Presiding Bishop*)

DIOCESE OF SOUTH FLORIDA
P.O. Box 790
WINTER PARK, FLORIDA
32789

September 20, 1966

THE RT. REV. JOHN E. HINES, D.D.
Episcopal Church Center
815 Second Avenue
New York, New York 10017

DEAR JOHN:

I am enclosing herewith a copy of the Presentment which will be formally and officially sent to you under Canon 56, Section 2, on October 1st. This is in accordance with our recent conversations concerning Jim Pike and his extremely bothersome teaching.

I am writing to him today personally and I enclose herewith a copy of that letter.

At the same time I am sending this material to all the bishops of the Church, inviting one and all to join the Committee of Bishops for the Defense of the Faith.

Praying the guidance of the Holy Spirit for you and all of us in this most important and difficult matter, I am, with affectionate regards,

                        Faithfully yours
                        (*Signed*) HENRY I. LOUTTIT
                        BISHOP OF SOUTH FLORIDA

APPENDIX

(*Letter to the Bishops*)

DIOCESE OF SOUTH FLORIDA
P.O. Box 790
WINTER PARK, FLORIDA
32789

September 20, 1966

TO THE BISHOPS OF THE
EPISCOPAL CHURCH IN THE U.S.A.

BRETHREN:

Would that I could write to each of you personally but the cost and time of secretarial assistance is prohibitive. Enclosed herewith you will find material concerning the retired Bishop of California, which is self-explanatory.

This is an invitation to each of you to join the Committee of Bishops for the Defense of the Faith. There is no membership fee, no dues, and no meetings. All that is necessary is for you to sign the enclosed Presentment, having your signature witnessed by two witnesses, as under the canon it must be signed and the signature verified, and return it to me as soon as possible.

For the last several years I have cringed each time I ordained a man, either deacon or priest. As I accepted his vows I cringed inwardly, knowing in fact that I was violating my own consecration vows. I am through cringing.

It seems to me that the time has come when we who are bishops of the Church of God must stand up and be counted. Either we are a college of bishops of the Catholic Church who are bound under our consecration vows to banish and drive away from the Church all erroneous and strange doctrine contrary to God's Word or we are a group of individualists who either disbelieve or who in the interest of harmony violate our consecration vows.

This is a serious matter I full well know and I pray the guidance of the Holy Spirit for all of us. Obviously, those bishops who are already assigned to the Court for a Trial of a Bishop or the Court of Review of the Trial of a Bishop cannot prejudge the matter and sign the Presentment. You might, however, indicate in general your approval or disapproval of the stand taken by the Committee of Bishops for the Defense of the Faith.

With affectionate regards, I am

Faithfully yours,
(*Signed*) HENRY I. LOUTTIT
BISHOP OF SOUTH FLORIDA

P.S. Obviously, the Presentment was written by me as self-appointed Chairman of the aforesaid committee. It is based on research done by two canons on my staff and with the aid of the legal training of Bill Hargrave Consequently even those bishops who have assured me verbally that they would sign the Presentment, and all the bishops for that matter, may amend by emendation or addition this Presentment, thus making one that they in good conscience can sign. H.I.L.

(THE PRESENTMENT)

WHEREAS the Right Reverend James Albert Pike, J.S.D., S.T.D., D.D., J.U.D., LittD., LL.D., D.Hu.L., Hum.D., D.S.Litt., retired Bishop of California, has for the past several years held and taught publicly and advisedly (through both the written and spoken word) doctrine contrary to that held by this Church as set forth in the Creeds, the Catechism, the Offices of Instruction, and the Book of Common Prayer, and

WHEREAS this teaching has confused, not to say bewildered, many of the faithful laity of the Church, and

WHEREAS it becomes increasingly difficult to discipline the clergy who see one of their Right Reverend Fathers in God unwilling to discipline himself or to accept the kindly admonitions, criticisms, and suggestions of his fellow bishops given many times, both individually and corporately, and, moreover, see him continue to break his consecration and ordination vows by publicly proclaiming his erroneous and heretical views, and

WHEREAS this teaching jeopardizes our ecumenical conversations with our fellow Christians of the Eastern Orthodox, the Roman Catholic, and Conservative Reformed and Evangelical bodies,

THEREFORE the undersigned bishops of the Episcopal Church in the United States of America do herewith offer this presentment of charges to the Presiding Bishop under Article VIII of the Constitution of the Protestant Episcopal Church in the United States of America, and under Canons 53 and 56 of the General Convention of this Church, to wit:

1. Disloyalty to the Constitution of this Church;
2. Holding and teaching publicly and advisedly, doctrines contrary to that held by this Church;
3. Violation of the Constitution or Canons of the General Convention;
4. Any act which involves a violation of his ordination vows;
5. Conduct unbecoming a Clergyman;

To wit: In evidence of which is appended hereto information specified as necessary under provision of Canon 56, Sec. 3.

The following Bishops make this presentment.*

* The Bishop of Dallas later withdrew his signature. The Bishop of Long Island disassociated himself from certain parts of the presentment. The Bishop of Kentucky did not sign, though he promised to do so. The Bishops of Chicago and Montana are both recorded in Bishop Louttit's files as having reluctantly acceded to the use of their names after their names were published as signatories.

THE BISHOP OF LONG ISLAND
THE BISHOP OF TENNESSEE
THE BISHOP OF MONTANA
THE BISHOP OF GEORGIA
THE BISHOP OF ALBANY
THE BISHOP OF UPPER SOUTH CAROLINA
THE BISHOP OF DALLAS
THE BISHOP OF CHICAGO
THE BISHOP OF KENTUCKY
THE BISHOP OF NORTHERN CALIFORNIA

THE BISHOP OF FLORIDA, and

THE BISHOP OF SOUTH FLORIDA
Co-Chairmen (Self-appointed) of the Committee of Bishops to Defend the Faith

(Specification of Charges)

APPENDIX—PRESENTMENT OF THE RIGHT REVEREND
JAMES ALBERT PIKE, RETIRED BISHOP OF CALIFORNIA

CHARGE 1. That Bishop Pike has affirmed that this Church should *not* require belief in one God in three Persons as this Church has received the same; that in so saying, he has contradicted and denied the plain and inevitable meaning of Holy Scripture and the teachings of this Church.

OFFENSE: Violation of Article VIII, Constitution of this Church.
Violation of Canon 53, Sec. 1, (2) (4) (6) (8).

GROUNDS: From his book, A TIME FOR CHRISTIAN CANDOR, (Harper and Row, 1964) Bishop Pike states: (P. 123, 124):

"Is a conceptualized doctrine of the Trinity in fact needed in order to preserve the essentials of the Christian Faith? If the answer is no, then the Church's mission would be relieved of a heavy piece of luggage . . . obviously, an essential of the Faith should not be abandoned or played down, even if it does make conversion to, or understanding of, Christianity more difficult . . . The Church's classical way of stating what is represented by the doctrine of the Trinity has in fact been a barrier with the well educated and less educated alike. AND IT IS NOT ESSENTIAL TO THE CHRISTIAN FAITH." (Bishop Pike has this last sentence in italics).

The following is from the farewell sermon at Grace Cathedral upon Bishop Pike's retirement, reported in the newspaper, ARIZONA REPUBLIC, Phoenix, September 5, 1966: "Bishop James A. Pike, in his final pastoral sermon at Grace Cathedral, declared yesterday that he could not affirm the existence of an "all-powerful . . . all-good . . . all-knowing God." The article goes on: "His faith is boiled down to what he himself observes and reads about." And it goes on to quote the Bishop, "Do you look at the data? Do you look at what is? There is only one breadth—the secular. There is no supernatural. If something is true, it is natural. If it is not natural, it is not true."

The following is from an article in the NEW YORK TIMES MAGAZINE, August 14, 1966, by John Cogley (p. 16): Pike acknowledges that he no longer thinks of himself as a Christian apologist, or as a defender of the faith. "I am," he said in a recent interview, "No longer primarily concerned with the question: Is it True or isn't it True? What I am interested in now is: How can I make it convincing?"

. . . . He says, however, that he no longer blesses "in the Name of the Father, and of the Son, and of the Holy Spirit," but simply "In the name of God." "Whatever is applied to One of the Three, even according to the classical theology, is the work of all Three," he argues. "So why complicate the issue by invoking the Trinitarian formula?"

"I have jettisoned the Trinity, the Virgin Birth and the Incarnation," he told an editor of LOOK Magazine in his Cambridge flat in England recently. Further references may be adduced by perusal of the article itself, in the February 22 issue of LOOK, p. 25ff; as well there is more of interest in the New York Times article in their Sunday Magazine, p. 16, issue of August 4, 1966.

* * *

CHARGE 2. That Bishop Pike has affirmed that Holy Scripture does *not* affirm the Person of the Holy Spirit, and that the Apostles and the early Church knew nothing about it; they "never heard of it". . . .

OFFENSE: Violation of Article VIII, Constitution of the Church.
Violation of Canon 53, Sec. 1 (2) (4) (6) (8).

GROUNDS: From his book, A TIME FOR CHRISTIAN CANDOR Pages 124, 125; Bishop Pike writes: (re the Trinity)
"These considerations support this conclusion: 1. The apostles and the other first followers of the Way never heard of it . . . 2. All that can be said of the Holy Spirit can be said of God without attribution to a distinct Person in the Godhead . . ."

* * *

CHARGE 3. That Bishop Pike has denied the doctrine of this Church and of Holy Scripture as this Church holds the same, as regards the Second Person of the Godhead, the Eternal Son, and has contradicted the same doctrines of His Incarnation, and distorted the reasons for His being put to death.

OFFENSE: Violation of Article VIII, Constitution of this Church Violation of Canon 53, Sec. 1 (2) (4) (6) (8).

APPENDIX

GROUNDS: On pages 112, 113 of A TIME FOR CHRISTIAN CANDOR, Bishop Pike Writes:

"So in the revelation of Jesus Christ the uniqueness lies not in the fact of revelation or in the Source of what is revealed, but rather in the avenue of that Source's revelation—at the right time the right man related aright to Him who is ever there and ready to be revealed. He was totally open to the Source, the Ultimate Ground of all that is."

"His divinity is in the fullness of His true humanity, His total readiness to be a man, that is, the full, active vehicle of God's meaning and love. But this possibility is in all men. . . . Some man had in a measure shown this capacity before; some have shown it since. It is ever a possibility. But this possibility—in its fullness—would not have been an actuality until the *kairos* —the right time, the time when men were ready for God thus to be revealed, the time into which One could be born who would be ready. Israel in that century was the right time and place, and Jesus was ready. The one Source of all was recognized; the claim had already been recognized; and He, with the authority of the source, pushed the claim to the absolute limit. He did not deny the value of accepted rules in stating certain duties within the claim, but He honestly declared that the codified law of His day was inadequate to encompass the claim; indeed, He saw in the assertions of particular elements of the law the minimization of the overall obligation. He in effect ordered His own death."

(The reason for such a lengthy passage is that it encompasses all the specifications of the charge it is appended to—i.e. the inherent adoptionist view in refusing the definition of God the Son as an infant in the Incarnation; and related substitutionary matter in its place to explain Jesus' "vocation"; and the obvious avoidance of the plain reason of the account of His death, which was largely blasphemy, His being equated with God.) Cited also here as further grounds: from Bishop Pike's Book, WHAT IS THIS TREASURE, pages 60, 61, 62, where the Bishop not only distorts the reasons for Jesus being put to death, but assigns interpretation or contradictions to Holy Scripture that they do not bear: the several passages from pages 60–62 on who Jesus is: the declaration that St. Paul's passage in Philippian's 2ff is "apparent adoptionism"; and on page 63 his assertion: "in contrast to the Virgin Birth narratives which presuppose adoption at the time of conception or a prior status thereto."

On page 65, WHAT IS THIS TREASURE?: "Therefore we should endeavor to rethink and restate the answer to the old question, "What think ye of Christ?" in a way which preserves three things: (1) The fact of Jesus' full humanity and individuality as a human being (2) the fact that in the experience of the Christian Community Jesus is sensed as belonging to the ultimate dimension of reality, and (3) the fact that God Himself, as the Ultimate Ground of all being, is unchanging and universal in His reality and ways, and though He is through the teaching and lives of many, many human beings—and very conspicuously in some, and though each of these manifestations is special, nevertheless God *is not acting 'specially' at any time.*" This obviously is the Bishop's conclusion after examinations in the context of this chapter "Early assessments of Jesus," which examines the Holy Scriptures as to who Jesus is . . . and is his version of the doctrinal necessity of believing in "Incarnation." This obviously affects the possible operations of the Father, Son and the Holy Spirit.

To clinch the matter, on the next page, 66, he refers to his point 3 again: "It would have to be consistent with a sound view of God, particularly . . . in regard to the point (numbered 3) at the close of the last chapter: "what we see of reality in the operation of God in the image of Jesus must not be arbitrary or 'special' on God's part, no matter how 'special' we may regard Jesus.

And other distortions of Scripture: page 69 of WHAT IS THIS TREASURE: "If we assume that the 'exclusivist salvation' notion from the Fourth Gospel (purportedly supported by words from Jesus) did not really represent the true Jesus (but rather an early—and persistent—unfortunate development in the Christian Church) we yet have to deal with what one of the commentators has called a "Johannine bolt from the blue" which appears in two synoptic Gospels: "Everything is entrusted to me by my Father; and no one knows the Father but the Son and those to whom the Son shall choose to reveal Him" (Matt. 11:27; Luke 10:22).

Already referred to has been the contradiction in Judaism, reflected in the books of the Old Testament between a forum for universal salvation and an ethnic club. While the conversation with the Gentile woman might seem to indicate Jesus had opted for the latter, this is not at all clear: and certainly as we have seen, early organized Christianity followed the first alternative. But in the words attributed to Jesus there would seem to be support for the other kind of exclusivist salvation which has been the prevalent motif in organized Christianity, AS WE INDICATED IN CHAPTER 4, IT IS BAD ENOUGH FOR THE CHURCH TO HAVE HELD THIS VIEW SO LONG AND SO WIDELY, WITHOUT HAVING IT ATTRIBUTABLE TO THE CHURCH'S LORD. SINCE THIS TEXT IS SUI GENERIS (John 14:6—"No one comes to the Father but by Me) SO FAR AS THE RELATIVELY RELIABLE ACCOUNTS OF JESUS' TEACHING GOES. ONE CAN INDULGE WITH PLAUSIBILITY THE HOPE THAT THE WORDS ARE NOT AUTHENTIC . . ."

Another, Page 82: "The Resurrection of our Lord presents no special theological question. The Basic question is, does the individual personality survive into eternity? If the answer is yes, then of course this is true of Jesus."

On page 63, (on discussing the early General Councils) "Meanwhile the *bishops* had given *Jesus* equal place in the *new* trinity with the Father and *a* personified Holy Spirit."

From the NEW YORK TIMES MAGAZINE, August 14, 1966, by John Cogley, Religious News Editor of the TIMES: "Joseph, Mary's husband, Pike holds, was actually the natural father of Jesus."

From an article in LOOK MAGAZINE, February 22, 1966, on page 25ff: "That Jesus was man, though so perfect that God 'adopted' him, is the heresy of "adoptionism," for it denies that Jesus was God Incarnate. "My position," says Bishop Pike, "Is not even that traditional, for adoptionism presupposes a special act of God. I've rejected that God does special things. Jesus freely adopted the Messianic role. God was able to flow through because Jesus was more open" . . . Then how does Jesus differ from other good but mortal men, like Socrates or Buddha? The Bishop's distinction is in degree, not kind. "Jesus is still unique because God Who breaks through Him is unique, and Jesus is the standard by which all others are measured."

*   *   *

CHARGE 4: That Bishop Pike has further distorted or denied doctrines of salvation as regards the Son of God as taught by Scripture and the Book of Common Prayer of this Church.

OFFENSE: Violation of Article VIII, Constitution of the Church
Violation of Canon 53, Sec. 1 (2) (4) (6) (8)

GROUNDS: In his book, WHAT IS THIS TREASURE Bishop Pike writes, on page 38:

"A few examples are sufficient, from the Bible: 'No one can come to the Father except by Me.' (John 14:6). 'God so loved the world so much that He gave His only Son, that everyone who had faith in Him may not die but have eternal life.' (John 3:16) 'Everything is entrusted to me by my Father; and no one knows the Son but the Father, and no one knows the Father but the Son and those to whom the Son may choose to reveal Him.' (Matt. 11:27; Luke 1:22) . . . 'None can enter into the kingdom of God, except he be regenerate and born anew of Water and of the Holy Ghost.' (Book of Common Prayer, Page 273); . . . 'there is none other name under heaven given to man, in whom, and through whom, thou mayest receive health and salvation, but only in the Name of our Lord Jesus Christ.' (Book of Common Prayer, page 314).

Bishop Pike continues on Page 39: "The alternatives for reaction are clear: either (a) The New Testament and the preponderance of the teaching of the Church throughout the centuries is flatly wrong, or (b) that the God thus taught about either does not exist or is subhuman in morality—with the moral consequence that belief in Him (or if perchance such a god does exist, HE) is to be opposed."

*   *   *

CHARGE 5: That Bishop Pike affirms that beyond the ultimacy of God and His mighty acts, there is nothing else that is to be considered as essential, including (apparently) all that is spoken of in the Chicago-Lambeth Quadrilateral as *essential* to the Church.

OFFENSE: Violation of Article VIII, Constitution of the Church.
Violation of Canon 53, Sec. 1 (2) (4) (6) (8).

GROUNDS: On page 24 of A TIME FOR CHRISTIAN CANDOR, Bishop Pike writes:

> "There is only one *Ultimate* God as known and experienced in His over-all claim, His mighty acts. To make anything else ultimate is idolatry. Anything else: whether a particular doctrinal formulation, a particular book or books, a particular scheme of church government, a particular office or person, a particular ethical rule, a particular way of worship. *None of these is an essential of the Gospel.* (note: none of these are ultimate, by Bishop Pike's Christology, especially, but the Bishop said none are *essential* as well. . . .)

III. The Louttit-Pike Correspondence

DIOCESE OF SOUTH FLORIDA
324 NORTH INTERLACHEN AVENUE
P. O. Box 790
WINTER PARK, FLORIDA
32789

September 22, 1966

THE RT. REV. JAMES A. PIKE, D.D.
1055 Taylor St.
San Francisco, California 94108

DEAR JIM:
The enclosures are self-explanatory. You must realize I hate to do this to you or to any brother bishop. As a person and a fellow-Christian, I love you. Moreover, I have the greatest respect for your keen legally trained mind. But I must go on to say that I take a dim view of your theology. Indeed, having read everything that you have written over the years, I have come to the reluctant conclusion that on this subject about which you speak and write so constantly, you are not very knowledgeable.

Always I have defended your sincerity and believe now that you are speaking as your intellect demands you should. I would say your "conscience," but I am not at all sure that you believe in that faculty any more. Please believe that I just as sincerely believe that in this action I am being guided by the Holy Spirit (in whom you do not believe) who has been my constant companion, guide, and comforter since the days of my youth.

As you will note from the list of present members of the Committee of Bishops to Defend the Faith of the Church, I have talked with a great many bishops in recent weeks. All of us who are your friends, and I include myself as such a one, are of the unanimous opinion that for the best good of the Church and for your own best good, you should publicly concede that you can no longer in good conscience accept the teaching of the Church and consequently must renounce the ministry and ask for deposition. This asks a real sacrifice on your part, the sacrifice of that publicity which you so dearly love. But I am sure it is worth the price.

Be sure I pray God's blessing upon you and yours and ask His guidance for all of us in this most important matter.

With warm personal regards, I am

Faithfully yours
(Signed) HENRY I. LOUTTIT
BISHOP OF SOUTH FLORIDA

APPENDIX 211

P.S. Had you done the courtesy (as any other member of the House would have done) of advising me that you were preaching in St. Petersburg on Monday last, I should have gladly come down and talked to you about this matter personally. However, I learned too late that in direct violation of Canon 42, Sec 9(a) you were functioning as a bishop of the Church of God in the Diocese of South Florida. I did not have time to get in touch with you.

H. I. L.*

Box 4068, Santa Barbara, California 93103

September 28, 1966

CONFIDENTIAL

Dear Hank:

On September 28th I have just received your letter of September 22nd and its enclosures. Naturally this is quite a surprise to me and I have not had an opportunity to digest it. However, I find four things in your letter, which, quite apart from the merits of your main position, are denigrating to me personally and "I rise to a point of personal privilege." Since without any advance notice to me you sent your letter and material to all our brother bishops, I ask that you also circulate to them a withdrawal of these statements —with or without apology, as your own ethic demands.

1. You have judged me in the P.S. with violating Canon 42, Sec. 9(a). This section makes a clear distinction between episcopal acts within a jurisdiction which are to be performed at the request of the Bishop and call for his *consent*, and ministerial acts which call for *reporting*; and, of course, as a resigned Bishop I shall make periodic reports to those Bishops in whose Dioceses I have performed any ministerial act, especially in the Diocese of California for which I am Auxiliary Bishop; and I shall observe in any such acts the requirements of Canon 44, Sec. 4(a), which requires consent in advance before performing ministerial acts within anyone's parish boundaries. But you will note that this Canon has an exception: "This rule shall not apply to any Church, Chapel, or Oratory, which is part of the premises of an incorporated institution, created by legislative authority, provided that such place of worship is designed and set apart for the convenience and uses of such institution, and not as a place for public or parochial worship." What I did in your Diocese was give a public address in an auditorium at Florida Presbyterian College, addressed and had dialogue with the Benedictine Fathers of the faculty of St. Leo's College, and preached at a chapel service on the campus of Florida Presbyterian College. The first two are not ministerial acts

* There is uncertainty about when this letter, dated September 22, 1966, was actually dispatched to Bishop Pike. A mimeographed copy of it sent, with the presentment papers, to all bishops was dated two days earlier.

within the careful definition of Canon 44, Sec. 4(a), and the latter falls within the explicit exception in that Section. Because of that exception, in the years I have been speaking at universities and colleges, I have not felt it necessary or appropriate to procure advance consent or report such addresses to the various Bishops; but now that I have resigned my See I shall comply with Canon 42, Sec. 9(a), and send a report to Bishops in whose Dioceses I may preach at a collegiate chapel within the provision of the exception of Canon 42, Sec. 9(a). Though no time is specified in Canon 42, Sec. 9(a) within which one should file such a report, please regard this letter as serving as such a report.

2. You describe me as "the retired Bishop of California." I am not retired. This is made clear by my letter to the Presiding Bishop which he distributed to all of you, and by his official notice following your consents. I have *re-signed* the post of Diocesan and continue in quite active work suitable for the ministry of a Bishop, both as a Staff Member at the Center for the Study of Democratic Institutions and as Auxiliary Bishop of the Diocese of California (by action of the Ecclesiastical Authority and the Diocesan Convention pursuant to Canon 42, Sec. 9 (a)). Further examination of the Canons will show you and your advisors that "retired" and "resigned" do not mean the same thing.

3. You state that I should have renounced the ministry and asked for deposition. While deacons and priests may so do, a Bishop may not. If you will examine the Canons, you will find that there is no provision for a renunciation of the ministry by Bishops; deposition can only come after the judicial procedure called for in the Canons, even if the given Bishop wished to be deposed. It is quite unfair of you to judge me for not taking a step which I am totally unable to take.

4. More serious, ethically speaking, is your passing judgment on my motives, when, in connection with your declaration that I should have sought deposition, "this asks a real sacrifice on your part, the sacrifice of that publicity that you so dearly love." In the first place, I would rather imagine that my renouncing the ministry (were that possible—and it is not) and my subsequent deposition would be attended by considerable publicity, whether I wanted it or not. And further, there is no reason to believe that my continued writing and speaking, as a person, and as a member of the Center for the Study of Democratic Institutions, as a member of the faculty of the University of California at Berkeley, as Chairman of the California Advisory Committee to the U.S. Civil Rights Commission, etc., would be free of publicity. But, quite apart from the fact that your statement makes any sense, your judgmentalism is a violation of one of the more serious norms of Christian ethics. We are entitled in appropriate cases to pass judgment on other person's actions or to disagree with their statements. We are not entitled to judge their motives. We have some guidance on this from the Bible, "Judge not and ye shall not be judged," and St. Paul's comment, "I judge no man, not even myself." The point is that even on the basis of a thorough psycho-

analytical report as to the operation of a person's conscious and unconscious motivations, we cannot be sure as to anyone else, or even as to ourselves in this regard. I am not conscious of a desire to seek publicity for its own sake; I am conscious of the recognition of the appropriateness of the communication of what one believes to be sound ideas and calls for action. I do not seek out the press except in the case of occasional prepared statements when an expressed position is called for; they tend to cover, on their own initiative, most occasions of my speaking. But I will not myself make a final assessment of my motivations since there is One "unto whom all hearts are open, all desires known, and from whom no secrets are hid," and that neither you nor I would think that that One is the Bishop of South Florida or I.

When I have had an opportunity to study the material which you have sent, both in its present form and in such form as it may take when it is officially filed with the Presiding Bishop, I shall have more to say. The only comment I will make about the charges is that in the Appendix, you have used hearsay evidence, including a quotation from the N.Y. Times Magazine, which has already run a Letter to the Editor from me correcting the statement, and a garbled quotation from the *Arizona Republic* which I have not seen before, and which quotes me both incorrectly and out of context. I will stand on what I have written in my books.

With every good wish,

Sincerely yours,
(*Signed*) JAMES A. PIKE

The Bishop of South Florida
Copies to the Bishops of the Church

DIOCESE OF SOUTH FLORIDA
324 NORTH INTERLACHEN AVENUE
P.O. BOX 790
WINTER PARK, FLORIDA
32789

October 3, 1966

Personal and Confidential

THE RT. REV. JAMES A. PIKE, STD
Box 4068
Santa Barbara, California 93103

DEAR JIM:
Thank you for your confidential letter of September 28. Let me say first of all that I have no false notions that I know more about canons than do you. I consider you an expert in the subject. I use them seldom and conse-

quently refer to them very infrequently. After all I prefer to think that the Church lives under the grace and not under the law.

Concerning your paragraph number one. I was not demanding really any canonical procedure. I merely suggested that as a brother bishop you might have the courtesy to advise us when you are functioning in our dioceses. There is no way possible to separate Word from Sacrament. When a bishop speaks he speaks as a bishop in the Church of God, wherever he speaks, regardless of canons.

Concerning your paragraph number two. I have searched the canons and can find no provision for an "auxiliary bishop."

Your paragraph three shows clearly your knowledge of the canon and your lack of knowledge of theology. All of us who have been ordained deacon, priest or bishop are deacons through all eternity, priests through all eternity, and bishops through all eternity, whether good or bad, deposed, resigned or active. All you need to do is renounce your ministry as deacon and priest and ask to be deposed. There was really no need to provide in the canon for a bishop renouncing the ministry and asking for deposition.

Four, I really was somewhat judgmental about your obsession for publicity. But then that is an occupational hazard which we all must fight. It seems to me that I remember on one occasion you passed serious judgment on the daughter of President Johnson when she left the communion of the Anglican Church to become a Roman Catholic. If the reports are correct, this judgment of yours was sent out over the racing track wires in order to hit the Sunday papers. It was most embarrassing to me and I am sure to most of the Church. I have in all of my ministry worked on the assumption that the Roman Catholic Church was a Christian body. Always in counseling couples wanting to be married, I urged that they unite on church affiliation and prayed that they would be faithful. Fortunately or unfortunately, this means that over the years I have encouraged a few of our communicants to become Roman Catholics rather than have a marriage split on religion. Then for you as a brother bishop to speak for the Church put me in a very difficult position with my own people and many, many Roman Catholics whom I love.

Jim, I am sure you will believe me when I say that there is nothing personal in this whole matter. You and I happen to believe different things and I pray for God's guidance and blessing for you, all the members of the House of Bishops and myself.

With affectionate regards, I am

Faithfully yours
(Signed) HENRY I. LOUTTIT
BISHOP OF SOUTH FLORIDA

Dictated by the Bishop and
signed in his absence by:
ALBERT C. MORRIS
Canon to the Ordinary

APPENDIX 215

Box 4068, Santa Barbara, California 93103
October 7, 1966

CONFIDENTIAL

DEAR HANK:

Thank you for your letter. I am glad that you have conceded that I did not violate the canon law in my talks at the Roman Catholic and Presbyterian colleges in your area.

I am surprised that, as unfamiliar with the canons as you modestly claim to be, you assert that a search of the canons reveals to you no basis for the designation of Auxiliary Bishop which describes my episcopal functioning in the Diocese of California. You didn't have to search: I cited the Canon in my last letter to you; and in fact it is the same Section you said in your first letter I had violated! The appropriate passage of Canon 42, Sec. 9, reads as follows: "A Bishop whose resignation has been accepted may perform episcopal acts at the request of any Bishop . . . He may also be given . . . an honorary seat in the Cathedral of the Diocese, if there be one (I am an Honorary Canon) or *such honorary appointment as may be designated* by the Convention of the Diocese with the consent of the Bishop." Acting under this Canon, the Diocesan Convention which elected my successor, in concurrence with the Ecclesiastical Authority (the Standing Committee), designated me as it did because I am now one of the fifty or so auxiliary ministers (perpetual deacons, worker priests and now one worker-priest in the purple) of the Diocese of California. This is not like an honorary degree; I have the same confirmation schedule I always had—two Churches a Sunday. It is honorary in the English usage of the word: it is without stipend.

What really disturbs me about your letter is your faulting me for my procuring from the Vatican on the Tuesday following my protest a position against the heretofore common practice in this country of Roman Catholic rebaptizing of Episcopal accessions—getting the American practice in line with the declaration of Vatican II and with the agreement the week before at the consultation of Roman Catholic and Episcopal bishops and theologians. You say:

"I really was somewhat judgmental about your obsession for publicity, but then that is an occupational hazard which we all must fight. It seems to me that I remember on one occasion you passed serious judgment on the daughter of President Johnson when she left the communion of the Anglican Church to become a Roman Catholic. If the reports are correct, this judgment of yours was sent out over the racing track wires in order to hit the Sunday papers. It was most embarrassing to me and I am sure to most of the Church. I have, in all of my ministry, worked on the assumption that the Roman Catholic Church was a Christian body. Always in counselling couples wanting to be married, I urged that they unite on church affiliation and prayed that they would be faithful. Fortunately or unfortunately, this means that over the years I have encouraged a few of our communicants to become

Roman Catholics rather than have a marriage split on religion. Then for you, as a brother Bishop, to speak for the Church put me in a very difficult position with my own people and many, many Roman Catholics whom I love."

There are any number of things wrong with this:

1. In my sermon (and this was made clear in the press), I praised Luci for her independence in making her own religious decision.

2. I did not judge Luci's *motives*; I protested the *action*. My criticism was the denigration of our baptisms. I would presume that our ordination and consecration vows would require that we regard our baptisms as indubitably valid. Were you more concerned about the criticism of some of your Roman Catholic friends (apparently ill-informed ones, unaware of Vatican II, the Vatican statement on the Tuesday following my sermon and the widespread support of my position in the Roman Catholic press) than about the integrity of your own Church's Sacrament of Baptism? Here you are distinguished from one of the signers of your proposed presentment, Don Hallock, who, as chairman of the Episcopal contingency at the Episcopal-Roman Catholic conference the week before the rebaptism in question, stated to the press his objection to Luci's rebaptism on precisely the same ground. Both of us spoke for our Church's established position and for the official Roman Catholic position as well. It is precisely because the Roman Catholic Church is a Christian Church as you point out, and we are a Christian Church, that a baptism is recognized across the board.

3. As to the use of the race track wire, when I read in Saturday morning's paper of the rebaptism, I prepared, with the counsel of a Roman Catholic theologian, the portion of my sermon for the next day at the Cathedral which would deal with this matter, and in seeking to implement the release of it I found that the Diocesan Communications Officer, Mr. Howard Freeman, was in Sacramento serving one of his old accounts, the annual California State Fair. Handy to him for expeditious dispatch of the sermon was the teletype also used for racing results. I fail to see the significance of your critique on this point.

4. I too believe in religious unity in marriage, as you can see from my *If You Marry Outside Your Faith* (Harper & Row), used by clergy for counselling in this field, including Roman Catholic ones, basic portions of which were issued in a Forward Movement pamphlet. But in the fulfillment of the ideal of religious unity in marriage, I am more loyal to our Church than your statement would suggest you are. In my book I quote in full (pp. 91–93) from the Lambeth Resolution and Report and from the 1949 General Convention Resolution, as to the duty of the Anglican party not to contract out of religious training of his or her children, and I urge equal consideration by the couple of the two Churches as a basis of a mutual decision, after mature study as to which one of the two Churches in which they should unite, if possible, on a basis of truth-decisions, rather than an automatic yielding of the Episcopal fiance to the canonical requirement of the Roman Catholic Church. In this concern I am in line with the Archbishop of Canterbury's widely publicized statements over the past year. Further, as

you must know, the mixed marriage problem is part of the official dialogue between representatives of the Roman Catholic and other Churches in several countries.

Speaking of publicity, I will get the following off my chest. The Canons permit you to conjoin with at least two other bishops to cause the Presiding Bishop to appoint a small investigating committee. You first lined up a dozen co-presenters. But this was not enough to satisfy you. You released your material to the press before the filing date (and *I* learned about it first from the press!) and you circularized all the members of what, under the Canons, is the final Court which is called upon to act impartially on a basis of the whole record (after the action of four other bodies—the investigating committee, the Board of Inquiry, the Trial Court and the Court of Appeal), and whose two-thirds vote would result in sanctions. You were not only eager to place the judges of this final Court in a pre-judging position but you even invited the members of the two other Courts to indicate to you their affirmative reaction to your charges. You have recently even released to the press your original personal letter to me with its denigrating statements which go beyond the charges in your proposed presentment— when I had declined to release either your letter or my answer, sharing the latter only (as I do this letter) with our brother bishops. In addition, you have wired at least some of the non-signing bishops asking how, if they do not sign, they can face their "conservative" members. All this is not what our carefully drafted canonical provisions contemplate. You say in your letter we should go by grace not law. The way you have been going about this is *neither* grace nor law. I feel violated.

With every good wish,

Sincerely in Xto,
(*Signed*) JAMES A. PIKE

The Bishop of South Florida
Copies to Bishops of the Church

DIOCESE OF SOUTH FLORIDA
324 NORTH INTERLACHEN AVENUE
P.O. BOX 790
WINTER PARK, FLORIDA
32789

October 14, 1966

THE RT. REV. JAMES A. PIKE, D.D.
P.O. Box 4068
Santa Barbara, California 93103

DEAR JIM:

Thank you very much for your two mimeographed replies to my personal letters to you dated September 20 and October 3. And I am even more grateful that you have willingly relinquished your noncanonical title of

Auxiliary Bishop of California. This was confusing both to the public and our own people. I do thank you for taking this step.

I have come to the conclusion, and I hope you will agree with me, that our exchange of correspondence with our splitting of hairs concerning points of disagreements as to canons and doctrine is getting somewhat silly. Therefore, I would suggest that when you publicly reply to this epistle that we call a truce until the meeting of the House of Bishops where we will have the benefit of all of our brethren's advice.

I read with some amusement your threat to sue me for libel. I only attended the University of Miami Law School one month hearing lectures on torts and contracts, which bored me no end. You, I understand, have an earned doctorate in jurisprudence. You should know that under the Florida Statutes only a criminal charge is libelous per se. In all other cases, you have to prove damage, which my legal advisers tell me is difficult indeed to do.

In any case, in order to make it easier for you and your attorneys, I give you herewith the law firms that I have retained to defend me, if that become necessary, and to work on the prosecution of your case, if you insist on coming to trial. They are as follows:

Cadwalader, Wickersham and Taft, 1 Wall St., New York City
Winderweedle, Haines and Ward, Box 257, Winter Park, Florida
Burns, Middleton, Rogers & Farrell, P.O. Box 2637, Palm Beach, Fla.
Fisher and Wilsey, 275 Fourth St., No., St. Petersburg, Fla.

You will rejoice with me, I know, that the Rev. Charles L. Winters, Professor of Systematic Theology at Sewanee, and I are forming a committee of theologians to translate the doctrine of the Church into Twentieth Century American prose. At the present moment some of the faculty of the School of Theology at the University of the South are preparing a Chalcedonian statement in modern American which I hope to be able to present to the House of Bishops when they meet. We are hopeful of getting representation from all of the faculties of the theological seminaries and schools of the Episcopal Church. It is our plan to hold a symposium some time next summer (the cost of which is being underwritten by a friend of the Church) probably at Sewanee to work on this most important matter which you, in a sense, pioneered.

Please know, Jim, that I think that you have made a very valuable contribution to the Church by making us all think through once again our theological positions. More than that, you have stimulated a real interest among many lay people in theology. I have a few more years than you in the ministry and in the episcopate. But I was happy indeed to have you join me and stand shoulder to shoulder with me in our fight for civil rights even though at times we may have disagreed as to methods as I am not really enthusiastic about demonstrations.

Looking forward to seeing you at Wheeling and with affectionate regards, I am

                        Faithfully yours in Christ
                        (*Signed*) HENRY I. LOUTTIT
                        BISHOP OF SOUTH FLORIDA

P.S. Since dictating the above I found the copy of your second letter which I had mislaid. My criticism of the Luci Baines Johnson affair is simply that I believe the bishops of the Roman Catholic Church who were at the Vatican Council are quite qualified and have the authority to censure and admonish their own priests. It seems to me somewhat presumptuous for an Anglican bishop who did not attend the Vatican Council to tell the world what the Church of Rome should do.

I truly apologize that you were not at home to receive my air mail, special delivery, registered, return receipt requested personal letter to you. I thought I had it timed so you would read the personal letter before your brother bishops saw it or it was known to the press. My memory is that your letter was mailed on Friday, though possibly it could have been Saturday. I know the letter to the other bishops was mailed on Saturday and it was the following Wednesday when I felt certain you must have received my epistle that I gave it to the Associated Press. In this I erred and for this I am sorry.

                                                        H.I.L.

IV. The Wheeling Documents

(*Excerpted from the Minutes of the House of Bishops,
Wheeling, West Virginia, October 23–27, 1966*)

At pp. 26–28
—The majority statement censuring Bishop Pike*

Statement

1. The fact has been widely publicized that a number of Bishops of the Episcopal Church have been prepared to initiate a formal trial of Bishop James A. Pike. Those who contemplated this action did so because they were deeply troubled by certain utterances of Bishop Pike which they believed to be contrary to the clear teaching of this Church on basic aspects of our faith.

2. When all of our Bishops were notified of this contemplated action, many were convinced that it should not be taken without an opportunity for corporate consideration by the House of Bishops. The action was postponed; and the meeting in which we are now engaged has given an opportunity for formal and informal consultation on the part of those of us present.

3. This Statement, adopted by a majority of the House of Bishops, seeks to embody briefly the conclusions we have reached.

4. It is our opinion that this proposed trial would not solve the problem presented to the Church by this minister, but in fact would be detrimental to the Church's mission and witness.

5. This judgment does not as such represent any legal opinion on our part for or against any charges which might be brought against Bishop Pike.

6. Many considerations have led us to this conclusion. We recognize that ideas and beliefs can not be constrained by laws and penalties. This "heresy trial" would be widely viewed as a "throw-back" to centuries when the law, in Church and State, sought to repress and penalize unacceptable

---

* The following requested their names be completely disassociated from the censure: the Bishops of Pennsylvania, Southern Ohio, Western Massachusetts, Washington, Vermont, Missouri, Western New York, Rochester, Mexico, Harrisburg, Nevada, New Hampshire, Massachusetts, Southwestern Virginia, Newark, and Indianapolis; the Bishop Coadjutor of Central New York; and the Suffragan Bishops of Washington, Massachusetts (Burgess), Newark, Michigan (Myers), and California.

opinions. It would spread abroad a "repressive image" of the Church, and suggest to many that we are more concerned with traditional propositions about God than with faith as the response of the whole man to God. The language and the mysteries of the Christian faith are inescapably hardened when dealt with in legal terms. We believe that our Church is quite capable of carrying the strains of free inquiry and of responsible, and even irresponsible, attempts to restate great articles of faith in ways that would speak in positive and kindling terms to men of our own time. And we are confident that the great majority of our clergy and people are gratefully loyal to our good inheritance in a Church catholic, evangelical and open.

7. Having taken this position regarding a trial, nevertheless, we feel bound to reject the tone and manner of much that Bishop Pike has said as being offensive and highly disturbing within the communion and fellowship of the Church. And we would disassociate ourselves from many of his utterances as being irresponsible on the part of one holding the office and trust that he shares with us.

8. His writing and speaking on profound realities with which Christian faith and worship are concerned are too often marred by caricatures of treasured symbols and at the worst, by cheap vulgarizations of great expressions of faith.

9. We are more deeply concerned with the irresponsibility revealed in many of his utterances. He has certainly spoken in a disparaging way of the Trinity, for example, and suggested that a conceptualized doctrine of the Trinity is a "heavy piece of luggage," of which the Church might well be relieved. Yet he knows well that a Triune apprehension of the mystery of God's being and action is woven into the whole fabric of the creeds and prayers and hymnody of our Episcopal Church, as it is into the vows of loyalty taken by our clergy at their ordination. It is explicit in our membership in the World Council of Churches and in our consultations on Church union with other major Churches. To dissect it out of the stuff of our shared life in Christ would indeed be a radical operation, and to suggest such surgery is totally irresponsible.

10. Mature and competent theologians have always known that the language of profound faith presents special problems. Silence is often more expressive of "the knowledge of God" than facile speaking. But men must seek to find words, symbols, metaphors and parables to express their faith if they are to communicate and share it. The language of faith is frequently open to unimaginative and literalistic interpretations. Ancient terms and formulas may cease to speak to men in later times. There is constant need for reinterpretation and recasting, especially in a time of such rapid intellectual and social change as ours. For this task there must be freedom, responsible freedom. But this calls for sensitive pastoral care and for patient and reverent penetration into what hallowed word-forms have been trying to say. We find too little of this pastoral concern and of this patient and reverent penetration in many of Bishop Pike's utterances on the most sensitive themes.

11. At the last meeting of this House, Bishop Pike affirmed his loyalty to the Doctrine, Discipline, and Worship of this Church and expressed his concern for the episcopal brotherhood he shares with us. We welcomed that assurance and the hope it gave that the dynamic leadership with which he is endowed might be used in such a way as to strengthen our corporate life and witness. Nothing so troubles us now as the sense shared by most of us that this hope was vain.

12. This is a hard thing to say—perhaps as hard as what Bishop Pike has said of beliefs treasured in the Church in whose service he and we have been joined and honored. Doubtless he would declare that he intended "to speak the truth in love." We would say the same—indeed we would acknowledge gratefully and sincerely that there has been so much in his ministry among us in which we rejoice.

13. Finally, we do not think his often obscure and contradictory utterances warrant the time and the work and the wounds of a trial. The Church has more important things to get on with.

The Bishop of Virginia moved to amend the Statement, by striking, from the last sentence of paragraph 9, the words "and" and "totally."

Motion Carried

The Bishop of Albany proposed that the period following the last word of paragraph 12 be deleted; that a comma be substituted therefor; and that a new clause be added, to read as follows:

> and we take this action aware of our common need for redemption, forgiveness and love.

Bishop Dun, for the Committee, accepted the foregoing addition to the document.

No action necessary

At pp. 31
—A statement of the minority

We minister in a time of rapid change in which many people are deeply disturbed. Old cherished foundations are being shaken and the hope of what is to be is not yet clear. This is an exciting time in which to live and a time of great adventure. It is a time for the young and for those who can speak to the young.

Bishop Pike has been disturbing, admittedly. Often in his dialogues with the faithless, with youth, with adherents of other religious faiths, he has spoken precipitously and with some risk. He would have preferred more time for consideration, but the pace of our day does not allow us such time. We believe it is more important to be a sympathetic and self-conscious part of God's action in the secular world than it is to defend the positions of the past, which is a past that is altered with each new discovery of truth.

At the Anglican Congress in Toronto in 1963 we explored the new frontiers that face the Church in its mission in our day. We happily agreed that there are frontiers of political and social and technological and theological thought and action confronting Christ's Church; and that our mission is to pierce them. Few of us have done so, in large part because of the risk involved and because of the danger of the task. Bishop Pike has faced, often hurriedly, the demands, intellectual and theological, of our time in history, and we commend him for doing so. If he has to be a casualty of the Christian mission in our day we regret that this is so. We would rather hope that the Church may accept the cost and the risk and the joy of moving on in its ministry to all that is to be.

* Subscribed to by the Bishops of Washington, Indianapolis, Mexico, Nevada, Missouri, Pennsylvania, Rochester, Vermont, Western Massachusetts, New Hampshire, Western New York, Southwestern Virginia, Newark, Massachusetts, Harrisburg, and Southern Ohio; the Bishop Coadjutor of Central New York; and the Suffragan Bishops of Washington, Massachusetts (Burgess), Michigan (Myers), California, and Newark.

At p. 32
—Bishop Pike's demand for investigation

TO THE PRESIDING BISHOP:

WHEREAS, There are in circulation rumors, reports, and allegations, affecting my personal and official character; namely,

a. The draft presentment circulated by the Bishop of South Florida and his associates to the Bishops and to the press, the telegrams sent to the Bishops by the Bishop of South Florida, his additional press statements and letters to the Bishops;

b. The charges of the Bishop of Montana in the Chicago *Tribune*;

c. The conclusions drawn by the *Ad Hoc* Committee, with three of my accusers as members, without opportunity for me to be in dialogue with them and present data, by the censure of the House of Bishops on October 25 as to my conduct as a clergyman, my professional competence as a theologian, my pastoral concern, and my integrity, and comments made in the course of the discussion; and

WHEREAS, I have sought the advice of at least two Bishops of this Church; Therefore,

Pursuant to Canon 56, Section 4, of the Canons of the General Convention, I demand investigation of said rumors, reports, and allegations, and such further steps as may become appropriate under the Canons.

Wheeling, W. Va.
Oct. 25, 1966

                I consent:
                (*Signed*) Bishop-elect of California
                (*Signed*) Bishop of Indianapolis
                (*Signed*) Resigned Bishop of California

APPENDIX

At pp. 44
—The Stokes resolution

WHEREAS, Christian truth requires constant re-thinking and re-stating in every age, and particularly in this age; and

WHEREAS, None of us can be satisfied with the clarity of his faith, or his ability to express it, or his courage to witness to it in moral and social as well as theological issues; and

WHEREAS, Neither hasty re-thinking of traditional statements, nor frightened questioning of those who challenge them, will suffice for the deeper consideration required of the whole Church; and

WHEREAS, The Roman Catholic Church has shown that a great Church can re-think publicly and with freedom, not only the expressions of its faith, but also its total life and mission in our day; and

WHEREAS, These times call for a major re-examination by our Church, not only of its theological stance, but also of its structure, worship, and total life and call, also, for encouragement and co-ordination of the work of many Committees and Commissions now studying different aspects of its life; now, therefore, be it

RESOLVED, That this House request the Presiding Bishop to appoint a committee to develop a Council of this Church, which shall include a cross section of the Church's lay and clerical membership and draw on the best wisdom available to help re-think, re-structure, and renew the Church for life in the world today; and that this committee report at the next meeting of the House.

Key to symbols: A = absent   Y = yes or aye   R = refused to answer
                P = present   N = no or nay   U = unknown
                S = signed

† = conditioned upon qualifications or limitations
‡ = voidable for want of canonical authorization

All data reported in this table furnished by the bishop to which it is attributed except where a symbol is enclosed in parentheses —( )—to indicate a source other than the named bishop.

* member of Court for Trial of a Bishop
** member of Court for Review of Trial of a Bishop

Name	See or Other Status	attendance	presentment	censure	minority statement
(as of October 25, 1966)					
Bennett, Granville Gaylord	Rhode Island, Res. Bp.	U	U	U	
Strider, Robert Edward Lee	West Virginia, Res. Bp.	U	U	U	
Sterrett, Frank William	Bethlehem, Res. Bp.	U	U	U	
Juhan, Frank Alexander	Florida, Res. Bp.	A	Y‡	A	
Campbell, Robert Erskine, OHC	Liberia, Res. Bp.	A	Y‡	A	
Mitchell, Walter	Arizona, Res. Bp.	P	N	Y	
Thomas, Albert Sidney	South Carolina, Res. Bp.	U	Y‡	U	
Sturtevant, Harwood	Fond du Lac, Res. Bp.	U	Y‡	U	
Littell, Samuel Harrington	Honolulu, Res. Bp.	U	U	U	
Hobson, Henry Wise	Southern Ohio, Res. Bp.	A	N	A	

Name (as of October 25, 1966)	See or Other Status	attend-ance	present-ment	censure	minority state-ment
Scarlett, William	Missouri, Res. Bp.	A	N	A	
*Gooden, Robert Burton	Los Angeles, Res. Suffr.	A	N	A	
Sherrill, Henry Knox	Res. Presiding Bishop	(A)	U	(A)	
Goodwin, Frederick Deane	Virginia, Res. Bp.	R	R	R	
Bentley, John Boyd	Alaska, Res. Suffr.	P	U	(N)	
Salinas y Velasco, Efrain	Mexico, Res. Miss. Bp.	(A)	U	(A)	
Gribbin, Robert Emmet	Western No. Car., Res. Bp.	A	U	A	
Clingman, Charles	Kentucky, Res. Bp.	A	N	A	
Ziegler, Winfred Hamlin	Wyoming, Res. Bp.	P	Y‡	A	
Lawrence, William Appleton	Western Mass., Res. Bp.	R	N	(N)	
Roberts, William Payne	Shanghai, Res. Miss. Bp.	R	R	R	
Carpenter, Charles Colcock Jones	Alabama	P	U	(Y)	
Tucker, Beverley Dandridge	Ohio, Res. Bp.	A	N	A	
**Peabody, Malcolm Endicott	Central N.Y., Res. Bp.	U	N	U	
Kirchhoffer, Richard Ainslie	Indianapolis, Res. Bp.	(A)	D	(A)	
McKinstry, Arthur Raymond	Delaware, Res. Bp.	A	N	A	
Blankingship, Alexander Hugo	Cuba, Res. Miss. Bp.	P	N	Y	
**Gray, Walter Henry	Conn., Bp.	P	D	(Y)	
Craighill, Lloyd Rutherford	Anking, Res. Miss. Bp.	(A)	N	A	
Conkling, Wallace Edmonds	Chicago, Res. Bp.	A	N	(A)	
**Loring, Oliver Leland	Maine	P	D	U	
Powell, Noble Cilley	Maryland, Res. Bp.	P	N	Y	
Mason, Wiley Roy	Virginia, Res. Suffr.	U	U	U	
*Hart, Oliver James	Penn., Res. Bp.	U	D	D	
Page, Herman Riddle	Northern Michigan	A	N	A	
**Heistand, John Thomas	Harrisburg, Res. Bp.	P	Z	U	
Jones, Everett Holland	West Texas	A	N	A	
Voegeli, Charles Alfred	Haiti, Miss. Bp.	P	H	H	

Walters, Sumner Francis Dudley	San Joaquin, Miss. Bp.	P	U	(Y)
Kennedy, Harry Sherbourne	Honolulu, Miss. Bp.	P	Y	Y
Pardue, Austin	Pittsburgh	P	U	(Y)
Dun, Angus	Washington, Res. Bp.	(P)	(N)	(Y)
Horstick, William Wallace	Eau Claire	A	Y	A
Gesner, Conrad Herbert	South Dakota, Miss. Bp.	P	Y	Y
Gooden, Reginald Heber	Canal Zone, Miss. Bp.	P	N	Y
Louttit, Henry Irving	South Florida	P	Y	Y
Mason, Charles Avery	Dallas	P	Y	Y
Banyard, Alfred Lothian	New Jersey	U	N	U
Wright, Thomas Henry	East Carolina	P	U	Y
Hines, John Elbridge	Presiding Bishop	P	U	U
*Moody, William Robert	Lexington	P	U	Y
Emrich, Richard Stanley Merrill	Michigan	P	N	A
Sawyer, Harold Everett	Erie, Res. Bp.	A	(N)	N
Barton, Lane Wickham	Eastern Oregon, Miss. Bp.	P	N	Y
**Quarterman, George Henry	North Texas	P	N	Y
Bayne Jr., Stephen Fielding	Vice President, Exec. C'l.	P	Y‡	Y (s)
Bowen, Harold Linwood	Colorado, Res. Bp.	U	N	U (s)
Donegan, Horace William Baden	New York	P	N	Y
Gunn, George Purnell	Southern Virginia	P	U	Y
Hall, Charles Francis	New Hampshire	P	N	(Y)
Hunter, James Wilson	Wyoming, Miss. Bp.	P	N	N
Bloy, Francis Eric Irving	Los Angeles	P	N	Y
Scaife, Lauriston Livingston	Western New York	P	N	Y
Gordon Jr., William Jones	Alaska, Miss. Bp.	P	N	N
Hubbard, Russell Sturgis	Spokane, Res. Bp.	P	N	Y
Henry, Matthew George	Western No. Car.	A	N	A
West, Edward Hamilton	Florida	P	N	Y
Higley, Walter Maydole	Central New York	(P)	(Y)	(Y)
Sherman, Jonathan Goodhue	Long Island	P	N	Y
Campbell, Donald James	Los Angeles, Res. Suffr.	P	Y†	Y
Jones, Girault McArthur	Louisiana	A	N	A
Claiborne, Randolph Royall	Atlanta	P	N	Y

Name	See or Other Status	attend-ance	present-ment	censure	minority state-ment
(as of October 25, 1966)					
Gibson Jr., Robert Fisher	Virginia	P	N	Y	
*Street, Charles Larrabee	Chicago, Res. Suffr.	P	U	U	
Miller, Allen Jerome	Easton, Res. Bp.	P	(N)	Y	
Burroughs, Nelson Marigold	Ohio	P	U	Y	
Krischke, Egmont Machado	Southern Brazil, Miss. Bp.	(A)	(N)	(A)	
Stark, Dudley Scott	Rochester, Res. Bp.	A	U	A	
Welles, Edward Randolph	West Missouri	P	N†	Y	
**Smith, Gordon V.	Iowa	P	U	U	
Campbell, Wilburn Camrock	West Virginia	P	Y‡	Y	
Burrill, Gerald Francis	Chicago	P	Y†	Y	
Baker, Richard Henry	North Carolina	A	(N)	A	
Lichtenberger, Arthur	Res. Presiding Bishop	A	N	A	S
*Hatch, Robert McConnell	Western Mass.	P	Y	N	
Watson, Richard Simpson	Utah	P	U	Y	
Swift, Albert Ervins	Puerto Rico, Miss. Bp.	P	U	U	
Richards, David Emrys	Central America, Miss. Bp.	P	N	Y	
Powell, Winslow Robert Chilton	Oklahoma	P	Y	Y	
Hallock, Donald Hathaway Valentine	Milwaukee	P	N	N	
Kellogg, Hamilton Hyde	Minnesota	P	N	U	
Crittenden, William	Erie	P	U	Y	
Noland, Iveson Batchelor	Louisiana, Coadj.	P	N	Y	
Ogilby, Lyman Cunningham	Philippines, Miss. Bp.	P	N	Y	
Higgins, John Seville	Rhode Island	P	Y	Y	
Warnecke, Frederick John	Bethlehem	P	N	N	
Brady, William Hampton	Fond du Lac	P	N	N	S
Stark, Leland William Frederick	Newark	P	U	(Y)	
Murray, George Mosley	Alabama	A	(N)	A	
McNeil, Dudley Barr	Western Mich., Res. Bp.				

Rose, David Shepherd	So. Virginia, Suffr.	P	U	U	
Lickfield, Francis William	Quincy	P	Y	(Y)	s
Blanchard, Roger Wilson	Southern Ohio	P	N	N	
Sherrill, Edmond Knox	Central Brazil, Miss. Bp.	(A)	U	(A)	
Brown, Allen Webster	Albany	P	Y	Y	
Cabanban, Benito Cabanban	Philippines, Suffr.	A	(N)	A	
Cadigan, George Leslie	Missouri	P	N	N	s
Creighton, William Forman	Washington	P	N	N	s
Millard, George Richard	California, Suffr.	P	N	N	s
Wright, William Godsell	Nevada, Miss. Bp.	P	N	(N)	s
Bennison, Charles Ellsworth	Western Michigan	P	Y	Y	
Kellogg, Paul Axtell	Dominican Republic, Miss. Bp.	P	(N)	U	
Wetmore, James Stuart	New York, Suffr.	P	N	N	
Curtis, Ivol Ira	Olympia	P	(N)	U	
Chilton, Samuel Blackwell	Virginia, Suffr.	P	(N)	Y	s
Fraser Jr., Thomas Augustus	North Carolina	P	(N)	U	
DeWitt, Robert Lionne	Pennsylvania	P	N	N	
Thayer, Edwin Burton	Colorado, Suffr.	P	Y‡	Y	s
Temple, Gray	South Carolina	P	Y	R	
Butterfield, Harvey Dean	Vermont	P	N	N	
Rauscher, Russell Theodore	Nebraska	P	Y	U	
Gilson, Charles Packard	Honolulu, Res. Suffr.	A	U	A	
Brown Jr., Dillard Houston	Liberia, Res. Miss. Bp.	P	U	U	
Allin, John Maury	Mississippi	P	Y	Y	
Hutchens, Joseph Warren	Connecticut, Suffr.	P	(N)	(Y)	
Duncan, James Loughlin	South Florida, Suffr.	P	Y‡	Y	
Hargrave, William Loftin	South Florida, Suffr.	P	Y‡	Y	
Thomas, William S.	Pittsburg, Suffr.	P	U	(Y)	
Kinsolving III, Charles James	N. M. & S. W. Tex.	(A)	U	U	
Mosley, J. Brooke	Delaware	P	N	Y	
Marmion, William Henry	Southwestern Virginia	P	N	N	
Marmion, Charles Gresham	Kentucky	P	N†	Y	s
Harte, John Joseph Meakin	Arizona	P	Y	Y	
Minnis, Joseph Summerville	Colorado	P	Y	Y	

Name	See or Other Status	attend-ance	present-ment	censure	minority state-ment
(as of October 25, 1966)					
Crowley, Archie Henry	Michigan, Suffr.	P	N	Y	
Stuart, Albert Rhett	Georgia	P	Y	Y	S
Stokes, Anson Phelps	Massachusetts	P	N	N	
Vander Horst, John	Tennessee	P	N	Y	
Doll, Harry Lee	Maryland	P	N	Y	
Dicus, Richard Earl	West Texas, Suffr.	P	N	Y	
Goddard, Frederick Percy	Texas, Suffr.	P	N	Y	
Brown, Robert Raymond	Arkansas	P	U	U	
Lewis, Arnold Meredith	Western Kansas, Miss. Bp.	P	N	Y	
Carman, James Walmsley Frederic	Oregon	P	N	Y	
Honaman, Earl Miller	Harrisburg, Suffr.	(A)	U	(A)	
Simoes, Plinio Lauer	S. W. Brazil, Miss. Bp.	P	U	U	
Turner, Edward Clark	Kansas	A	Y	A	
Sterling, Chandler Winfield	Montana	A	Y†	A	
Lawrence, Frederic Cunningham	Massachusetts, Suffr.	P	N	N	S
Foote, Norman Landon	Idaho, Miss. Bp.	P	U	U	
Craine, John Pares	Indianapolis	P	N	N	
Haden, Clarence Rupert	No. California	P	Y	Y	
Saucedo, Jose Gaudalupe	Mexico, Miss. Bp.	P	(N)	(Y)	S
McNairy, Philip Frederick	Minnesota, Suffr.	P	N	Y	
Esquirol, John Henry	Connecticut, Suffr.	P	U	U	
Corrigan, Daniel	Vice President, Exec. C'l.	P	Y	(Y)	
MacLean, Charles Waldo	Long Island, Suffr.	(P)	(N)	(N)	
Sanders, William Evan	Tennessee, Coadj.	P	U	U	
Montgomery, James Winchester	Chicago, Coadj.	P	N	Y	
Chambers, Albert Arthur	Springfield	P	N	Y	
McCrea, Theodore Harper	Dallas, Suffr.	P	Y	Y	
Burgess, John Melville	Massachusetts, Suffr.	P	U	U	S
Longid, Edward Gaudan	Philippines, Suffr.	P	N	N	

Barrett, George West	Rochester				
Putnam Jr., Frederick Warren	Oklahoma, Suffr.	P	(N)	U	
Klien, Walter Conrad	Northern Indiana	P	Y	Y	
Pinckney, John Adams	Upper South Carolina	P	Y	Y	S
Moore Jr., Paul	Washington, Suffr.	P	N	N	
Rivera, Leonardo Romero	Mexico, Suffr.	U	U	U	
Sauceco, Melchor	Mexico, Suffr.	P	U	U	
Rath, George Edward	Newark, Suffr.	P	N	N	
Cole, Jr., Ned	Central New York, Coadj.	P	N	N	S
Reed, David Benson	Columbia, Miss. Bp.	P	N	Y	S
Bailey, Scott Field	Texas, Suffr.	P	U	U	
Myers, Chauncie Kilmer	California, Bp.-elect	P	N	N	S
Rusack, Robert Claflin	Los Angeles, Suffr.	P	N	Y	
Selway, George Rhys	Northern Michigan	P	N	Y	
Reus-Froylan, Francisco	Puerto Rico, Miss. Bp.	P	N	N	
Wong, James Chang Lee	Taiwan, Miss. Bp.	P	U	U	
Masuda, George Theodore	North Dakota, Miss. Bp.	P	U	U	
Richardson, James Milton	Texas	P	U	U	
Gross, Hal Raymond	Oregon, Suffr.	P	(N)	(N)	
Davidson, William	Western Kansas	P	Y	Y	
Wiencke, Albert	New Jersey, Suffr.	P	N	N	
Gates, William Fred	Tennessee, Suffr.	P	N	N	
Barnds, William Paul	Dallas, Suffr.	P	U	U	
Stevenson, Dean Theodore	Harrisburg	P	(N)	(N)	S
Hall, Robert Bruce	Virginia, Coadj.	P	U	U	

Totals: 190

P 146	Y 37	Y 82	S 22
A 32	N 102	N 33	
R 2	R 2	A 32	
U 12	U 51	R 3	
		U 42	

VI. Relevant Provisions of the Constitution and Canons of the Episcopal Church

CONSTITUTION
ADOPTED IN GENERAL CONVENTION
IN PHILADELPHIA, OCTOBER, 1789,
AS AMENDED IN SUBSEQUENT GENERAL CONVENTIONS

ARTICLE I.

SEC. 2. Each Bishop of this Church having jurisdiction, every Bishop Coadjutor, every Suffragan Bishop, and every Bishop who by reason of advanced age or bodily infirmity, or, who under an election to an office created by the General Convention has resigned his jurisdiction, shall have a seat and a vote in the House of Bishops. A majority of all Bishops entitled to vote, exclusive of Bishops who have resigned their jurisdiction or positions, shall be necessary to constitute a quorum for the transaction of business.

ARTICLE II.

SEC. 6. A Bishop may not resign his jurisdiction without the consent of the House of Bishops.

. . . . .

ARTICLE VIII.

No person shall be ordered Priest or Deacon to minister in this Church until he shall have been examined by the Bishop and two Priests and shall have exhibited such testimonials and other requisites as the Canons in that case provided may direct. No persons shall be ordained and consecrated Bishop, or ordered Priest or Deacon to minister in this Church, unless at the time, in the presence of the ordaining Bishop or Bishops, he shall subscribe and make the following declaration:

"I do believe the Holy Scriptures of the Old and New Testaments to be the Word of God, and to contain all things necessary to salvation; and I do solemnly engage to conform to the Doctrine, Discipline, and Worship of the Protestant Episcopal Church in the United States of America."

ARTICLE IX.

The General Convention may, by Canon, establish a Court for the trial of Bishops, which shall be composed of Bishops only.

The General Convention, in like manner, may establish or may provide for the establishment of Courts of Review of the determination of diocesan or other trial Courts.

The Court for the review of the determination of the trial Court, on the trial of a Bishop, shall be composed of Bishops only.

The General Convention, in like manner, may establish an ultimate Court of Appeal, solely for the review of the determination of any Court of Review on questions of Doctrine, Faith or Worship.

None but a Bishop shall pronounce sentence of admonition, or of suspension, deposition, or degradation from the Ministry, on any Bishop, Presbyter, or Deacon.

CANONS

AS AMENDED, ADOPTED, AND CODIFIED IN GENERAL CONVENTION, 1943 AND SUBSEQUENTLY AMENDED

CANON 42
Of Duties of Bishops

Sec. 8 (a). If the Bishop of a Diocese, or a Bishop Coadjutor, shall desire to resign his jurisdiction, he shall send in writing to the Presiding Bishop his resignation with the reasons therefor. This communication shall be sent at least thirty days before the date set for a regular or a special meeting of the House of Bishops. The Presiding Bishop shall without delay send a copy of the communication to every Bishop of this Church having ecclesiastical jurisdiction, and also to the Standing Committee of the Diocese of the Bishop desiring to resign, in order that the Standing Committee may on behalf of the Diocese be heard either in person or by correspondence upon the subject. The House during its session shall investigate the whole case, and by a majority of those present accept or refuse the resignation.

(b). If said resignation shall have been tendered more than three months before a regular or special meeting of the House of Bishops, the Presiding Bishop shall communicate the same, together with any statement from the Standing Committee of the Diocese concerned, to every Bishop of this Church having jurisdiction in the United States; and if a majority of such Bishops shall consent to the resignation, the Presiding Bishop shall, without delay, notify the resigning Bishop and the Standing Committee of the Diocese concerned, of the acceptance of such resignation and the termination of said Bishop's jurisdiction, effective as of the date fixed. He shall also order the Secretary of the House of Bishops to record the same, effective as of the date fixed, to be incorporated in the Journal of the House.

Sec. 9 (a). A Bishop whose resignation has been accepted may perform episcopal acts at the request of any Bishop of this Church, having ecclesiastical jurisdiction, within the limits of his jurisdiction. He may also be given an honorary seat in the Convention of the Diocese, with voice, but without vote, and an honorary seat in the Cathedral of the Diocese, if there be one, or such honorary appointment as may be designated by the Convention of the Diocese with the consent of the Bishop. He shall report all ministerial acts to the Bishop and to the Diocese in which such acts are performed.

(b). A Bishop who ceases to have episcopal charge shall still be subject in all matters to the Canons and authority of the General Convention.

(c). A Bishop who has resigned his jurisdiction with the consent of the House of Bishops, may, at the discretion of the Bishop of the Diocese (or Missionary District) in which he chooses to reside, be enrolled among the Clergy of that Diocese (or Missionary District), and become subject to its Canons and regulations; and if he accept any pastoral charge or ministerial appointment within the Diocese (or Missionary District) he may be accorded a seat and vote in the Diocesan Convention (or Convocation) according to its canonical provisions for the qualification of Presbyters. The same shall apply to a resigned Bishop who continues to reside within the jurisdiction in which he formerly served as Bishop; *Provided*, that, the Bishop seeking to be counted among the Clergy of a Diocese and to sit in its Diocesan Convention is not at the same time exercising his right (under Article I., Section 2) to vote in the House of Bishops.

CANON 44

Of Ministers and Their Duties

Sec. 4 (a). No Minister of this Church shall officiate, either by preaching, reading prayers in public worship, or by performing any other priestly or ministerial function, in the Parish, or within the Cure, of another Minister, without the consent of the Minister of that Parish or Cure; or of one of its Churchwardens if, in his absence or disability, the Minister fail to provide for the stated services of such Parish or Cure.

ECCLESIASTICAL DISCIPLINE

CANON 53

Of Offenses for Which Bishops, Presbyters, or Deacons May Be Tried

Sec. 1. A Bishop, Presbyter, or Deacon of this Church shall be liable to presentment and trial for the following offenses, viz.:

(1). Crime or immorality.

(2). Holding and teaching publicly or privately and advisedly, any doctrine contrary to that held by this Church.

(3). Violation of the Rubrics of the Book of Common Prayer.

(4). Violation of the Constitution of the General Convention.

(5). Violation of the Constitution or Canons of the Diocese or Missionary District to which he belongs.

(6). Any act which involves a violation of his Ordination vows.

(7). Habitual neglect of the exercise of his Ministerial Office, without cause; or habitual neglect of Public Worship, and of the Holy Communion, according to the order and use of this Church.

(8). Conduct unbecoming a Clergyman;

Provided, however, that in the case of a Presbyter or Deacon charged with this offense, before proceeding to a presentment, the consent of three-fourths of all the members of the Standing Committee or Council of Advice of the Diocese or Missionary District in which the Presbyter or Deacon is canonically resident shall be required.

Upon a Presbyter or Deacon being found guilty, such Presbyter or Deacon shall be admonished, or shall be suspended or deposed from the Sacred Ministry, as shall be adjudged by the Trial Court, except as provided in Canon 64, Sec. 3.

Sec. 2. In the case of a Bishop, Presbyter, or Deacon convicted in a Court of Record of any crime or misdemeanor involving immorality, or against whom a judgment has been entered in a Court of Record in a cause involving immorality, it shall be the duty of the Presiding Bishop, in the case of a Bishop, and in the case of a Presbyter or Deacon, of the Standing Committee of the Diocese or of the Council of Advice of the Missionary District in which he is canonically resident, to institute an inquiry into the matter. If in the judgment of either there is sufficient reason for further proceedings, it shall be their duty to present him, or to cause that he be presented, for trial.

Sec. 3. No presentment shall be made or conviction had for any offense, unless the offense shall have been committed within five years immediately preceding the time of the presentment, except that in a case of a conviction in a Court of Record exercising criminal jurisdiction as aforesaid, a presentment may be made at any time within one year after such conviction notwithstanding five years may have elapsed since the commission of the offense.

CANON 55

Of Courts, Their Membership and Procedure

(c) Court for the Trial of a Bishop

Sec. 14 (a). There shall be a Court for the trial of a Bishop constituted as follows: The House of Bishops shall choose three Bishops to serve as judges of said court for a term of three years, three Bishops to serve as aforesaid for a term of six years, and three Bishops to serve as aforesaid for a term of nine years, and thereafter at each General Convention the House of Bishops shall choose three Bishops to serve as aforesaid for the term of nine years, in place of those whose term of office shall then have expired.

(b). The Court is vested with jurisdiction to try a Bishop who is duly charged with any one or more of the offenses specified in Canon 53.

(c). Not less than six of said judges shall constitute a quorum, but any less number may adjourn the Court from time to time.

(d) The Court of Review of the Trial of a Bishop

Sec. 15. There shall be a Court of Review of the Trial of a Bishop, which shall be composed of Bishops only and shall be constituted as follows:

The House of Bishops shall choose three Bishops who shall serve as Judges of the Court of Review of the Trial of a Bishop for the term of three years; three Bishops to serve as aforesaid for the term of six years; and three Bishops to serve as aforesaid for the term of nine years, and thereafter at each General Convention the House of Bishops shall choose three Bishops to serve as aforesaid for the term of nine years in place of those whose term of office shall then have expired.

Sec. 16. The said Court of Review is vested with jurisdiction to hear and determine appeals from the determination of the Court for the Trial of a Bishop.

Sec. 17. Not less than six Judges shall constitute a quorum and the concurrence of six Judges shall be necessary to pronounce a judgment, but any less number may adjourn the Court from time to time.

(e) Of Membership in Courts

Sec. 18 (a). No person shall sit as a member of any Court who is a presenter of charges or is related to the accused or either of them by affinity or consanguinity in a direct ascending or descending line, or as a brother, uncle, nephew, or first cousin, nor shall any Bishop, nor any Presbyter, nor any Layman of the Diocese or Missionary District in which the trial was had be competent to sit on an appeal from the decision on such trial, nor shall any Bishop, Presbyter, or Layman who for any reason upon objection made by either party is deemed by the other members of the Court to be disqualified.

(b). The death, permanent disability, resignation, or refusal to serve as a member of any Court or Board of Inquiry shall constitute a vacancy in the Court or Board of Inquiry.

Notices of resignations or refusals to serve shall be given as follows:

(1). By any Bishop chosen to serve as a member of the Court for the Trial of a Bishop or of the Court of Review of the Trial of a Bishop; written notice sent to the Presiding Bishop.

(2). By the President of the Court of Review of the Trial of a Presbyter or Deacon; written notice sent to the President of the Provincial Synod.

(3). By a Presbyter or Layman of such Court; written notice sent to the President of said Court.

(4). By a Presbyter or Layman appointed to a Board of Inquiry; written notice sent to the Presiding Bishop.

(c). If any Presbyter appointed to a Board of Inquiry or to any of the Courts shall become a Bishop, or any Layman appointed to a Board of Inquiry or to any of the Courts shall become a Presbyter before the final disposition of the charge, he shall thereby vacate his place as a member of the Board or Court.

Sec. 19. Vacancies occurring in any of the Courts or Boards may be filled as follows:

(1). In the case of disqualification of any Judge of any Court, the remaining Judges of the said Court shall appoint a Judge to take the place of the one so disqualified in that particular case.

(2). In the case of a vacancy in the Court for the Trial of a Bishop or in the Court of Review of the Trial of a Bishop the remaining Judges thereafter shall have power to fill such vacancy until the next General Convention when the House of Bishops shall choose a Bishop to fill such vacancy. The Bishop so chosen shall serve during the remainder of the term.

(3). In the case of death, permanent disability, resignation, or refusal to serve, or the removal from the Province of the Bishop appointed as a member of the Court of Review of the Trial of a Presbyter or Deacon, the President of the Provincial Synod shall give written notice thereof to the Bishop with jurisdiction senior by consecration in the Province. Thereupon the Bishop so notified shall become a member of the Court until a new appointment shall be made. If in a particular case the Bishop so appointed is unable or unwilling to serve as a member of the Court he shall notify the President of the Provincial Synod of this fact, who shall thereupon appoint the Bishop with jurisdiction next senior by consecration in that Province.

(4). In case a vacancy shall exist in the membership of the Court of Review in any Province, among the clerical or lay members originally chosen, or in case any of them shall be disqualified or unable to sit in a particular case, the President of the Court shall appoint other Presbyters or Laymen residing in the Province to fill such vacancy and to sit as members of said Court.

(5). In the case of a vacancy for any cause in the Board of Inquiry the Presiding Bishop shall appoint another Presbyter or another Layman, as the case may be, to act as a member of the Board, who, upon acceptance of appointment, shall become a member of the Board.

All of the provisions of the Canons relating to persons originally appointed as members of the several Courts or Boards of Inquiry or Commissions, shall apply to those persons appointed in succession to the persons originally appointed, and all proceedings which may have been taken on any cause pending at or prior to such appointment, shall have the same force and effect as if the appointee had been a member of the Court, Board, or Commission, when such cause was commenced, and such appointee may participate in the continuing hearing and determination of the said cause.

If the term for which a member of a Court, Board, or Commission was chosen shall have expired during the course of a hearing or trial, said member shall notwithstanding be competent to act in the cause until the termination of the trial or hearing.

(f) Of Procedure

Sec. 20 (a). The procedure in Diocesan Courts shall be as provided by the Canons of the respective Dioceses or Missionary Districts.

(b). The Court for the Trial of a Bishop and the Court of Review of the Trial of a Bishop shall from time to time elect from its own membership a Presiding Judge who shall hold office until the expiration of the term for which he was chosen Judge. If in any proceeding before said Courts the Presiding Judge is disqualified or is for any cause unable to act, the Court shall elect a Bishop as Presiding Judge *pro tempore*.

(c). The several Courts shall appoint clerks and if necessary assistant clerks, who shall be Presbyters of this Church, to serve during the pleasure of the Court.

The several Courts may appoint not less than two nor more than three lay communicants of this Church, learned in the law, as assessors. They shall have no vote. It shall be their duty to give the Court an opinion on any question, not theological, upon which the Court or any member thereof, or either party, shall desire an opinion. If a question shall arise as to whether any question is theological, it shall be decided by the Court by a majority of the votes.

The several Courts may adopt rules of procedure not inconsistent with the Constitution and Canons of this Church, with power to alter or rescind the same from time to time.

Sec. 21. In the conduct of investigations preliminary to presentments, as well as in all trials, the laws of the civil jurisdiction in which such investigation or trial is had, so far as they relate to evidence, shall be adopted and taken as the rules by which said Board of Inquiry, Commission, or Court, shall be governed, and trials shall be conducted according to the principles of the common law as the same is generally administered in the United States, except in those Dioceses where Ecclesiastical Courts are provided for by Constitution or Statute, in which case the same shall govern.

No determination or judgment of any Court shall be disturbed for technical errors not going to the merits of the cause.

The several Courts shall keep a record of all their proceedings.

Sec. 22. The various Courts shall permit the accused to be heard in person or by counsel of his own selection, provided every such counsel shall be a communicant of this Church, but in every trial or investigation the several Courts may regulate the number of counsel who may address the Court or examine witnesses.

The President, or any other member of the several Courts, shall upon application of either the Church Advocate or the accused issue subpoenas for witnesses, but before doing so the person who issues the same shall first be satisfied that the testimony sought to be adduced is material and that the witness is one whom the Court would be willing to hear upon the trial, otherwise he may refuse to issue the same.

When the several Courts are not in session, if there is a vacancy in the office of the President, the Bishop who is senior by consecration shall perform the duties of the office of President.

If in the course of a trial it becomes necessary to take the testimony of

APPENDIX 239

absent witnesses, it may be taken upon a commission as such commissions are authorized by the common law in the jurisdiction in which the trial takes place, and in case there is ground to suppose that the attendance of a witness at the forthcoming trial cannot be obtained, it shall be lawful for either party to apply to the Court if in session, or, if not, to any member thereof, who shall thereupon appoint a Commissioner to take the deposition of such witness; and such party desiring to take such depositions shall give the opposite party reasonable notice of the time and place of taking depositions, accompanying such notice with the interrogatories to be propounded to the witness, whereupon it shall be lawful for the other party within six days after such notice to propound cross-interrogatories and such interrogatories and cross-interrogatories, if any be propounded, shall be sent to the Commissioner, who shall thereupon proceed to take the testimony of such witness and transmit it under seal to the Court. Such testimony shall be preceded by a written declaration of the witness similar to that of a witness testifying in person before the Court for the Trial of a Bishop.

In any Diocese in which the Civil Government shall have authorized the Ecclesiastical Courts therein to issue subpoenas for witnesses or to administer an oath, the Court shall act in conformity to such law.

Provided, however, that no deposition shall be taken, or read at the trial, unless the Court shall deem such testimony to be material and also have reasonable assurance that the attendance of the witness cannot be procured, and the several Courts shall have power to limit the scope of the testimony and the number of witnesses to be examined and whose depositions shall be taken.

Sec. 23. Where a presentment of a Bishop is made by any three Bishops of this Church exercising jurisdiction, they may select a Church Advocate as legal adviser. The Presiding Bishop upon the receipt of written charges or written demand under the provisions of Sections 3 or 4 of Canon 56 shall at the same time that the Board of Inquiry is appointed as provided in Section 5 of said Canon 56 appoint a Church Advocate to act as the legal adviser of the Board.

CANON 56.
Of Presentments
(b) Of a Bishop

Sec. 2. A Bishop may be presented by any three Bishops of this Church exercising jurisdiction, for holding and teaching publicly or privately and advisedly, doctrine contrary to that held by this Church. Such presentment shall be in writing, signed and verified by the Bishops presenting, and shall be delivered to the Presiding Bishop.

Sec. 3. A Bishop may be charged with any one or more of the offenses specified in Canon 53, other than that of holding and teaching doctrine contrary to that held by this Church, by three Bishops or ten or more male communicants of this Church in good standing, of whom at least two shall be Presbyters; one Presbyter and not less than six communicants shall belong to the Diocese or Missionary District of the accused, or, in case the accused have no jurisdiction, to the Diocese or District in which he has domicile. Such charges shall be in writing, signed by all the accusers, sworn to by two or more of them, and shall be presented to the Presiding Bishop of the Church. The grounds of accusation must be set forth with reasonable certainty of time, place, and circumstance.

Sec. 4. Whenever a Bishop shall have reason to believe that there are in circulation rumors, reports, or allegations affecting his personal or official character, he may, acting in conformity with the written advice and consent of any two Bishops of this Church, demand in writing of the Presiding Bishop that investigation of said rumors, reports, and allegations be made.

Sec. 5. The Presiding Bishop, upon the receipt of such written charges or such written demand, shall summon not less than three nor more than seven Bishops, and, unless a majority of them shall determine that such charges, if proved, would constitute no canonical offense, they shall select a Board of Inquiry of five Presbyters and five Laymen, none of whom shall belong to the Diocese of the accused, of whom eight shall form a quorum.

The Board of Inquiry shall investigate such charges, or the said rumors or reports, as the case may be. In conducting the investigation, the Board shall hear the accusations and such proof as the accusers may produce, and shall determine whether, upon matters of law and of fact, as presented to them, there is sufficient ground to put the accused Bishop on his trial.

The testimony shall be stenographically reported, and shall be preserved in the custody of the Presiding Bishop or in the archives of the House of Bishops. The proceedings of the Board of Inquiry shall be private.

Sec. 6. If in the judgment of the majority of the whole Board of Inquiry, there is sufficient ground to put the said Bishop upon trial, they shall cause the Church Advocate to prepare a presentment, which shall be signed by such of the Board as shall agree thereto, and which shall be transmitted with the certificate of the determination of the Board to the Presiding Bishop.

If a majority of the whole Board shall determine that there is not sufficient ground to present the accused Bishop for trial, it shall forward the charges and a certificate of the finding thereon to the Presiding Bishop. He shall send the same to the Secretary of the House of Bishops, by him to be deposited in the archives of the House; and a true copy of these papers shall be given to the accused Bishop. No further proceeding shall be had by way of presentment on such charges, except that any communicant of this Church in good standing may make and present to the Presiding Bishop his affidavit alleging the discovery of new evidence as to the facts charged and setting forth what such evidence is; and upon the receipt thereof the Presiding Bishop shall decide whether the affidavit does or does not state grounds which in his opinion are sufficient for reopening the case. If the Presiding Bishop shall be of opinion that the affidavit states grounds sufficient to justify reopening the case, he shall reconvene the Board, which shall determine, first, whether as a matter of fact the evidence set forth in such affidavit is really new evidence and not merely cumulative; and if the Board shall find that the evidence so tendered is new, it shall proceed to receive and to consider such evidence, and any further evidence that it may deem proper to receive; and in the light of all the evidence the Board shall determine whether there are sufficient grounds for presentment. If the Board, by a majority of its members, shall decide that there is any such sufficient ground, it shall certify its decision as in this Canon heretofore provided.

Sec. 7. In case a majority of the whole Board shall fail to find either that there is, or that there is not, sufficient ground to present the accused Bishop for trial, it shall certify the fact of its inability to agree upon any such finding to the Presiding Bishop, who, at the request of the accused Bishop, may select a new Board in the manner provided in Section 5, who shall consider the case *de novo*.

Sec. 8. In case any presentment shall be made to the Presiding Bishop as hereinbefore provided, he shall at once transmit the same to the President of the Court for the Trial of a Bishop, and shall cause a true copy of the presentment to be served upon the accused Bishop, in the manner provided in Canon 54.

Sec. 9. In case the Presiding Bishop shall be either an accuser or the accused, or shall otherwise be disabled, his duties under this Canon shall be performed by the Bishop who, according to the rules of the House of Bishops, becomes its Presiding Officer in case of the disability of the Presiding Bishop of the Church.

CANON 57.
Of the Trial of a Bishop

Sec. 1 (a). When the President of the Court for the Trial of a Bishop shall receive a presentment, he shall call the Court to meet at a certain time and place, said time not to be less than two nor more than six calendar months from the day of mailing such notice, and at a place within the Diocese or Missionary District of the accused Bishop, unless the same be of such difficult access, in the judgment of the President of the Court, that reasonable convenience requires the appointment of another place; and in case the accused have no jurisdiction, at a place within the Diocese or Missionary District in which he has his domicile. With said notice, he shall send to each member of the Court a copy of the presentment.

Sec. 3. The accused being present and the trial proceeding, it shall be conducted in accordance with Secs. 20, 21, and 22 of Canon 55. The accused shall in all cases have the right to be a witness on his own behalf, subject to cross-examination in the same manner as any other witness. No testimony shall be received at the trial, except from witnesses who have signed a declaration in the following words, to be read aloud before the witness testifies and to be filed with the records of the Court.

Sec. 6. A Bishop found guilty upon a presentment for crime or immorality shall not, after the rendering of such judgment, and while the same continues unreversed, perform any episcopal or ministerial functions, except such as relate to the administration of the temporal affairs of his Diocese or Missionary District.

After the entry of final judgment, the President of the Court shall appoint a time and place not less than 60 days thereafter for pronouncing sentence. At the time and place appointed, if the accused shall not have an appeal pending in the Court of Review of the Trial of a Bishop, or the action of the Court of Review has not made it unnecessary for the Trial Court to proceed to pronounce sentence, the President of the Court or a member thereof designated in writing by a majority of the members thereof to do so, shall in the presence of the accused, if he shall see fit to attend, pronounce the sentence which has been adjudged by the Court, and direct the same to be recorded by the Clerk.

CANON 58.

Of Appeals to the Court of Review of the Trial of a Bishop

Sec. 1. A Bishop found guilty of any offense shall have the right to appeal from the judgment of the Trial Court to the Court of Review of the Trial of a Bishop; and in the case of a Bishop presented for holding and teaching doctrine contrary to that held by this Church, the Church Advocate shall have a like right to appeal.

Sec. 2. Unless within sixty days from the date of entry of judgment in the Trial Court the appellant shall have given notice of the appeal, in writing, to said Court, to the party against whom the appeal is taken, and to the President of the Court of Review of the Trial of a Bishop, assigning in said notice the reasons of appeal, he shall be held to have waived the right of appeal, although in its discretion the Court of Review of the Trial of a Bishop may entertain and hear an appeal not taken within such prescribed period.

The President of the Court of Review upon receiving the notice of appeal shall appoint a time within 60 days thereafter for hearing the appeal and fix the place of the hearing, and at least 30 days prior to the day appointed written notice of such time and place shall be given by him to the other members of the Court and also to the appellant and appellee.

Sec. 3. Upon notice of appeal being given, the Clerk of the Trial Court shall send to the Clerk of the Court of Review of the Trial of a Bishop a transcript of the record, including all the evidence, certified by the President and Clerk of the said Court, and the Clerk shall lay the same before the Court at its next session.

Sec. 4. No oral testimony shall be heard by said Court, nor, except by permission of the said court shall any new evidence be introduced in said hearing.

Sec. 5. The Court of Review of the Trial of a Bishop may affirm or reverse any judgment brought before it on appeal, and may enter final judgment in the case, or may remit the same to the Trial Court for a new trial, or for such further proceedings as the interests of justice may require; *Provided, however,* that if the accused shall have been found not guilty by the Trial Court upon any of the charges and specifications upon which he has been tried other than that of holding and teaching doctrine contrary to that held by this Church, the Court of Review of the Trial of a Bishop shall have no power to reverse said findings; and, *Provided, further,* that sentence shall not be imposed upon a Bishop found guilty of holding and teaching doctrine contrary to that held by this Church unless and until the said findings shall have been approved by a vote of two-thirds of all the Bishops canonically assembled in said House, and entitled to vote.

Sec. 6. If the Court of Review of the Trial of a Bishop shall enter final judgment in the case, and if by said judgment the accused shall be found guilty of any of the charges or specifications upon which he has been tried, the Court of Review of the Trial of a Bishop shall determine the sentence, which shall be either admonition, suspension, as defined by the Canons of this Church, or deposition. Before sentence is passed the accused shall have the opportunity of being heard, if he have aught to say in excuse or palliation. The sentence shall be pronounced by the Presiding Bishop, or such other Bishop as the Presiding Bishop shall designate, who shall thereupon give the notices thereof required by Canon 64.

Sec. 7. In case of appeal, all proceedings in the Trial Court shall be stayed until such appeal be dismissed by the Court of Review of the Trial of a Bishop, or the said case be remitted by the said Court to the Trial Court. Should the appellant fail to prosecute his appeal before the said Court at the first session thereof, after the entry of the appeal, at which the same could be heard, the appeal may be dismissed for want of prosecution. In case the said Court dismiss the appeal, the Clerk of the Court shall immediately give notice of such dismissal to the Trial Court.

The appellant may waive his appeal at any time before a hearing thereof has begun before the Court of Review of the Trial of a Bishop. After said hearing has begun, he may waive his appeal only with the consent of the Court. In case the appeal is waived or dismissed, the Trial Court shall proceed as if no appeal had been taken.

CANON 59.

Of a Minister in any Diocese or Missionary District Chargeable with Offense in Another

Sec. 2. If a Minister shall come temporarily into any Diocese or Missionary District, under the imputation of having elsewhere been guilty of any of the offenses within the provisions of Canon 53, or if any Minister, while sojourning in any Diocese or Missionary District, shall so offend, the Bishop, upon probable cause, may admonish such Minister and inhibit him from officiating in said Diocese or Missionary District. And if, after such inhibition, the said Minister so officiate, the Bishop shall give notice to all the Ministers and Congregations in said Diocese or Missionary District, that the officiating of said Minister is inhibited; and like notice shall be given to the Ecclesiastical Authority of the Diocese or Missionary District to which the said Minister belongs, and to the Recorder. And such inhibition shall continue in force until the Bishop of the first-named Diocese or Missionary District be satisfied of the innocence of the said Minister, or until he be acquitted on trial.

VII. Data on the "Bayne Committee"
(*The Presiding Bishop's mandate*)

EXECUTIVE COUNCIL/THE EPISCOPAL CHURCH
815 SECOND AVENUE, NEW YORK, N.Y.
10017/TN 7-8400

DOUGLAS A. BUSHY
Public Relations Officer

NEW YORK, N.Y., *January 12*—The Rt. Rev. John E. Hines, Presiding Bishop of the Episcopal Church, today appointed a committee of bishops, priests, laymen and a theologian not an Episcopalian to advise him in relation to the theological situation with which the Episcopal Church is faced. This situation includes some of the perplexing questions implicit but not resolved in the session in which the House of Bishops in Wheeling, W. Va., sought to deal with the issues raised for the Church by the possibility of a presentment against the resigned bishop of California, the Rt. Rev. James A. Pike, on the part of a group of bishops. The committee has been requested to report to the Presiding Bishop who will then make appropriate use of the findings to help clarify some of the issues upon which there is widespread misunderstanding and outright disagreement among many Church people. The findings could serve as a resource for the exploratory committee called for by a House of Bishops resolution looking towards a possible council of renewal in the Episcopal Church. The committee will be asked to direct its attention to the following issues:

1. The theological situation today: the form of the problems as now posed, the various alternative opportunities and the state and prospects of the dialogue within our own Church.
2. The scope of legitimate openness in our Church for theological reformation, in the light of what yardsticks may be available to test given affirmations or non-affirmations of theologians and others, whether episcopal, presbyterial or lay writers and speakers.
3. The permissible breadth and variety of modes and manners of statement in our time, considering the ever widening generation gap and the rapid change in thought forms and style of communication.
4. The subject of "Anglican comprehensiveness" as regards limits, if any, beyond which a spokesman may not take himself without, as a matter of integrity, renouncing the position of authority in the "order" to which he has come.

APPENDIX

5. The issue as to what extent problems, doubts and new or radical positions should be shared with the laity, with the risk of disturbing some of them.
6. The scope of freedom in the Church in all these matters, modes of official judgments with special attention to the place of the ecclesiastical equivalent of "due process" in the decision-making procedures on the part of appropriate deciding bodies.
7. The nature of "heresy" in the light of the increasingly complex relationships and interaction between "Faith" and scientific knowledge such as has been, and is being, evidenced today.
8. The role of responsible bodies, such as the House of Bishops, in interpreting a wise and effective stance under the umbrella label "Defenders of the Faith," and including an appraisal of the possible Church-wide and world-wide effect of presently provided canonical procedures with reference to a trial for heresy.

The members of the advisory committee are as follows:

THE RT. REV. STEPHEN F. BAYNE, Chairman
Vice-President, Executive Council

THE RT. REV. EVERETT H. JONES
Bishop of West Texas

THE RT. REV. GEORGE W. BARRETT
Bishop of Rochester

LOUIS CASSELS
Religion Editor, United Press International

THE REV. DR. THEODORE P. FERRIS
Rector, Trinity Church, Boston

THE REV. DR. JOHN M. MACQUARRIE
Professor, Union Seminary

THE REV. DR. ALBERT T. MOLLEGEN
Professor, Virginia Theological Seminary

THE REV. DR. CHARLES P. PRICE
Minister, Memorial Church, Harvard University

THE REV. DR. PAUL S. MINEAR
Visiting Professor, Yale Divinity School

PROFESSOR GEORGE SHIPMAN
University of Washington, Seattle

DR. DAVID L. SILLS, EDITOR
International Encyclopedia of Social Sciences

(BISHOP PIKE'S RESPONSE)

Statement of Bishop James A. Pike, theologian-in-residence, Center for the Study of Democratic Institutions from Richmond, Va. where he is engaged *in a four-day teaching mission under the auspices of the Episcopal clergy of the city.*

In the light of the Presiding Bishop's creative—indeed historic—step which gives a comprehensive opportunity to move toward a consensus regarding the issues of which the draft heresy presentment and the House of Bishops censure has made me for the time being a focus, I am quite content that the Presiding Bishop delay further—indeed until after this new committee does its work and he issues his statement—the appointment of the first of the bodies involved in the canonical judicial process which the above-named charges required me to initiate after the vote at Wheeling. The committee—in the open, I trust, and with adequate hearing of data and views—will be confronting the nature of the current theological revolution in which I, among many, am participating; the norms of judging the degree of permissibility of exploration in public of a relevant theology for today; and the question of due process in the making of official judgments, if and when necessary, about those engaged in this essential task. The data and views presented and the conclusions of this committee and of the Presiding Bishop could be of inestimable guidance to the one to five consecutive judicial bodies which could be called upon to make decisions in the particular controversy, the implications of which affect so many in the Church, clergy and lay. Further, the work of this committee and the Presiding Bishop's declaration will assist Churchmen at all levels—from theologians to those whom some patronizingly call "the little people"—better to interpret (supportively or critically) the one to five canonical adjudications which may be called for. Still more important, the fruit of this effort will lay down a platform (or at least the highlighting of the relevant issues) for the major council for renewal initiated by the House's resolution and which would be convened after the Seattle General Convention. It would seem that for our Church the new Reformation may be really underway.

I know I will be joined by many in commending the Presiding Bishop's statesmanship and sensitivity to the needs and prospects of our Church in our day, which this step demonstrates.

January 12, 1967

(*Bishop Bayne's interpretation of the Committee's task*)

THE NATIONAL COUNCIL
Episcopal Church Center, 815 Second Avenue, New York 17, N.Y.
TN 7-8400

February 11, 1967

DEAR JIM:

I'm glad I could catch you before you set out on your wanderings. It was obviously important for us to clear the date of April 29th with you, and I'm glad it is possible for you. We can write later about travel time, etc.

First, let me enclose a copy of the letter which is going out to the eighteen people we have asked to serve as consultants for us. It outlines in general what we hope they will do, in the memoranda we are asking for.*

I did not mention in the letter, for obvious reasons, what I talked with you about—namely that we also wanted four of the consultants to come to Boston to talk with the Committee privately about the memorandum they had written. We don't expect them to read their papers to us! But we thought it would be essential that we go into all these matters in greater depth with a selected group of the consultants, in an informal and entirely private way. At the moment we have identified four whom we want to see. Perhaps there will be more as time goes on; but I doubt if we can manage many more than four in the time available.

Of course our report has got to cover an awfully wide field, if we are to fulfill the terms of reference John Hines has given. But I believe, as I said in my form letter, that the three questions will take us over the first threshold and will expose further issues and areas of discussion helpfully. If they are to be published, as I hope most of them will, they ought to be fairly brief. But certainly in your case—indeed in any case—if they really want more than 5 thousand words, I hope they will take them.

Let me know of anything more I can helpfully write you about this next meeting. As soon as we have a place selected, I'll let you know that; it will be in Boston, and of course we will be responsible for your travel and hospitality.

Yours ever,
(Signed) STEPHEN F. BAYNE, JR.
The Rt. Rev. Stephen F. Bayne, Jr.

THE RT. REV. JAMES A. PIKE, S.T.D.
Memorial Union
University of Wisconsin
Madison, Wisconsin 53706

cc to Santa Barbara

* The following letter was enclosed:

THE NATIONAL COUNCIL
Episcopal Church Center, 815 Second Avenue, New York 17, N.Y.
TN 7-8400

February 11, 1967

DEAR PAUL:

As you know, the Presiding Bishop has appointed an Advisory Committee to give him counsel as to theological debate within the Church—the liberties and responsibilities essential to it and whatever limitations or obligations may be encountered in it. Indeed the terms of reference of this Committee are extremely broad, covering practically every aspect of theological dialogue.

The Committee consists of three bishops—Bishop Barrett of Rochester, Bishop Jones of West Texas and myself; four presbyters—Dr. Theodore Ferris of Boston, Dr. John Macquarrie of Union Seminary, Dr. Theodore Mollegen of the Virginia Seminary and Dr. Charles Price of Harvard; one theologian from a sister church in the Consultation on Church Union, Professor Paul S. Minear; and three laymen—Mr. Louis Cassels (religion editor of United Press International), Professor George Shipman (University of Washington) and Dr. David Sills, editor of the International Encyclopedia of Social Sciences.

We have just completed a brief organizing meeting to plan our work. Almost at once we agreed that it would be most important to us to have the help of a representative group of consultants, especially in respect to certain specific aspects of the problem. So far we have identified eighteen people, including yourself, as those we particularly want to assist us. The help we want is this: Will you—can you—by April 1st next, write me a paper giving your response to three questions? The paper probably shouldn't be longer than 4 or 5 thousand words (but more, or less, if you feel it appropriate). All of them will be studied by the Committee, of course, but we hope also to print them, if that is practicable and agreeable, as an appendix to our report. But we feel such publication would be a significant contribution to a debate of considerable ecumenical as well as Episcopalian concern. The three questions are these:

1. What obligations does the Church have for encouraging theological inquiry and social criticism? What procedures should it provide to fulfill those obligations?

2. What obligations should be assumed by those who participate in theological inquiry and social criticism?

3. What is heresy? How should the Church define, detect and deal with it?

The work of the Committee, no doubt, must range beyond these areas. But the questions seem to us to hold the core of our immediate task, and the answers will be immensely helpful to us. I cannot promise any reward, alas, except such pleasure as you might find in assisting the Committee to prepare a sensible and perhaps important guide for the Church in a time of great perplexity and yet also great promise. I sincerely hope you can and will do this for us.

Faithfully yours,
(*Signed*) STEPHEN F. BAYNE, JR.
The Rt. Rev. Stephen F. Bayne, Jr.

THE RT. REV. PAUL MOORE, JR., S.T.D.
Episcopal Church House
Mount St. Alban
Washington, D.C. 20016

VIII. Bibliography of Works of James A. Pike

Title	Publisher	Date
Cases and Other Materials on New Federal and Code Procedure	Callaghan	1939
Administrative Law (with Fischer)	Matthew Bender	1941
The Faith of the Church (with Pittenger)	Seabury	1951
Beyond Anxiety	Scribner	1953
If You Marry Outside Your Faith	Harper & Row	1954
Roadblocks to Faith (with Krumm)	Morehouse	1954
Doing the Truth	Doubleday	1955
	The Macmillan Co.	1965
The Church, Politics and Society (with Pyle)	Morehouse	1955
Modern Canterbury Pilgrims (editor of)	Morehouse	1956
Man in the Middle (with Johnson)	Seabury	1956
The Next Day	Doubleday	1957
A Roman Catholic in the White House (with Byfield)	Doubleday	1960
Our Christmas Challenge	Sterling	1961
A New Look in Preaching	Scribner	1961
Beyond the Law	Doubleday	1963
A Time for Christian Candor	Harper & Row	1964
Teen-Agers and Sex	Prentice-Hall	1965
What Is This Treasure	Harper & Row	1966
You and the New Morality	Harper & Row	1967
If This Be Heresy	Harper & Row	1967

Notes

PART ONE

1. From a letter of Bishop Pike to Dr. McCrady dated February 12, 1953.
2. From a conversation between the authors and Bishop Louttit over several days in March, 1967. All other statements of Bishop Louttit in this book—unless otherwise attributed—are from that same conversation.
3. Text of telegram to Bishop Pike from the graduating class, 1953, School of Theology, University of the South, dated February 13, 1953.
4. From a six-hour tape recording made by Bishop Pike with the authors over several days in December, 1966 and January, 1967. All other statements by Bishop Pike in this book—unless otherwise attributed—are from that same tape.
5. *Time* magazine, November 11, 1966, p. 58.
6. See Bibliography of Works of James A. Pike, Appendix. Through 1966 *The Faith of the Church* had sold 31,000 copies in hard cover and 108,000 copies in paperback.
7. See Bibliography of Works of James A. Pike, Appendix, for full list of titles he published during this period.
8. The thirteen articles in that series were subsequently collected and edited by Harold E. Fey under the title *How My Mind Has Changed* (Cleveland and New York: Living Age Books, World Publishing Co., 1960). Bishop Pike's contribution, somewhat revised from its periodical version, begins on p. 170.
9. *Ibid.*, p. 186.
10. *Ibid.*, pp. 176, 182.
11. The "Pastoral Letter" issued by the House of Bishops November 16, 1960 (*Journal of the General Convention*, PECUSA, 1961, Secretary to the House, 815 Second Ave., New York City), p. 123.
12. *Ibid.*, p. 123.
13. *Ibid.*, p. 120.
14. *Ibid.*, p. 123–24.

15. *Christianity Today,* January 16, 1961.
16. *New York Times,* January 29, 1961.
17. *Ibid.*
18. *Ibid.,* February 3, 1961.
19. *Journal of the General Convention,* 1961, *op. cit.,* pp. 406–407.
20. *Ibid.,* p. 407.
21. *Ibid.,* p. 240.

22. Dean Pike's election took place February 4, 1958, on the sixth ballot, on which he received 221 lay votes (193 required) and 57 clergy votes (56 required) during a meeting of the diocesan convention.

23. From a questionnaire returned to the authors by Francis Eric Irving Bloy, Bishop of Los Angeles. It is interesting to note that a judgment of ecclesiastical annulment had been entered with respect to Bishop Pike's first marriage by Bishop Bloy's predecessor, the late Dr. Bertrand W. Stevens, 2nd Bishop of Los Angeles.

24. The text of Dean Coburn's consecration sermon was supplied to the authors by Bishop Pike.

25. *Episcopal Church Annual* (New York: Morehouse–Barlow Co.), 1959, pp. 20–21; 1966, p. 14.

26. From the text of an address delivered by Bishop Pike to his diocesan convention on February 1, 1965.

27. The Stated Clerk of the Presbyterian Church USA is the chief executive officer of that denomination.

28. Bishop Newbiggin used a liturgy of the Church of South India, a union of the same four denominations initially involved in COCU.

29. Published ultimately as *A Time for Christian Candor.* See Bibliography of Works of James A. Pike, Appendix.

30. Robinson, John A. T., *Honest to God* (Philadelphia: Westminster Press, 1963).

31. Pike, *op. cit.,* pp. 99 ff.
32. *Ibid.,* p. 124.

33. This image of Bishop Pike as an airplane under attack from the ground brings to mind that in the armed services chaplains are sometimes called "skypilots."

34. Pike, *op. cit.,* pp. 120–30.
35. *Ibid.,* pp. 131–41.

36. *Journal of the General Convention,* PECUSA, 1964, Secretary to the House, 815 Second Ave., New York City, pp. 262–64. Following certain amendments the use of "Protestant" became in a sense optional, but in practice it has disappeared from general use.

37. From the text of the sermon as provided to the authors by Bishop Pike.

38. *Time* magazine, October 22, 1964, p. 88.

39. The full text of the statement was provided by its author, William Stringfellow.

40. *Journal*, 1964, *op. cit.*
41. *Ibid.*, pp. 59–60. Cf. also p. 155. In effect, the House of Deputies rejected the position paper, and it stands, therefore, as an action of the House of Bishops only.
42. *Ibid.*, x–xi.
43. *Ibid.*, pp. 144, 167, 372.
44. *Ibid.*, p. 62.
45. *Ibid.*, p. 66.
46. The text as received by Bishop Pike. It is undated.
47. From a communication received by Bishop Pike several days after his son's death. It is undated.
48. In his conversations with the authors Bishop Louttit adverted many times to Father Brunton, somewhat defensively it seemed to them, as though he wished to disassociate himself from the actions of the priest and to disassociate that priest from his own actions.
49. *Arizona Republic*, August 25, 1965, p. 7.
50. From a letter to Bishop Pike dated August 18, 1965, signed Dr. Remus F. Muray, who was, at the time, a priest from Hungary.
51. From a letter to the editor of the *Living Church* dated August 18, 1965, signed Charles Agneau.
52. Bishop Pike has also noted that the Feast of the Annunciation happened to fall in 1965 on March 25 or "nine months to the day before Christmas." A concern with precision is typical of the Bishop—a consequence, perhaps, of his training in law.
53. It is doubtful that Bishop Pike would today fully subscribe to these remarks. He has, for example, more recently denied of God that he is omniscient or indeed "omni"-anything.
54. *Minutes of the Special Meeting of the House of Bishops*, PECUSA, 1965, Secretary to the House, 815 Second Ave., New York City, p. 33.
55. *Ibid.*, p. 6.
56. *Ibid.*, p. 6.
57. *Journal*, 1964, *op. cit.*, pp. 125–26.
58. *Ibid.*, pp. 247–48–conforming with Lambeth, 1920 and 1930.
59. *Minutes*, 1965, *op. cit.*, pp. 5, 9–10, and 24–30.
60. The actions of the bishops at St. Louis and at Glacier Park seem to mean that deaconesses already in orders had already been ordained, but that in future a special service for their ordination would be followed. The service Bishop Pike conducted for Mrs. Edwards was not, then, an ordination, but rather a service in recognition of her ministerial status, a point he made plain at the time in the sermon he delivered. The authors confess that they are perplexed as to the meaning of all these events and uncertain as to the actual status of deaconesses now in the Episcopal Church. Questions arise which merit clarification by the bishops: Are deaconesses ordained or aren't they? Is the service adopted at Glacier Park a service of ordination? If not, what is it? Does it apply retroactively to all deaconesses—dead or alive—or

only to deaconesses ordered after Glacier Park? If the latter is the case, was Bishop Pike right to "recognize" Mrs. Edwards in the way he did? If he was right should not all pre-Glacier deaconesses—living at least—be similarly recognized? At Glacier Park the bishops said the actions at St. Louis had "clarified" a status of deaconesses "that was already theirs." The authors find less clarity rather than more.

61. From an article by John Cogley in the *New York Times* Sunday "News of the Week in Review" section, July 11, 1965.

62. *New York Times*, July 5, 1965.

63. *Ibid.*, July 7, 1965.

64. *Ibid.*

65. *Ibid.*, July 5, 1965.

66. *Ibid.*

67. MRI was officially accepted by the General Convention at St. Louis in 1964. See *Journal*, 1964, *op. cit.*, pp. 209, 722–30, 156, 324–30, and 172.

68. Father Brunton sent copies of these letters to Bishop Pike, and it is to the copies that reference is made. Neither letter was dated.

69. Letter to Bishop Harte dated September 21, 1965, signed by Bishop Pike; letter to Bishop Louttit dated January 6, 1966, signed by David J. Baar; letter to Father Baar dated January 13, 1966, signed by Bishop Louttit.

70. From the text of an address delivered by Bishop Pike to the council of the Diocese of California, February 4, 1966.

71. *Ibid.*

72. *Look* magazine, February 22, 1966.

73. More recently the Bishop has said, in effect, that he affirms the ongoingness of human personality after death and sees no reason to deny that estate to Jesus—a conception of the Resurrection some bishops might regard as insufficient.

74. The pertinent rubric from the service for Holy Communion as given in the *Book of Common Prayer* reads, in part: "Then shall the Priest first receive the Holy Communion in both kinds himself, and proceed to deliver the same to the Bishops, Priests, and Deacons, in like manner, (if any be present,) and after that, to the People also in order, *into their hands*, all devoutly kneeling." [Italics added.]

75. Letter to the editors of *Look* magazine, dated March 8, 1966, signed by Bishop Pike, with a copy to Bishop Hines. The letter was never printed in *Look*. Bishop Hines promptly sent copies to the various metropolitans. He did not send copies to other bishops until after the meeting of the House of Bishops at Wheeling nine months later.

76. See Bibliography of Works of James A. Pike, Appendix. As of the end of February, 1967, *Treasure* had a total sale of 17,560 copies; as of the same date, *Candor* (published November, 1964) had a total sale of 25,726 copies.

77. The referendum, the Bishop notwithstanding, passed by a 2–1 majority, but was subsequently declared unconstitutional by the California Supreme Court.

78. From a letter with enclosure to Bishop Pike dated April 20, 1966, signed by the rector, Graham N. Lesser, the senior warden, Robert A. Lane, and the junior warden, Thomas Woode, of Trinity Episcopal Church, Hayward, California. It should be added that there is good reason to believe that the vestry of Trinity Church were also influenced by social issues.

79. *Daily Review*, Hayward, California, May 10, 1966, pp. 1–2.

80. *Ibid.*, April 27, 1966, p. 1.

81. *New York Times*, April 16, 1965.

82. *Time* magazine, May 20, 1966.

83. *Ibid.*

84. *Ibid.*

85. See Bibliography of Works of James A. Pike, Appendix.

86. The Bishop's investigations of the latter subject tentatively suggests an inverse relationship: for example, that there tends to be more race discrimination among churchgoers than among people who never or seldom attend church.

87. *San Francisco Chronicle*, September 6, 1966, p. 1.

88. This discussion of the meeting of the fourth province bishops is based mainly on the recollections of Bishop Louttit.

89. *New York Times*, October 26, 1966.

90. *Ibid.*

91. *Ibid.*

92. *St. Petersburg Times*, section on "News of Religion," September 24, 1966, pp. 1 and 2.

93. Telegram to Bishop Louttit dated September 30, 1966, from Bishop Burroughs.

94. Telegram to Bishop Louttit dated September 30, 1966, from Bishop Emrich.

95. From a letter to Bishop Louttit dated September 29, 1966, signed by Bishop Dun.

96. From a letter to Bishop Louttit dated September 26, 1966, signed by Bishop Hines.

97. As told to the authors by Bishop Louttit and confirmed by Bishop Mosley.

98. Telegram from Bishop Louttit to some 30 bishops dated September 30, 1966.

99. Telegram to Bishop Louttit dated September 29, 1966, from Bishop Hines.

100. From a letter to Bishop Hines dated October 1, 1966, signed by Bishop Louttit.

101. For this account of the October 3, 1966 meeting the authors depend upon what was told to them by Bishop Louttit and confirmed to them by Bishop Hines.

102. From a letter to Bishop Louttit dated September 29, 1966, signed by Bishop Peabody.

103. Telegram from Bishop Louttit dated October 3, 1966, to some bishops.

104. From a letter to Bishop Louttit dated October 6, 1966, signed by Bishop Wright.

105. The question of how many bishops actually signed the presentment is riddled with confusions. Newspaper accounts range from 24 to 32. Bishop Louttit believes there were ultimately 28. Various bishops signed and later withdrew; others never specifically withdrew but indicated that they did not wish to be considered as having signed. Many bishops agreed to sign over the telephone but actually never signed anything. Canon law requires that signatures to a formal presentment be witnessed. Few signatures were, in fact, witnessed, but on the other hand the presentment was never *formally* filed. Some of the putative signatories were retired; under the canons their signatures would be invalid on a filed presentment. It is clear, in any event, that between 25 and 35 bishops did associate themselves with the presentment in one way or another.

106. *Chicago Tribune*, October 5, 1966.

107. In conversations with the authors Bishop Sterling has more recently expressed the belief that the presentment and the censure of Bishop Pike were unfortunate.

108. Petition of the Association of Episcopal Clergy dated October 5, 1966, signed by all members of its board of directors. No action was taken by the bishops at Wheeling on this petition.

109. From a letter to Bishop Pike dated October 7, 1966, signed by Father Allen. Another letter to Bishop Pike dated October 13, 1966, signed by the Reverend John H. Gill, then director of the Community Project of Holyrood Church, New York City, concluded with this not untypical sentiment: "There are many of us sheep who hope you will long remain among the shepherds." Not a few clergy—some from other churches—indicated in letters to Bishop Pike that should he be driven from the Church they would feel obliged to leave with him.

110. *Religious News Service* dispatch from Durham, N.C., dated October 10, 1966.

111. *Ibid.*

112. The text of this statement, dated October 13, 1966, was provided to the authors by Bishop Donegan.

113. From a letter to Bishop Pike dated October 19, 1966, signed by Bishop Allin.

114. From a letter to all bishops dated October 18, 1966, signed by Bishop Hines.

115. *New York Times*, October 19, 1966.

116. *Ibid.*

117. This explanation of the composition of the committee fails to account for the inclusion of Bishop Warnecke, who was not a member of the Theological Committee.

118. From a letter to the authors from the bishop in question. Because he is retired and has long argued that retired bishops should not directly involve themselves in the business of the House this particular bishop specifically requested that he remain anonymous.

119. Bishop Emrich had greater success with a similar move against another priest—Father Malcolm Boyd—who had suggested on a radio program that Jesus had organs like other men including even a penis. So outraged was Bishop Emrich by this astounding proposition that he publicly rebuked Father Boyd and arranged for his dismissal as chaplain at Wayne State University in Detroit. Bishop Emrich's success in this discipline is explicable when it is noted that as Bishop of Michigan he was, at that time, Father Boyd's episcopal superior. Father Boyd is now attached to the Diocese of Washington, and, as a member of the staff of the Episcopal Society for Cultural and Racial Unity (ESCRU), serves as chaplain-at-large to all American universities and colleges.

120. *Minutes of the Special Meeting of the House of Bishops*, PECUSA, 1966, Secretary to the House, 815 Second Ave., New York City, p. 18.

121. From a letter to Bishop Pike dated October 7, 1966, signed by Bishop Campbell. In a long letter to the authors dated March 20, 1966, Bishop Campbell set forth his understanding of many episodes at Wheeling. He denies that he formally inhibited Bishop Pike from speaking under Episcopal auspices in his diocese. He notes that his letter to Bishop Pike did not "invoke" the pertinent canon—Canon 59, Section 2 (see Appendix for text)—but only "mentioned" it. This is true, but the authors fail to find the distinction meaningful since, in fact, the two invitations Bishop Pike had received from Episcopal auspices in Wheeling were withdrawn as a direct result of Bishop Campbell's initiative.

On Sunday evening, October 23, 1966 Bishops Campbell and Pike had a length private conversation which persuaded the former that the latter was innocent of Bishop Louttit's charges. Bishop Campbell, therefore, though he had joined in the presentment, decided that, should it be formally filed, he would withdraw his name. The two bishops issued on October 24, 1966 a statement clarifying the dispute concerning the inhibition. The two bishops also worked on a statement that would define the "irreducible minimum of doctrine necessary" to comply with the Oath of Conformity. That effort was not completed, nor, according to Bishop Campbell, was it pursued on the floor out of deference to Bishop Stokes' resolution calling for a committee to study church doctrine.

122. *Minutes*, 1966, *op. cit.*, pp. 8 and 14.
123. *Ibid.*, pp. 8–9.
124. *Ibid.*, p. 10.
125. *Ibid.*, pp. 10 and 18.
126. *Ibid.*, p. 13.
127. *Ibid.*, p. 17.

128. *Ibid.*, pp. 17–21.
129. *Ibid.*, p. 21.
130. *Ibid.*, p. 26.
131. *Ibid.*, pp. 26–28.
132. All statements—unless otherwise attributed—in the following recapitulation of the censure debate are taken from the transcript of a tape recording of that debate made on the scene by the Canadian Broadcasting Corporation.
133. *Minutes*, 1966, *op. cit.*, p. 28. (The 1966 *Minutes* appear to be in error as to the order in which various motions were offered and voted upon, in that the CBC tape—*op cit.*—shows an order radically different.)
134. *Ibid.*, pp. 28–29. (The minutes indicate the motion was made by the Bishop of Washington, but, in fact, it was made by the *Suffragan* Bishop of Washington.)
135. Bishop Stark actually voted *against* the censure, one of a few bishops whose minds changed in the course of the debate.
136. *Minutes*, 1966, *op. cit.*, p. 29.
137. *Ibid.*, p. 29.
138. The minutes—p. 29—explain this action differently but inaccurately.
139. According to Bishop Campbell the crozier had been requested by an associate of Bishop Pike (Bishop Pike denies knowledge of this), and Bishop Hodges complied, not wishing to offend the Bishop of West Virginia.
140. Bishop Allin's letter was so long he could not complete reading it in his allotted three minutes. The last paragraph of the letter is quoted earlier in this book, p. 71.
141. *Minutes*, 1966, *op. cit.*, p. 30.
142. *Ibid.*, p. 28. (The minutes place this motion in the afternoon session, but the minutes are in error.)
143. *Ibid.*, p. 30.
144. *Ibid.*, p. 28. (The minutes also erroneously place this motion in the afternoon session.)
145. Quotation is as read by Bishop Pike.
146. *Minutes*, 1966, *op cit.*, pp. 30–31.
147. *Ibid.*, pp. 35–37.
148. The highlight of the evening's entertainment was provided by a group of Roman Catholic nuns who sang, among other things, "Getting to Know You."
149. It was Bishop Chambers of Springfield who called the grace "Jewish" and "not Christian"; it was Bishop Brown of Albany—in his diocesan newsletter—who called it "untrinitarian."
150. This is the text of the controversial grace: "O, blessed art thou, O, Lord God of our fathers, King of the universe, who bringeth forth the fruit of the vine; blessed art thou, O, Lord God of our fathers, King of the universe, who bringeth forth bread from the earth; blessed art thou, O, Lord God of our fathers, King of the universe, who puteth compassion into the hearts of men."

PART TWO
FIRST: *Dogma, Doctrine and Discipline*

1. The United Church of Christ authorized such a creedal statement in 1959, while the United Presbyterian Church undertook similar action in 1967.
2. *Minutes of the House of Bishops*, New York, October 18, 1924, p. 411 f.
3. *Minutes of the House of Bishops*, Dallas, November 5, 1923, p. 466.
4. *Ibid.*, pp. 470–71.
5. Theodore Schroeder, *Concerning the Heresy Trial of Rt. Rev. William Montgomery Brown* (New York: Truth Seeker, 1924), pp. 17–18.
6. *Creeds and Loyalty* (New York: The Macmillan Co., 1924).
7. From a carbon copy of the address obtained from the Rev. Lester Kinsolving, *The San Francisco Chronicle*.
8. See *New York Times*, March 7, 1967.
9. William Lawrence (the Rt. Rev.), *Fifty Years* (Boston: Houghton Mifflin, 1923), p. 81.
10. *Minutes*, Dallas, November 5, 1923, p. 471. See Hugh M. Jansen, "A Threatened Heresy Trial in the Twenties," *Anglican Theological Review*, Winter, 1967.
11. Edward Bushnell, *The Narrow Bed* (Galion, Ohio: Bradford Brown Educational Co., 1925), p. 23. Bushnell, a Presbyterian layman, was one of Bishop Brown's counsel. He disagreed with Brown's doctrinal views, but was so outraged by usurpation of legal process in the case that he was moved to write this review of the Brown trial.
12. *New York Times*, March 7, 1967.
13. Alexander Allen, *Freedom in the Church* (New York: The Macmillan Co., 1907), p. 216.
14. *Ibid.*, p. 216–7.
15. The singing of creeds has been mandatory at the Cathedral, at missions, and in parishes on occasions of episcopal visitations while Pike was Bishop of California.
16. See Louttit–Pike Correspondence, Appendix III.
17. Bishop Louttit's impression that a "Chalcedonian statement in modern American" was under way is evidently based upon a conversation he had with a Sewanee theological professor, the Rev. Charles Winters, during a visit of Professor Winters to the 1966 clergy conference of the Diocese of South Florida. Bishop Louttit thought Professor Winters had agreed, on behalf of his faculty, to the scheme Bishop Louttit described in his October 14, 1966 letter to Bishop Pike. Professor Winters has a quite different recollection, and the Very Rev. George M. Alexander, Dean of the School of Theology at the University of the South, wrote Bishop Louttit on October 17, 1966 to indicate there had been some misunderstanding, that the Sewanee faculty had not agreed to the "Chalcedonian-in-American" project, but that they

did favor a much broader theological inquiry and renewal within the Episcopal Church.

18. Anthony Towne, "In Defense of Heresy," *Christian Century*, January 11, 1967, p. 47. Queries what dignity the Articles of Religion have. The *Book of Common Prayer* uses the term "established" in designating the status of the Articles, which would appear less binding than "adopted," or "promulgated," "enacted."

19. As transcribed live by the Canadian Broadcasting Corp., October 25, 1966, at Wheeling, W. Va. Hereinafter cited as CBC tape.

20. John D. Covert and Austin F. Anderson, "The Case Against the Reverend Lee W. Heaton" (Fort Worth: Trinity Church, undated). Cf. Hugh M. Jansen, *op. cit.*

21. Allen, *op. cit.*, p. 10.

22. Stephen F. Bayne, *Dogma and Reality* (New York: Trinity Church, 1964), p. 3.

23. *Ibid.*, pp. 4–5.

24. *Ibid.*, p. 5, emphasis added.

25. The Rt. Rev. William Crittenden, Bishop of Erie.

26. Bushnell, *op. cit.*, pp. 27–29. Bishop Brown was conditionally consecrated by Archbishop William H. Francis, Metropolitan of the Old Catholic Church in the U.S., in June, 1925. Conditional consecration is similar to conditional baptism—the issue raised in Luci Baines Johnson becoming a Roman Catholic—in that the act is performed in case a prior consecration was ineffectual. Bishop Brown's conditional consecration occurred before the meeting of the House of Bishops which was to hear his appeal from the sentence of deposition imposed upon him by the ecclesiastical courts, and appears to have incensed many Episcopal bishops and probably explains why, when the House convened in October, 1925, Brown received no hearing. The Old Catholic Church traces its origins to the ancient Church of the Netherlands founded in the seventh century. In 1871, after papal infallibility was decreed, the Old Catholic Church was organized in protest against that dogma. Its episcopal orders are acknowledged as *valid* by all Catholic traditions, but are regarded by Roman Catholics as *illegally conferred* because the Old Catholic Church is schismatic in refusing to accept papal infallibility.

27. *Doctrine in the Church of England* (London: S.P.C.K., 1938), p. 9.

28. *Ibid.*, p. 12.

29. *Ibid.*, p. 10.

30. *Ibid.*, pp. 17–18.

SECOND: *Heresy and Due Process*

1. Zeigler v. Railroad Co., 58 Ala. 599.

2. *New York Times*, October 30, 1966.

3. E. A. Vastyan, "Chaplain Thinks Due Processes Were Violated by Bishops," *Witness*, December 8, 1966, p. 3.

4. From a letter to Bishop Hines from the Rev. William B. Eastern, November 7, 1966.
5. *New York Times*, October 30, 1966.
6. Bishop Campbell of West Virginia claims he did not formally invoke the canon providing for inhibitions against Bishop Pike. His letter to Pike, dated October 7, 1966, contains, however, this sentence: "This decision of mine is in accordance with Canon 59, Section 2." Campbell was a signer of the Louttit presentment. Bishop Bloy caused the withdrawal of an invitation to Bishop Pike to preach in a parish within the Diocese of Los Angeles, but the matter was handled by telephone. Bloy voted for the censure.
7. Bishop Mason of Dallas and Bishop Harte of Arizona.
8. Algernon Crapsey, *The Last of the Heretics* (New York: Alfred A. Knopf, 1924), p. 261.
9. *Ibid.*, p. 262.
10. *Ibid.*, pp. 262–63.
11. Edwin A. White and Jackson Dykman, *Annotated Constitution and Canons of the Protestant Episcopal Church* (Greenwich, Conn.: Seabury Press, 1954), Vol. II, p. 344.
12. *New York Times*, October 27, 1966; cf. *Washington Post*, October 27, 1966, p. 43.
13. Letter to Bishop Hines from Bishop Pike, November 4, 1966.
14. From transcript of press conference of Bishop Hines, January 14, 1967, made by a reporter for the *San Jose Mercury*.
15. Statement by Bishop Hines released to press January 12, 1967; cf. *Episcopalian*, March, 1967, pp. 36–37.
16. Statement by Bishop Pike released to press January 12, 1967.
17. Members of the committee, in addition to Bishop Bayne, are Bishop Everett Jones, Bishop George Barrett, Louis Cassels, Dr. Theodore Ferris, Dr. John Macquarrie, Dr. Albert Mollegan, Dr. Charles Price, Dr. David Sills, Prof. George Shipman, Dr. Paul Minear.
18. Interview with Bishop Hines, March 20, 1967. For documents on "Bayne Committee" see Appendix VII. It may be questioned whether Bishop Bayne interprets the mandate of the committee much more broadly than Bishop Hines has stated.
19. Bushnell, *op. cit.*, p. 51.
20. See Appendix II.
21. Canon 56, Sec. 2, see Appendix VI.
22. Dr. Sam Shepard, for example, was freed because of prejudicial publicity after having been convicted of murder.
23. *Washington Post*, October 27, 1966, p. 43.
24. Interview with Bishop Hines, March 20, 1967.
25. CBC tape.
26. In an interview with the authors, April 14, 1967.
27. Letter to Bishop Dun from Bishop Pike, undated.
28. Frank M. Brunton, "Pike and His Peers." Brunton does not usually

date his doggerel, though it is often possible to identify events which have provoked him to write a particular piece.

THIRD: *The Fraternity of Bishops*

1. *Chicago Tribune*, October 5, 1966.
2. From a letter of Bishop Bennison to the clergy of Western Michigan, September 15, 1965.
3. Bishop Gordon of Alaska, in a note to the authors responding to questions submitted to all bishops. Emphasis added.
4. *Look*, February 22, 1966.
5. Bishop Hallock of Milwaukee in the *Milwaukee Churchman*, November, 1966.
6. Letter to Bishop Louttit from Bishop Kennedy, October 5, 1966.
7. William Stringfellow spent part of February, 1966 in Vietnam surveying the ministry of the churches to the Vietnamese. Some of the findings of that visit have been published through the Associated Church Press.
8. According to the priest-in-charge of the Episcopal Church in Saigon requests for funds to build a school for Vietnamese children have met only with demurrers, as of February, 1966.
9. From a letter to Bishop Louttit from George M. Sheldon, Lt., CHC, USNR, October 5, 1966.
10. Letter of Bishop Butterfield to Bishop Louttit, October 13, 1966; CBC transcription.
11. In a note to the authors responding to questions submitted to all bishops.
12. Statement of Bishop Donegan to the Council of the Diocese of New York, October 13, 1966. The statement was circulated to all bishops and released to the press.
13. Letter to the Presiding Bishop from Bishop Pike, May 9, 1966.
14. In a note to the authors responding to questions submitted to all bishops.
15. Letter of Bishop Bloy to the clergy of Los Angeles, September 28, 1966.
16. Bishop Pike had been invited to preach at St. Paul's Church, Ventura on July 9, 1961 by the rector, the Rev. William A. Gilbert, and had accepted the invitation. It was withdrawn in late March, 1967 on instructions from the offices of Bishop Bloy. Since no formal inhibition had been promulgated, Bishop Pike reported the matter to the Presiding Bishop and requested clarification from Bishop Bloy on March 28, 1967.
17. CBC transcription.
18. From a letter to Bishop Pike from Judge Seals.
19. *Arizona Republic*, February 12, 1967.
20. This and the immediately preceding quotations and citations are from letters received by Bishop Pike or Bishop Louttit, as the case may be.

NOTES 263

21. *St. Petersburg Times*, October 2, 1966.
22. This and the immediately preceding quotations and citations are from letters received by Bishop Louttit.
23. *Ibid.*
24. Miss Mohr wrote this in Lent, 1966. It was sent with her cover letter and other verses to the bishops named on October 16, 1966.
25. Bishop Pike has been privy to such councils, including chairmanship of the California Advisory Committee to the U.S. Civil Rights Commission, appointment by President Kennedy to the Food for Peace Council, as an advisor about Hungarian refugee problems during the Eisenhower administration, *et al.*
26. From a letter to Bishop Pike from Sister Hugo, O.P., November 1, 1966.
27. Bishop Brown made repeated appeals for reinstatement, the final one at the 1937 General Convention. He died October 31, 1937.
28. Statement of Bishop Burroughs at Trinity Cathedral, Cleveland, October 30, 1966. Burroughs voted for the censure.
29. *Cleveland Plain Dealer*, October 31, 1966, p. 14.
30. One communicant of St. Thomas remarked: "Bishop Pike is the only one who can fill this church."
31. *Christian Century*, February 15, 1967.
32. From a letter to Bishop Hines signed by 61 E.T.S. students, November 8, 1966.
33. From a letter to Bishop Creighton from Bishop Mosley, November 10, 1966.
34. From a letter to Bishop Pike from Gertrude Behanna, November 11, 1966.
35. From a letter to Bishop Louttit from Bishop Cadigan, September 28, 1966.
36. From a letter of Bishop Pinckney to the people of his diocese, November 2, 1966.
37. As cited in the introit to this chapter.
38. From a letter to Bishop Mosley from Bishop Creighton, October 29, 1966.
39. Address to the convention, Diocese of Western Michigan, May 17, 1966.
40. *Minutes*, 1966, *op. cit.*, p. 21.
41. *Playboy*, October, 1966.
42. Letter to Bishop Pike from Prof. William Hamilton, October 30, 1966.
43. *Time*, October 22, 1964, p. 88.
44. In a note to the authors responding to questions submitted to all bishops.
45. *Ibid.*

46. Bushnell, *op. cit.*, p. 15.
47. *American Church News*, February 1967, p. 2.
48. From a letter to Bishop Hines, *et al.*, from the Rev. Messrs. Fowler, Daughtry, Williams, and Merrell, March 8, 1967.
49. From a letter to Bishop Pike from the Rev. William Easter, November 5, 1966.
50. This and the immediately foregoing quotations are excerpted from letters received by Bishop Pike.

FOURTH: *Social Radicalism and Heresy*

1. William Montgomery, Brown, *Communism and Christianism* (Galion, Ohio: Bradford-Brown Educational Co., 1920). On the title page is this inscription: "Banish the Gods from the Skies and Capitalists from the Earth and make the world safe for Industrial Communism."
2. Algernon Crapsey, *The Rise of the Working Class* (New York: Century, 1914).
3. Teletype to *Newsweek*, August 10, 1965; see also, *Newsweek*, August 30, 1965 and September 20, 1965.
4. Several bishops so replied to authors' inquiries.
5. Letter to Bishop Louttit from Dr. McNair, October 1, 1966.
6. *Churchman*, June, 1961, p. 16.
7. *Journal of Convention of the Diocese of South Florida*, 1955, pp. 56, 64.
8. *New York Times*, photostat, February 1956.
9. Letter of Bishop Louttit to clergy, July 13, 1964.
10. Letter of Bishop Louttit to clergy, June 22, 1964.
11. Interview with Bishop Louttit, March 13, 1967.
12. This and the immediately foregoing quotations are from letters to or by Bishop Louttit, as the case may be.
13. See Lester Kinsolving, "Episcopal Extremism," *Nation*, January 23, 1967, p. 108.
14. *New York Times*, photostat, October 1961.
15. Albert Thomas, retired Bishop of South Carolina. Bishop Moody of Lexington (Ky.), a member of the Court for the Trial of a Bishop, is on the same board.
16. Brunton, "Pike on Sex."
17. Recorded interview taped by the National Broadcasting Company October 14, 1966. Hereinafter cited as NBC interview.
18. Letter to Bishop Louttit from the Rev. David Baar, January 6, 1966.
19. Letter to Fr. Baar from Bishop Louttit, January 13, 1966.
20. Dispatch from Wheeling, October 24, 1966.
21. For a more extensive discussion of this, see William Stringfellow, *Dissenter in a Great Society* (New York: Holt, Rinehart & Winston, 1966), chap. 4.

22. See Appendix I.
23. *San Francisco Chronicle*, October 25, 1966.
24. From a letter to Bishop Pike from Augustus Graydon, Esq., October 13, 1966.
25. *Berkeley Gazette*, September 13, 1965.
26. Acts 5.38–39.
27. From a letter of the Rev. William Penfield, October 12, 1966.
28. From a letter to Bishop Louttit from the Rev. Richard Shacklett, September 24, 1966.
29. CBC tape.
30. *Los Angeles Times*, September 23, 1966, p. 1.
31. *Associated Press* dispatch from Durham, N.C., October 10, 1966.
32. *Dallas Morning News*, February 9, 1966.
33. From a letter to Bishop Pike from Dean Usher, August 20, 1965.
34. In his regular radio program broadcast at various times by different stations.
35. From a letter to the authors from the Rev. Paul Urbano, April 3, 1967.
36. Brunton, "Dedicated to the House of Bishops."
37. Letter to Bishop Harte from Bishop Pike, September 21, 1965. Bishop Harte merely forwarded this letter to Bishop Louttit. Neither acted upon it. Bishop Harte appointed Brunton as *locus tenens* at a parish in Tempe, Arizona, adjacent to Arizona State University, sometime in 1966. Subsequently, after the censure, the clericus of the central deanery of Arizona took the unusual step of unanimously requesting Harte to withdraw Brunton's license to officiate as a priest. Bishop Harte demurred, though he did not renew Brunton's temporary appointment at Tempe.
38. *Detroit Free Press*, October 14, 1966.
39. *San Francisco Chronicle*, October 19, 1966.
40. NBC interview.
41. *Ibid.*
42. *The Arizona Republic*, October 15, 1966.
43. Brunton, "Pike and Julius Caesar."
44. Letter of Prof. George Forell to the authors, April 11, 1967.
45. *Nation*, January 23, 1967, p. 108.
46. *Ibid.*, p. 106.
47. *Witness*, May 19, 1966, p. 7; February 16, 1967, p. 7.
48. *Nation*, January 23, 1967, p. 107.
49. Letters to the Rev. John Morris, Executive Director of ESCRU from Bishop Bayne, November 13, 1959; December 17, 1963; December 30, 1963.
50. *Indianapolis Star*, January 18, 1967, as reprinted in the *Christian Challenge*, February, 1967, p. 1.
51. *Ibid.*
52. *Christian Challenge*, February, 1967, p. 3.
53. *Ibid.*, pp. 2, 4.

54. *Ibid.*, p. 3.
55. *New York Times*, October 1, 1961.
56. From the jacket of John Hines, *Thy Kingdom Come* (New York: Seabury, 1967).
57. In conversation with one of the authors.
58. *Report of the Special Committee*, Diocese of Louisiana, January 25, 1967, p. 1.
59. *Christian Challenge*, February, 1967, p. 2.
60. *Report of the Special Committee*, p. 3.
61. *Ibid.*, p. 4.
62. *Churchwork*, December, 1966, p. 1.
63. Statement of Bishop Pike, October 27, 1966.

A Homily

1. Letter to the authors dated January 17, 1967, signed by Bishop Juhan.
2. *Churchman*, April, 1961, p. 4.
3. See Bibliography of Works of James A. Pike, Appendix.

www.ingramcontent.com/pod-product-compliance
Lightning Source LLC
Chambersburg PA
CBHW050338230426
43663CB00010B/1901